Intersecting Boundaries

University of Minnesota Press
Minneapolis • London

Intersecting Boundaries

The Theatre of Adrienne Kennedy

Paul K. Bryant-Jackson and Lois More Overbeck, editors

Published by the University of Minnesota Press
2037 University Avenue Southeast, Minneapolis, MN 55414
Printed in the United States of America on acid-free paper

"Diverse Angles of Vision: Two Black Women Playwrights," by Margaret B. Wilkerson, is reprinted by permission of *Theatre Annual*, copyright 1985 by the University of Akron. John Falconieri, owner/editor; Wallace Sterling, executive editor. The quotations on page 88 are from *Prosa, Dramen, Verse*, by Reinhard Goering, copyright 1961 by Albert Langen Verlag, and are used by permission.

Library of Congress Cataloging-in-Publication Data

Intersecting boundaries : the theatre of Adrienne Kennedy/Paul K.
   Bryant-Jackson and Lois More Overbeck, editors.
       p.   cm.
    Includes bibliographical references and index.
    ISBN 0-8166-2015-6 (alk. paper). — ISBN 0-8166-2016-4 (pbk. :
alk. paper)
     I. Kennedy, Adrienne—Criticism and interpretation. I. Bryant
-Jackson, Paul K. II. Overbeck, Lois More.
    PS3561.E4252Z73 1992
    812'.54—dc20   91-41271
                                                            CIP

The University of Minnesota is an
equal-opportunity educator and employer.

To my parents, Paul Keith and Cecelia Bryant Jackson, and my sister, Cecelia Jones. Also to James D. Engstrom

—Paul K. Bryant-Jackson

To my family, James, Kristen, Andrew, and Jonathan Overbeck

—Lois More Overbeck

Contents

Preface

Paul K. Bryant-Jackson and Lois More Overbeck

The publication of Adrienne Kennedy's collected plays, *Adrienne Kennedy in One Act* (1988), as well as the appearance of *People Who Led to My Plays* (1987), *Deadly Triplets* (1990), *The Ohio State Murders* (workshop production, 1990), and *She Talks to Beethoven* (1991), has generated renewed critical interest in her oeuvre and opened discussion about the relationships among her plays. The glimpses into Kennedy's life afforded by *People Who Led to My Plays* and "A Theatre Journal" (in *Deadly Triplets*) encourage consideration of her experiences as shaping influences on the plays, especially because she has said that "autobiographical work is the only thing that interests me."[1] Until recently, criticism has largely dealt with plays as they appeared; now with the plays of the 1960s to 1980s gathered in a collected edition, the definition of an oeuvre is possible and stimulates questions of how Kennedy's writing as a whole is to be situated within multiple, even conflicting, dramatic traditions and theatrical movements. Looking at the plays through the various lenses of critical theory is made more complex and compelling by the issues of race, class, and gender that are embedded in the images and structures of Kennedy's plays. And finally, as with every playwright, there are the questions of dramaturgy and interpretation that arise as the plays are realized in performance.

Gerald Freedman, who directed *Cities in Bezique* (1969) and the workshop productions of *The Ohio State Murders* (1990, 1991), has written, "Adrienne Kennedy...uses theater materials to create a poem constructed of complex emotions and layers of time and reality that create a prism of refraction—story, event and character filter through by indirection, impression, and consciousness on the edge of awareness."[2] As the multiple perspectives represented in this volume imply, no single approach is adequate to inform the many and changing facets of Kennedy's work. These essays and interviews represent a dynamic collage whose impressions and conclusions overlayer each other; whether in corroboration or tension, the analyses and discoveries of these approaches demonstrate the need to immerse in the plays themselves rather than trying to force congruence with a theory or position outside of them. Indeed, the difficulty of Kennedy's plays lies both in their resistance to codification and the compelling way they wrap "around the mind like strange tendrils."[3] As the first book-length study of Kennedy's challenging and significant contribution to American theatre, the intent of this collection is to introduce her plays in their variety and to suggest critical strategies that will support fuller study and production of her works.

Part I, "The Life in the Work," begins with an interview with Paul Bryant-Jackson and Lois Overbeck in which Adrienne Kennedy talks about her vision in evolutionary terms. She also describes the solitary position of an African-American writer who finds her words as the only defense in a society that appears to be socially regressive. Werner Sollors, through a discussion of the autobiography, *People Who Led to My Plays*, connects Kennedy's vision and her middle-class childhood in a mixed neighborhood in Cleveland, as well as the racial experiences she endured while visiting relatives in Georgia during segregation. Sollors then traces the influence of popular culture in Kennedy's developing imagination. In "The Life of the Work," Overbeck draws upon programs, interviews, and reviews to sketch a prolegomenon of the production history of Kennedy's plays and points to the need for a more comprehensive record of the text performed and the playwriting process itself.

The essays in Part II, "Intersecting Dramatic Traditions," place Kennedy alongside movements of theatre history with which her plays have affinity. In "Kennedy's Travelers in the American and African Continuum," Bryant-Jackson considers the multicultural origins of Kennedy's dramaturgy, placing her against the traditions of the transcendentalism of Whitman and Emerson, West African ritual, twentieth-century absurdist theatre, and African-American women's writing. He concludes that Kennedy's work for theatre demands the use of multiple and simultaneous critical lenses to appreciate her contribution to the theatre. In "Diverse Angles of Vision: Two Black Women Playwrights," Margaret B. Wilkerson shows that both Lorraine Hansberry and Adrienne Kennedy reveal the "personal self as it engages the social and political world." Although ultimately at question for both playwrights is "what it means to be a black woman," Hansberry's dramaturgical treatment is "journalistic" and "dialectical," whereas Kennedy's is "imagistic" and "poetic."

Elinor Fuchs, in "Adrienne Kennedy and the First Avant-Garde," sees the early plays as mysteria, or mystery plays, a modern form first pioneered in the one-act plays of the international symbolist movement at the turn of the century. Kennedy's hermetic, static dramatic worlds inhabited by doomed characters have much in common with the early plays of Maeterlinck, while her split, prismatic characters can be traced to the symbolist Strindberg of *To Damascus, Part I.* Applying the lens of German expressionism to Kennedy's theatre, William Elwood finds several common denominators; among them are "spirit as primary locus for the dramatic action; mutability of forms; event as subject of articulation, rather than narrative form; the creation of a perception of reality through the orchestration of words, sounds, and images in modal relationships not limited to the scientific laws of cause and effect; manipulation of time." He considers the writings of Kokoschka, Hasenclever, and Toller in analogy with Kennedy's style, and notes a divergence from the German expressionist texture in the decidedly African texture of Kennedy's work.

Robert Scanlan undertakes a structural, formal analysis of Kennedy's *Funnyhouse of a Negro,* eschewing its reputed postmodernist label by demonstrating "a pattern of accumulating sense that...can be seen as a straightforward act of mimesis." He argues for a directorial approach to the play as a "performance sequence," which though composed of three types of segments (stage effects, scenes, and *écriture*) "does not alter the fact that a single action line underlies them all." Scanlan argues that "the material is so potent—especially in the overall historical context in which it emerged—that it is often difficult to keep a strict attention on form alone," yet "Kennedy has governed 'the unity and sequence of events' precisely by her control of the plot."

In Part III, "Changing Boundaries," the challenge of Kennedy's writing is met with critical interpretations of the plays that are also self-reflexive. Kimberly W. Benston's "Locating Adrienne Kennedy: *Prefacing the Subject*" responds semiotically to the "ceaseless self-interrogations" of Kennedy's work as it eludes and deflects application of conceptual or thematic coherence. Looking at Kennedy's prefatorial statements to *People Who Led to My Plays, Adrienne Kennedy in One Act,* and *Deadly Triplets,* Benston takes as his subject Kennedy's "'own' taking of herself as subject in writing." He finds that the prefaces offer "an interminable series of inscriptions upon the act of self-representation" that offer a "meditation on the problems of repetition, quest, dissimulation, and self-origination" that haunt the plays. He asks, "Is the author, then, merely a per-sona, a mask through which language(s) (whose? from where?) speak(s)?"

Elin Diamond's reading of Adrienne Kennedy underscores a difficulty confronted by a reader whose mimetic assumptions of "stable subject position" cannot account for a necessarily syncopated relationship to the plays and the playwright. Diamond insists that she cannot represent Kennedy's truths or the truths of her text, but rather the "otherness constructed for me by her texts." Examining syncopation in and with *Funnyhouse of a Negro*, *The Owl Answers*, *A Movie Star Has to Star in Black and White*, and *People Who Led to My Plays*, Diamond illumines disjunctions of race and gender both in the plays and in critical discourse, "not in black and white, but in black…white."

Rosemary Curb's "(Hetero)Sexual Terrors in Adrienne Kennedy's Early Plays" focuses on Kennedy's decentered subjects "as conscious sites of [heterosexual] invasion and colonization." Considering fear of rape; dualism and guilt; and loss of history, ancestry and identity, Curb's study of *Funnyhouse of a Negro*, *The Owl Answers*, *A Rat's Mass* and *A Lesson in Dead Language* shows how "Kennedy's layering of theatrical devices deconstructs the false simplicities of gender representation" and foregrounds sexuality in a matrix of oppression with race and gender.

In her essay "Kennedy's Body Politic: The Mulatta, Menses, and the Medusa," Jeanie Forte shows how Kennedy's protagonists resist racist assimilation and, at the same time, frame and deconstruct history and perceptions of race. While observing that Kennedy's texts seem "quintessential" in a postmodern age ("fragmented, decentered, nonlinear, marked by marginality and alterity, begging for comprehension and simultaneously defying it"), Forte also notes that Kennedy's protagonists are historicized. They are "not just victims of white oppressive culture," but embody resistance to it through "graphic violence at the specific site," the body.

In "A Spectator Watching My Life," Deborah Geis argues that the tension between a desire for and confrontation with cultural models experienced by Clara in *A Movie Star Has to Star in Black and White* "embodies the ambivalent spectatorial status of the African-American woman whose subjectivity risks being undermined by her identification with an exclusionary cultural apparatus." The inability of Clara's "*histoire* to fit her *discours*" is reflected by "the subversiveness of Kennedy's narrative strategy," namely the "refusal" of the movie images to cohere into a romantic or narrative self.

In an interview with herself, bell hooks examines Kennedy's work, which "problematizes the question of identity and black subjectivity."

Kennedy's focus on the place of black thinkers in a white world, her writing "about the way race informs the construction of a female's identity in a way that few women writers have," and her "creative daring" challenge the audience to expand its vision of what is dramatically possible.

Finally, Part IV of the collection, "Performance as a Collaborative Art," explores Kennedy on the stage. Through a series of interviews with directors, performers, and dramaturgs, Kennedy's plays are discussed as organic works for the theatre. Howard Stein interviews two directors who are central to Kennedy's early work: Michael Kahn, who directed the original *Funnyhouse of a Negro* and the Kennedy adaptations of Euripides commissioned by Juilliard, *Electra* and *Orestes*; and Gaby Rodgers, who directed *A Lesson in Dead Language* and *An Evening with Dead Essex*. In the interview, Kahn speaks of how he was drawn to the imagery and symbolism of *Funnyhouse*, and he also explores "primitive myth" as a source of the power of Kennedy's plays. Gaby Rodgers talks about the complexities of directing *Essex* as a white woman and, in the process, articulates a *lehrstücke* experience that occurred during the production period. Rodgers draws important gender connections that she shared with Kennedy during the production period of *Lesson*. As do all of the theatre artists interviewed here, Rodgers comments on the accumulation and repetition of image in Kennedy's plays, discussing it in a theoretical sense.

In his interview with Paul Bryant-Jackson, Gerald Freedman, director of *Cities in Bezique* and the workshop productions of *The Ohio State Murders*, draws an important connection between Kennedy's writing and recent developments in the theatre, such as the work of Robert Wilson. Freedman also talks about the challenge of concretizing Kennedy's elusive and leitmotific image on the stage from the perspective of action. Freedman and Jackson explore the nonwestern aspects of Kennedy's theatricality and dramaturgy. Finally, Freedman discusses the kind of response he hopes to engender in an audience when he directs a Kennedy play.

Performer and director Billie Allen talks with Paul Bryant-Jackson and Lois Overbeck about the complexities of building a character when conventional approaches to developing a character do not apply. She speaks of the need to physicalize Kennedy's characters: "Understanding [Sarah] created a different kind of body for me because she was very depressed, [and] did not have very much…self-esteem, yet, she has a certain fantasy, and in her fantasy she was chatting with those queens, and [in acting the part] you have your back arched, and you have your fan and your airs, and that was wonderful." Allen also discusses how Kennedy's language allows the character to come alive on the stage. Finally, speaking as a performer and a director of *Funnyhouse of a Negro*, Allen concludes that "these are director's plays."

David Willinger, who directed Kennedy's *Diary of Lights* (1987), writes about his experience directing, with Joseph Chaikin, the adaptation of Adrienne Kennedy's plays, *Solo Voyages* (1985), which featured Robbie McCauley as the single actor. His story of the distillation of passages from *The Owl Answers*, *A Rat's Mass*, and *A Movie Star Has to Star in Black and White* and the evolution of this performance underscores Kennedy's dramaturgy and elaborates the methods of Chaikin's staging of her work. In Willinger's interview with Robbie McCauley, she discusses this production as well as her performances in Kennedy's *A Movie Star Has to Star in Black and White* (directed by Chaikin) and *Cities in Bezique*.

Leaders of contemporary experimental theatre in this country, among them Edward Albee, Herbert Blau, Robert Brustein, Joseph Chaikin, Joseph Papp, Ellen Stewart, and David Wheeler, have regarded Kennedy's talent with appreciation and have encouraged her work. Her writing has found performance among companies or movements that have significantly altered the nature of American theatre: from Barr, Wilder, and Albee's "Theatre 1964" to Chaikin's Open Theater, from La Mama's experimental stage to the Interart Theatre. While the dramaturgy of surreal-expressionist-poetic theatre has placed Kennedy within a theatrical avant-garde in America, her subjects profoundly challenge the problematics of race, culture, gender, and class. Kennedy's writing is not easy nor does it "fit" in any neat arrangement of either theatre or social history, but her plays are compelling for their innovativeness and their honesty.

This collection of criticism encompasses Kennedy's oeuvre for the theatre and explores her innovative dramaturgy in the context of its intersections with traditions, theory, and performance. It is intended to raise questions for further study,[4] even as her writing continues to challenge theatre artists, audiences, and critics.

Notes

1. Adrienne Kennedy, "Growth of Images," *Drama Review* 21 (Dec. 1977): 41.

2. Gerald Freedman, "Director's Notes," New York Shakespeare Festival Public Theatre, *Cities in Bezique*, 1969.

3. Clive Barnes, quoted in "The Week's New Plays," *New York Times*, Jan. 19, 1979, sec. D, 27.

4. Of great use to future studies of Kennedy's work will be the documents acquired in 1992 by the Harry Ransom Research Center at the University of Texas at Austin. Housed there are drafts and notes for all of Kennedy's plays, treatments and proposals for adaptations of her works, and extensive clipping files covering the years 1954–the present.

Acknowledgments

The editors wish to thank the librarians of Columbia University, Emory University, Georgia State University, the University of Georgia, the New York Public Library, the Billy Rose Theatre Collection at Lincoln Center, the Baldwin Burroughs Collection at Spelman College, and the Juilliard School; Serge Moglat, archivist at the New York Shakespeare Festival, the Public Theater; and Doris Pettijohn, archivist at La Mama E.T.C. We appreciate the assistance of the press office of the Mark Taper Forum, the Great Lakes Theater Festival in Cleveland, and the Yale School of Drama.

We give special thanks to the contributors for their insights and for the collaborative spirit with which they engaged in this volume. We are grateful to Edward Albee, Simone Benmussa, Catharine Carver, Terry Cochran, William Coco, Ruby Cohn, Ann Colcord, Johnnetta Cole, Pauline Drake, Martha Fehsenfeld, Robert LaVigny, Ruth Simmons, and David Wheeler for their interest in and support of this project. For help with Italian translations, our thanks to Aurora Pastore; for transcribing interviews, our appreciation to Ruby Pace Byrom. The editors and staff of the University of Minnesota Press have been encouraging and professional in every aspect of the preparation of this book, and we appreciate their guidance.

The editors began their work on Adrienne Kennedy's theatre as members of the National Endowment for the Humanities Summer Seminars for College Teachers (1987): Lois Overbeck attended Herbert Blau's seminar,

"Performance Theory: Modern Drama and Postmodern Theater" (University of Wisconsin—Milwaukee), and Paul Bryant-Jackson attended Howard Stein's seminar, "The American Playwright: 1920–1980" (Columbia University). Paul Bryant-Jackson also thanks the Bush Foundation for two Faculty Research and Development Grants (1989, 1990, Spelman College) and Spelman College for periodic leaves to complete the research.

PART I

The Life in the Work

1

Adrienne Kennedy: An Interview

Paul K. Bryant-Jackson and Lois More Overbeck

Adrienne Kennedy was interviewed by Bryant-Jackson and Overbeck on February 24, 1990, in Cambridge, Massachusetts.

ADRIENNE KENNEDY: Joe [Chaikin] is...very important because when people had totally forgotten about me, in the mid-seventies, Joe was one of the people saying quite extravagant things about me, and working on my plays at his workshops. What he did with *Movie Star* [1976] was a total moving image; it just never stopped moving. It was a masterpiece the way he did it.

LOIS OVERBECK: So it was choreography?

KENNEDY: No. It was the process of the Open Theater, Joe's troupe....Joe and Michael Kahn, as far as I'm concerned, played the biggest role in keeping my morale up and for keeping my work in front of people throughout the seventies. Michael interested Juilliard in commissioning me.

L. O.: What kind of a director was Michael Kahn with your work?

KENNEDY: Very painstaking. And even as a very young director, he had phenomenal insight and vision.

L. O.: Did you talk with him a great deal about the work?

KENNEDY: We talked for two years. You know it took Edward Albee two years to produce *Funnyhouse*. So in those two years, Michael and I had plenty of time to discuss the play. There was really a base there.

L. O.: We were very interested in the dramatization of Sarah, particularly because, in a sense, she stops speaking after the first third of the play,

3

but she is still there, and she "speaks" through the other voices. What is Sarah doing when she is on stage even though she no longer has a speaking part?

KENNEDY: Well that was one of the things that Michael worked on: what Sarah was going to be doing when she was not speaking. He anchored Sarah in her room.

L. O.: In the transition from the Albee workshop production of *Funnyhouse* to its production on the commercial stage, were you making changes?

KENNEDY: I had a script, an original script of *Funnyhouse*. And then when I went into the workshop at the Circle [in the Square], I (literally) took out the word "niggers." And I gave it to Michael. Then as it got closer to the production, he said, "Albee says you have another script, and that's the one we should do. You know, the script you handed in to get in the class." So I did the first one. After that the script remained exactly the same.

PAUL JACKSON: Do you think that...the interchange that you were having in the workshops affected the writing of *The Owl Answers* that you were doing at the time?

KENNEDY: No, I had already written *Owl Answers*.

L. O.: You do write about...the turning point at which you learned that you could take the many parts of the self and use them as characters.... In *Owl Answers*, characters are transformed by just stepping out of their costumes. We wanted to ask you more about the transforming of characters and metamorphosis.

KENNEDY: It's back to childhood—people turning into different people, different characters, feeling that you have a lot of characters inside of you, that's just so much a part of me. I've always been like that. I always just could very easily become a character in the movies or in a book.

L. O.: What about the Duchess of Hapsburg?

KENNEDY: You mean how did I choose her?

L. O.: Is it as parallel to Queen Victoria?

KENNEDY: No. Like most people, I have always been fascinated by royalty. Why are people royal? I mean, that just used to drive me out of my mind, you know. It's in *People Who Led to My Plays*. I saw the movie *Juarez*; it's about the Duchess of Hapsburg. Then my husband and I took a trip to Mexico and we saw Chapultepec Castle, where the Hapsburgs lived. Too, probably because Bette Davis had played her, she interested me.

L. O.: It is interesting, though, that the Duchess of Hapsburg and Queen Victoria did preside with power that was based on colonization.

KENNEDY: There are negative qualities about all of Sarah's personas, except Lumumba.

L. O.: A working title for this collection of essays on your work is *Transforming Margins.*

KENNEDY: Transforming is a great word.

P. J.: What about margins?

KENNEDY: Boundaries, I think boundaries is a good word, too. [To Paul:] I don't know what kind of black world you grew up in,…the kind I grew up in—I respected. But it really was a very rigid childhood. I wasn't allowed to speak, just arbitrarily; I had to speak when I was spoken to. I wasn't allowed to express what I was thinking. I had to say things that were correct in school and at home. So all these people were burning inside of me.

L. O.: We read in *Deadly Triplets* that you were writing a play called *Cities in Bezique.* But the bill done at the Public Theater was another play.

KENNEDY: Joe Papp commissioned me to write [a play]. It was called *Cities in Bezique.* I wrote it when I lived in London. It was horrible. And Joe, a very understanding person said, "Well, I don't really like the play very much. But I'd like to use the title." And he decided to do *The Owl Answers* and *A Beast's Story* and call it *Cities in Bezique.*

L. O.: So you just abandoned the other play?

KENNEDY: I trusted Joe. Joe likes writers. I have abandoned a lot of work: stories, novels, plays. I know that I am in fact working something out. It is not wasted.

L. O.: The several manuscript versions of *A Beast's Story* in the Archives of the Public Theater seem radically different from the one that was published.

KENNEDY: It's because I changed it so. *A Beast's Story* was just a total failure, as far as I'm concerned (the writing, not the production). I just think that I never got the play right. When Samuel French said they wanted to publish it, I just took it and chopped it in two. I am never going to let it get republished.

L. O.: Can you tell us about the production of *Rat's Mass* at La Mama?

KENNEDY: It was a very big success. Seth Allen directed and Mary Alice and Gilbert Price were the leads. Then later Ellen Stewart wanted an opera of it.

P. J.: What became of the opera?

KENNEDY: It ran for six weeks. It had exquisite music that Cecil Taylor wrote. But it didn't work as an opera. It could have been, what do you call that—a cantata. I was never able to make a book out of it that fit the great music that Cecil composed.

L. O.: You did the libretto and he did the music?

KENNEDY: Yes.

L. O.: You loved the music?

KENNEDY: Oh, entirely. The guy is a genius.

L. O.: What about the ballet you did for Jerome Robbins?

KENNEDY: Jerome Robbins had something called Theatre Lab. And I was one of the first writers, I think, that he commissioned. He had liked *Funnyhouse*.

L. O.: What did you write?

KENNEDY: That's when I first started to try to write about Malcolm X. I never finished it. Also I went to live in England.

L. O.: Tell us a bit more about *Sun*.

KENNEDY: The Royal Court asked me to write a play. I had been working on some material from drawings of Leonardo da Vinci. And that's how I wrote *Sun*.

L. O.: Your style is poetic—almost like a concerto, and the visual elements are so complex. Now, under the spell of performance art, perhaps there is a much more ready acceptance of this kind of theatrical performance.

P. J.: One of the things I really admire when I look at your work from a theatrical sense [is that] your plays demand a new acting approach. A lot of people are involved with method acting, and with realistic plays the method works very well—allows you time to prepare the necessary emotional transitions. But in your plays, emotional transitions often come back to back, and so you have to go somewhere else in terms of your ability to become that character.

KENNEDY: I see.

P. J.: And I think, it was really groundbreaking in 1964, in the sense that on many levels, the acting style had to catch up to the form.

KENNEDY: You are making me remember what Joe Chaikin used to talk about. He worked with Robbie [McCauley] on the monologues in the Winter Project, to explore them.

L. O.: Did you see the Paris production of *Funnyhouse*?

KENNEDY: I saw a rehearsal of it.

L. O.: Was the play quite different in French?

KENNEDY: Jean-Marie Serreau put the play in a very small area. Serreau was one of France's great directors. He had a wonderful troupe.

L. O.: There was a dominating white sculpture of Queen Victoria, and otherwise the set seemed very black. How did he direct "Sarah"?

KENNEDY: He wanted her to be still....Serreau loved my writing so much. And he talked about it intensely. And when I met Jean-Louis Barrault, he kissed my hand. [Laughter.]

L. O.: You must have been pleased. To have your work translated—

KENNEDY: *Funnyhouse* had already been on Radio Denmark and the BBC.

L. O.: Were you pleased with the BBC production?

KENNEDY: Oh sure, because Emlyn Williams narrated it.

L. O.: How could it be on the radio without the visual elements?

KENNEDY: He read the stage directions.

P. J.: When you teach playwriting, you have the students keep a journal of their dreams, which is different from a daily journal. May I ask why?

KENNEDY: Oh, I just have the students do things that I did over the years. I kept a dream journal for years.

L. O.: You have said that *Rat's Mass* came out of a dream.

KENNEDY: Definitely. That's in that article, "A Growth of Images." That was one of the strongest dreams I ever had, on a train from Paris to Rome.

P. J.: As the world changes, how does it impact upon the vision of writers, the playwriting student, perhaps yourself?

KENNEDY: I have been more haunted and obsessed in recent years with how the media treats blacks. I think I am even more concerned about that than, say, the Berlin Wall. I'm interested in the Berlin Wall, but on a different level. What I am interested in right now is how in the media, blacks have become very much identified with drugs and a lot of negative things, and I don't remember that being [so] in the forties or fifties or the sixties. I am really worried about that. I don't know how that happened. The average black family is hardworking and has a very high morality.

P. J.: Don't you think that there is an agenda; that is to say, there has to be a relationship between negative portrayal of blacks in the media and how the power structure wants them to be perceived?

KENNEDY: I totally agree. Yes, I certainly do.

P. J.: How then do you look at someone like Spike Lee?

KENNEDY: I am glad that Spike Lee was smart enough to make his movies. I am glad that he was smart enough to see a place for himself. I think that as a black person in America, you almost have to force yourself on society.

L. O.: It is not enough to believe in yourself and what you do?

KENNEDY: I think you have to feel, always, that there is a resistance to you. There is a resistance, and it is never going to let up. It never lets up. I feel that quite strongly. That any black person has to fight twice as hard to achieve anything.

L. O.: How did you come to write *An Evening with Dead Essex*?

KENNEDY: I read about Mark Essex in *Time* magazine [January 22, 1973], and I just got very interested in this quiet little guy who went berserk and shot those people.

L. O.: Did you see him as a victim of the culture?

KENNEDY: A victim and a hero....

L. O.: When did you write the play?

KENNEDY: About 1973.

L. O.: You saw that all these feelings were working inside of him, and then he just exploded?

KENNEDY: Yes. I feel tremendous rage against American society. I feel like Mark Essex. I *still* feel that.

P. J.: I think every African-American person feels like that from time to time.

L. O.: Is it a play trying to get at the essence of Essex?

KENNEDY: We only knew him from the newspaper.

L. O.: The newsclips?

KENNEDY: Yes, the news photographs, [interviews with] his mother. A lot of people liked Mark Essex around that time [1973].

P. J.: They knew where he was coming from.

KENNEDY: Yes.

L. O.: Gaby Rodgers directed the play in New York, and Robert Brustein produced the play at Yale?

KENNEDY: Yes.

L. O.: What happened with that production?

KENNEDY: It didn't work on a big stage. It had worked down in the bottom of the American Place Theatre because it was a rehearsal hall, and the play took place in a rehearsal hall. But when we put it on at Yale Repertory Theatre, it didn't work.

P. J.: In our conversation, you mentioned James Baldwin?

KENNEDY: I liked him a lot....He used his writing like bullets. And his essays meant so much to me when I read them. His essays filled in a lot of gaps...issues I was struggling with.

P. J.: What about *Lancashire Lad*? That seems to be very charming. I would love to see it.

KENNEDY: Oh, that was wonderful. I took sections of Chaplin's autobiography [My *Autobiography*, 1964], and made a theatre piece out of it. It was totally charming. But Lady Chaplin didn't want us to continue with the material.

P. J.: Could you tell us about *Black Children's Day*?

KENNEDY: George Bass asked me to come up and live at Brown for a year to see if I could write a play. That's how *Black Children's Day* came about. He wanted me to write about the history of blacks in Rhode Island. The play is about these children on a Sunday in May—Children's Day. It attempts to use the history of Rhode Island. I was told there were slave tunnels under Providence. The children put on a pageant of black history, and, at the same time,...there is a bombing that occurs in the city. It's too melodramatic. I'm not sure I'd go back to it. I never quite got the language right. But George liked it.

L. O.: You don't have an interest yourself in working more on it?

KENNEDY: No.

L. O.: It seems that you were not completely satisfied with much of the writing that was commissioned.

KENNEDY: That's not true. I was happy with *Electra* and *Orestes* at Juilliard and the Chaplin piece. And I'm happy with *The Ohio State Murders* that I am writing for Jerry Freedman at the Great Lakes Theater Festival.

L. O.: When you work on a commission, do you feel you are writing for someone else instead of yourself?

KENNEDY: No, I feel it's a challenge. It's a good discipline to have something finished at a certain time, and I'm often getting into a different world. For example, I lived in Providence for a year.

L. O.: You are immersing yourself in a different place?

KENNEDY: Yes.

L. O.: In *Deadly Triplets*, you say that you were always writing sketches. Do you think that the sense of the moment and of the scene is innate to your writing? There seems to be nuance and complexity suggested in a few strokes, always implying that there is more to be seen.

KENNEDY: I think that's the way I see life. I'm just haunted by billions of scenes and they are indelible.

P. J.: Do you think that is why, often in your plays, you have the scene go to black so that we might have that focus with the blackout on another scene?

KENNEDY: Maybe, I don't know. That's great. I see, sure. That *is* how I experience it. Yes, that is true.

L. O.: In cinematographic terms, it would be like the switching of the camera eye.

KENNEDY: That's right. But I *don't* experience things (it took me a long time to understand) like a Victorian novel.

L. O.: That is very important, the way of seeing—

KENNEDY: I do see black things all around scenes. It's true, it's really true. [Laughter.] And we're back to the movies again?

P. J.: What about the scenes of childhood that you write about in *People Who Led to My Plays*, the *Now, Voyager* home?

KENNEDY: I always saw rooms. My family existed in scenes, very vivid scenes....I often saw our family, [as] if they were in a play. (I wasn't that aware of that until maybe about ten years ago.)

L. O.: With regard to "scenes," what was the influence of movies, especially French movies?

KENNEDY: I saw French movies when I was a teenager. When I was in high school—a lot of kids took French. I never did. But my friends who took French would take me to these movies. And that is when I first saw *Children of Paradise* and *Devil in the Flesh*.

L. O.: Because you didn't speak French, do you think that you concentrated on the images in these films?

KENNEDY: Perhaps. However, those movies were great. There were subject matters, too, that I had never seen necessarily in American movies. I couldn't articulate it, but they were dealing with things I had never thought of. Later it was Fellini and Bergman.

L. O.: Which Bergman?

KENNEDY: *Through a Glass Darkly*, *Wild Strawberries*,...Antonioni's *L'Avventura*. They gave a validity to what I thought, because these were people in another country.

L. O.: You said that you lived in your imagination; did you feel different as a child?

KENNEDY: I don't think I felt different from my family at all. I was very proud of my family, because my father was in the newspaper a lot. I was very proud of my mother because she was so pretty. I loved my childhood friends. I never felt different.

...My parents were *very* interested in me. Now that I have raised two children, I really see that. They really did *so* many things for me. They were so interested that I did feel sometimes that I was strangled. It was very typical of that time.

P. J.: I remember that my sister and I would sort of hide and watch our parents and their friends when they had parties and club meetings. Did you do that too?

KENNEDY: Oh, sure.

P. J.: That reminds me of Paula Giddings's book [*When and Where I Enter*], and that whole club movement that she talks about which is absolutely integral to African-American women's interaction with each other and society.

KENNEDY: Yes, they had so many clubs.

P. J.: The bridge club was my personal favorite. What was your personal favorite?

KENNEDY: I liked the bridge club also. I watched my mother *preparing* for it. I liked the dishes, the bridge club tablecloths, the phone ringing, and what they all wore. What they served. That was thrilling, truly thrilling. There is a trilogy in that somewhere. [Laughter.] Those people truly fascinate me. I've never been able to capture those people. I admire

those people very much, that generation. Most of them are dead now.
[To Paul]...Don't you admire these people? They are fabulous people.
P. J.: Of course. They were wonderful, with their clubs and their sororities.
KENNEDY: And their formal dances. I don't think that's reached literature,
yet, do you? I wish I could write a book about those women. They were
perfectionists. They were raising children. They seemed to do very well
as wives. They played all those roles.
P. J.: And they even had time for everyone else's kids.
KENNEDY: Yes, they had a lot of time for their neighbor's kids. There was
something about the values of that time. It wasn't just middle-class
blacks. It was in American society. These people were working all the
time...my parents' friends. The wife was either a social worker or a teacher,
mostly a teacher. She was working. These people were keeping black
culture alive. And they were forging ahead financially at the same time.
They were doing both. And that is what is so amazing.

L. O.: Often in looking at your work, people notice the repetition—
KENNEDY: I think that is the spirituals. I love them.
P. J.: You have said that your neighborhood was both black and European.
KENNEDY: My piano teacher was from Warsaw....And Mt. Pleasant was
mainly Italian and black, but there were people from all the central
European countries. Most of the teachers had been born in Europe. I
only had one black teacher, Miss Shook.
L. O.: There was a great sense that education was the way to a better
life?
KENNEDY: We all seemed to have that.
L. O.: Your expectations?
KENNEDY: Tremendous expectations.
P. J.: Wasn't [it] also a part of the African-American experience (one of
the things that you bring out in *People Who Led to My Plays*) that you were
"forced" to be bicultural?
KENNEDY: Oh yes. You were forced, oh, definitely. But there was tremen-
dous respect for DuBois and Langston Hughes...so it wasn't one-sided.
L. O.: Your culture was rich—
KENNEDY: Yes. My parents went to those southern schools—Morehouse,
Atlanta University—these had a tremendous effect. And they took us to
the concerts and banquets. They were involved in achievement, black
achievement.

L. O.: As a young woman with two young children, writing as intensely
as you were—how did you do this?
KENNEDY: As people have remarked over the years, I am a very determined
person. And so, I just stayed up late at night, and I was always tired.

And the miracle is that my children…love my work; they are proud of it. I also feel as if I owe everything to my former husband, Joe Kennedy. He read everything I wrote; he was always encouraging me. He was always talking about the possibilities of things. There is no way I could have done it without him. Because he is the person that released me from this image of myself as simply somebody who might teach the second grade. [Laughter.] It was very important.

L. O.: How do you see your work changing?
KENNEDY: I don't know. I really don't. And I think that's important, that I not know. I always think I am not going to write another word. I don't have anything planned. I don't have any plans at all.

2

People Who Led to My Plays: Adrienne Kennedy's Autobiography

Werner Sollors

> O generations of men,
> look, look on your hopes!
> Look at your lives,
> cut down with failure and crossed with death.
> See, in endless long parade,
> the passing generations go,
> changing places, changing lives.
> The suffering remain.
>
> —Electra and Orestes, (Adrienne
> Kennedy's 1980 adaptation of Euripedes)

> Sometimes I feel like I never been borned,
> Sometimes I feel like I never been borned,
> Sometimes I feel like I never been borned,
> I know my time ain't long, I know my time ain't long
> O—Lawdy, I know my time ain't long.
>
> —"Motherless Child," spiritual

Adrienne Kennedy's highly acclaimed and often enigmatic plays have received various interpretations ever since *Funnyhouse of a Negro* was co-produced by Edward Albee at the East End Theatre in New York City on January 14, 1964, and won the prestigious *Village Voice* Obie award. Undoubtedly Kennedy's dramatic works incorporate materials from the author's life, her readings, and her cultural and social experiences. Kennedy said in an interview, "Autobiographical work is the only thing that interests me, apparently because that is what I do best."[1] The publication of Kennedy's experimental autobiography, *People Who Led to My Plays* (1987), makes possible a discussion of the author and her most important plays in the light of her own extensive autobiographical self-representation.[2] This approach does not set out to delineate (let alone establish) strictly "biographical facts" but to illuminate some specific threads out of which her work was spun.

People Who Led to My Plays, regarded by Ishmael Reed as a "new form of black autobiography," is an unusually stylized memoir. The book is arranged in a loosely chronological order and divided into six sections with such titles as "Elementary School, 1936–1943" or "Marriage and Motherhood, 1953–1960," yet there are only occasional stretches of straightforward first-person-singular narrative, and most of the work—to which the title of Kennedy's "musical without songs," *Diary of Lights* (1987), would be equally suited—can be described as a series of flashes of vignettes. Their format is always that of a reflection elicited by a topic (e.g., "*Nkrumah's face*"), and sometimes a sequence of themes is introduced by the phrase "*I remembered....*" The subjects of the various entries include family members, friends, imaginary characters, names of places, books, movies, and things. The sentences, paragraphs, or pages—about such topics as animal crackers, Harry Belafonte, Marlon Brando as rebel, Nat King Cole, Dick and Jane, Emerson, Anne Frank, Ben Franklin, Grandfather, Greek heroines, Rita Hayworth, Hitler, Langston Hughes, Jesus, the man in the moon, Monet, Mother's dreams, "Negroes," paper dolls, Socrates, the United States Army, Utrillo, West Africa, "White people," Richard Wright, and Zombies—form fragments of a great twentieth-century confession. At times, the observations are reminiscent of haiku or of William Carlos Williams; Kennedy writes, "*My mother and my face*: My face as an adult will always seem to be lacking because it is not my mother's face" (51). She remembers a history teacher: "*Mr. David*: Often I thought of his saying, 'All events are connected'" (81). Or she comments tersely, "*People in the constellations*: Wonder" (16). The varied entries give us a fuller understanding of the complex personal-familial, cultural, and sociohistorical forces that shaped the writer's consciousness.

Kennedy, who was born Adrienne Hawkins on September 13, 1931, in Pittsburgh, sketches memories of a family that transcended the American racial boundary between black and white and that retained strong connections between urban North and rural South. Vignettes of Italian-American schoolfriends and of the small frame or brick double houses in her neighborhood, for example, illustrate the mixed Jewish, Polish, Italian, and black section of Cleveland, where Kennedy's parents had moved from the town of Montezuma, Georgia. During her childhood years Kennedy and her brother Cornell took many train trips back to Georgia, and she remembers having to travel by Jim Crow car south of Cincinnati. She mentions that, like most "Negro" families in the town, her folks had both black and white relatives (22). Kennedy's maternal grandfather was a rich white peach grower[3] who told his granddaughter "stories about people in the town, both white and black" (20). Her maternal grandmother had died when her mother was three. Kennedy was particularly fascinated by stories of her mother Etta who—like Jane Eyre—had been sent away to boarding school. Other stories came from her father, C. W. Hawkins, a Morehouse College–educated social worker, and her hard-working, religious, black paternal grandmother, as well as her aunts, cousins, and neighbors. In one vignette, for example, she remembers spending some time with her brother at the house of a sixteen-year-old, Sarah Clara, who let Kennedy smell perfume and made her daydream about being a grown-up woman (35); and in other sketches she recollects small events associated with a "distant" cousin (23) or a great-uncle (24), often against the beautiful background of the southern landscape.

The earliest influences from the larger culture that Kennedy reflects upon come from religious experiences that are viewed aesthetically in retrospect. Several church visits north and south left very deep impressions. When, as an adult, she finds a reproduction of Giotto's fresco of the marriage of Joseph and Mary (from the Cappella Scrovegni at Padua), she thinks back on the holy processions she had imagined when walking with her "grandmother to the white wooden church...the golden red road, the blue sky, the neighbors walking ahead of us" (34), and henceforth associates Giotto's colors, the Georgia landscape, and the pictures on Sunday school cards (88). She remembers both parents reading aloud from the Bible, in which the psalms and the nativity seemed to play an especially important role. During her school years in Cleveland, Kennedy also played Mary in a fourth-grade Christmas play. She recites some of her prayers, but also remembers many nursery rhymes and fairy tales (The Pied Piper of Hamelin, Sleeping Beauty, and Snow White, which she also saw in the Disney movie version).

American popular culture exerted a great formative influence upon Kennedy, as it molded a generation of modern American writers from Donald Barthelme, Maxine Hong Kingston, and Ishmael Reed to Robert Coover, Toni Morrison, and Woody Allen. The whole Kennedy family enjoyed and laughed about comic strips such as Little Orphan Annie, Blondie, and Bringing Up Father and radio programs like the Jack Benny show; the children also tuned in to "Let's Pretend."

Going to the movies was perhaps the most important pastime. Kennedy writes about many, many Hollywood films of the 1930s and 1940s, from magical movies such as The Blue Bird (1940) and The Wizard of Oz (1939) to horror films like Dracula (1931), Frankenstein (1931), The Mummy (1932), or The Invisible Man (1933), among which Lon Chaney in The Wolf Man (1941) stood out to her as "the single most frightening movie monster" (16). She remembers enjoying melodramas such as Mildred Pierce

(1945), which invited her to imagine that she was the hard-working mother's (Joan Crawford's) evil daughter (Ann Blythe), or *Leave Her to Heaven* (1945), with the memorable scene in which an obsessive woman (Gene Tierney) drowns her husband's crippled brother in a beautiful lake. The playwright recalls being intrigued by films of psychological interest like *Gaslight* (1943), in which a wife (played by Ingrid Bergman) is driven insane by her husband, or *The Seventh Veil* (England, 1945), in which a concert pianist (Ann Todd) who cannot make up her mind which of three men to marry masks "her hidden thoughts, feelings and personae" (49). Political films like *Mrs. Miniver* (1942) and *Hitler's Children* (1943) inspired her to imagine the fearful scenario of the Nazis' coming to Cleveland.

She was fascinated by and identified with Bette Davis, in *The Little Foxes* (1941), for example, based on the play by Lillian Hellman, who was, significantly, "a woman and a playwright" (90). Most influential for Kennedy's work were Bette Davis's roles as Carlotta Maria Amalia, the Hapsburgian Empress of Mexico, in William Dieterle's lavish film *Juarez* (1939), and as Charlotte Vale, a mentally disturbed daughter of a good Boston family who goes on an ocean journey in Irving Rapper's *Now, Voyager* (1942). Some later films that left a mark in her plays are *A Place in the Sun* (1951) and *Viva Zapata!* (1952).

"Hollywood" was part of an imaginary cultural community in which Kennedy matured. She started reading the movie journal *Modern Screen* as a child during one of the visits in Montezuma; when her mother disapproved she hid the magazine under her mattress, where she also kept a secret diary, written "backwards," in code. As a teenager she had stacks of *Modern Screen* in her room and found out about "famous people" and about how stars were "discovered." To her, her mother looked like "a combination of Lena Horne and Ingrid Bergman" (50). Her mother told her that she had chosen her daughter's first name after the actress Adrienne Ames (10). After seeing *The Constant Nymph* (1944), in which Charles Boyer loves Joan Fontaine, who plays the part of Tessa, Kennedy secretly called herself Tessa "for a summer" (49). The book that Kennedy mentions most frequently in her memoir is *Jane Eyre*; the movie version, with Orson Welles as Rochester (1943), fascinated her so much that she not only dressed up like Joan Fontaine in a drama class and acted Jane's part (62–63) but also wrote Welles a fan postcard and received an autographed picture from the studio (44).

Kennedy's memoir also stresses that she grew up with significant exposure to Afro-American literature, music, and culture. She mentions that her father, whom she later associates with Patrice Lumumba (119), took her to a performance by Paul Robeson, read her poetry by Paul Laurence Dunbar, and told her stories of African-American heroes and heroines like W. E. B. Du Bois or Mary Bethune. Her mother "often sang when she cooked Sunday-morning breakfast: particularly 'Sometimes I Feel like a Motherless Child'" (97)

While Kennedy writes about the significance of successful black role models in the arts (such as Billie Holiday, Josephine Baker, Dorothy Dandridge, and Lena Horne, and later, Gwendolyn Brooks and Lorraine Hansberry), she sometimes uses the term "Negroes" or "White People" in quotation marks, in order to suggest the somewhat hypothetical nature of "race" as a category during her process of socialization. For example:

> It seemed that we as "Negroes" sang of sorrow. It seemed strange. In the church in Georgia that my cousins and I drove in the carriage to, the songs were even sadder. They were moans. Why did we "sing" of sorrow? (97)

Or :

> "*Negroes*": We were underdogs, and underdogs must fight in life. (11)

Or :

> "*White People*": They tried to hold you back. That implied a great challenge existed in life. (14)

She writes that a schoolteacher discouraged her from contemplating the career of a journalist because of her color. She recalls racial discrimination not only on Southern trains, but also in her Ohio State University dormitory. As much of her work demonstrates, she approached the complex web of black-white relations that extended into her own family honestly, without embellishments, but also without facile generalizations. The writer James Alan McPherson observed that many black Americans in Los Angeles may "have been just as much influenced by Hollywood's 'star system' of the forties and fifties as they have been by society's response to the color of their skins."[4] In its combined emphasis on the realms of popular culture and of race, *People Who Led to My Plays* suggests that McPherson's observation may apply to non-Californians as well.

It is noteworthy that Kennedy did not perceive the imaginary world of popular culture and the harsh social reality of American race relations in the World War II period as if they were necessarily at odds with each other. Different from authors like LeRoi Jones/Amiri Baraka, who, in the play J-E-L-L-O (1970), subversively identified with the black chauffeur Rochester (Eddie Anderson) against Jack Benny and his whole cast in order to make a political statement, Kennedy writes how her whole family had the happiest times listening to the Jack Benny show: "We all sat around the Philco radio on Sunday night, eating Neapolitan ice cream with its three flavors, and laughed at Jack, Rochester, Mary, Phil, Dennis and Carmichael, Jack

Benny's bear" (29). Her comment on *Gone with the Wind* (1939) is similarly poignant in its absence of racial politics, though not of irony: she merely notes that Leslie Howard "had an English accent. How wonderful!" (16). Yet she also writes the entry "*Sabu, Turhan Bey*: Two people in the movies who were *not* white" (8), and she remembers looking out of the dirty windows of a Jim Crow car, while at the same time clutching an issue of *Modern Screen* with a Clark Gable cover in her hand (33).

The entries about Kennedy's high-school and college years focus on how she intensified her intellectual pursuits, studied Latin, and read world literature from Greek tragedy, Plato, Virgil, Dante, and English Romantic poetry to Flaubert, Tolstoi, Chekhov, and Lorca. She remembers how her Aunt Martha, who stayed with the Hawkins family in Cleveland for two years, introduced her to Shakespeare. After seeing a performance of Tennessee Williams's *The Glass Menagerie* at the Karamu Theatre[5] in Cleveland when she was sixteen, she became increasingly interested in drama and the theatre, and read Williams, Arthur Miller, Eugene O'Neill, and Thornton Wilder.

Alluding to *Blue Bird*, the first film she mentions having seen, she writes about being with her future husband, Joseph C. Kennedy: "When my fiancé and I were together I knew I had found the Blue Bird of Happiness" (72). They were married in 1953, but her husband was soon drafted and sent to Korea. He later went to graduate school in New York; after the birth of their first son, the young mother studied creative writing with John Selby at Columbia University's School of General Studies and wrote unpublished autobiographical fiction as well as a play entitled *Pale Blue Flowers*. Kennedy became especially keen on modernism in literature, music, and the arts and read T. S. Eliot, Ezra Pound, Marcel Proust, Virginia Woolf, and a little Gertrude Stein; looked at paintings by Van Gogh, Cézanne, Picasso, and Pollock; and listened to Debussy, Miles Davis, Thelonious Monk, and Charlie Mingus (though she also comments upon Beethoven, Chopin, Puccini, Verdi, and Wagner, and uses Haydn in her second play, *The Owl Answers*). The modernist themes that elicit many of her observations are alienated artists, family drama, dreams, madness, and suicide; while the formal features to which she seems most attracted are fragmentation, nonlinear narrative, noncausal representation, and multilayered imagery.

Once she began to think of herself as a writer, many of her readings and other cultural experiences directed her toward her own life and her own voice. In response to William Faulkner she writes, "He reinforced what I, as a child, had felt in my visits to Georgia to see my grandparents: that the South was a strange mesh of dark kinship between the races" (98). Listening to Duke Ellington, she gets inspired to find the "immense poetry inside [her] life as an American Negro" (100), and seeing Picasso's painting *Guernica*, "the concept of placing [her] characters in a dream domain seemed more and more real to [her]" (100). The general reception of cultural materials has given way to particular appropriations and adaptations.

In her memoir, the years 1960 and 1961 are treated in the sixth and last section, entitled "A Voyage," and viewed as the artistic turning point of her life. She traces her breakthrough to 1960, when she was bound for Britain on the *Queen Elizabeth*, remembered Bette Davis's curative ocean journey in the film *Now, Voyager*, and was inspired to write the short story "Because of the King of France" on the ocean liner's stationery. What she remembers most about her writing was that in this story she experimented with different simultaneous settings and a new logic. It became her first published work and appeared in the tenth issue of the West African journal *Black Orpheus*, edited by Ulli Beier (116, 120–21)—under the pen name "Adrienne Cornell," her brother's first as the author's last name.

At this point Kennedy mentions reading African writers such as Wole Soyinka and Chinua Achebe, who were also being published in *Black Orpheus* (121). Under the entry "West Africa" she writes that during her stay in Ghana and Liberia she "started the lines of two plays, *Funnyhouse of a Negro* and *The Owl Answers*, and the lines had a new power, a fierce new cadence" (119). In the paragraph dedicated to "*Africans or the masks*" she explains, "Not until I bought a great African mask from a vendor on the streets of Accra, of a woman with a bird flying through her forehead, did I totally break from realistic-looking characters" (121). An earlier vignette had suggested that in Florence, at the Piazzale Donatello (the location of the English Cemetery), the memory of the Georgia neighbor Sarah Clara returned, and that Kennedy named two of her heroines Sarah and Clara (35).

The strands of Adrienne Kennedy's life and of her influences—from Georgia and Cleveland, Africa and Europe, from popular, Afro-American, and high modernist sources—became raw materials in her hands and were shaped into her most famous plays.[6] Reading *People Who Led to My Plays* not only opens many possible ways of reinterpreting Kennedy's one-act plays, but also offers insights into the open-endedness and unpredictability of literary influences.

Notes

I am grateful to Adrienne Kennedy for correspondence and conversations, to Alice Quinn for the galleys of *People Who Led to My Plays*, and to the late Nathan I. Huggins and to other members of the W. E. B. Du Bois Institute colloquium for comments.

1. "A Growth of Images," interview transcribed and edited by Lisa Lehman, *Drama Review* 21 (1977): 42.

2. Page references to *People Who Led to My Plays* (New York: Knopf, 1987) are given parenthetically in the text. For a new reading of Kennedy's major plays in the light of her autobiography, see my "Owls and Rats in the American Funnyhouse: Adrienne Kennedy's Drama," *American Literature* 63.3 (September 1991): 507–32.

3. In *People Who Led to My Plays*, Kennedy does not explicitly identify her grandfather by race (29); she did so, however, in an interview of March 1, 1975. See Yemi Ogunbiyi, "New Black Playwrights in America, 1960–1975: Essays in Theatrical Criticism" (Ph.D. diss., New York University, 1976), 130.

4. "On Becoming an American Writer," in *Varieties of Black Experience at Harvard*, ed. Werner Sollors, Thomas A. Underwood, and Caldwell Titcomb (Cambridge, Mass.: Harvard University Department of Afro-American Studies, 1986), 150.

5. Ogunbiyi, 129.

6. Kennedy's latest works for the stage, *The Ohio State Murders* and *She Talks to Beethoven*, show the more overtly political side of Kennedy's dramatic work, while continuing her familiar division of a lyrical persona into antithetical selves, a Nkrumah and a Beethoven, a Thomas Hardy and a Frantz Fanon, whereas the lyrical monologue, *The Film Club*, specifically continues Kennedy's exploration of the power of popular culture, the movies in particular and Bette Davis most especially.

3

The Life of the Work: A Preliminary Sketch

Lois More Overbeck

There are no consolidated archives of Adrienne Kennedy's manuscripts or of the production history of her plays. Many of the plays had their first appearance in workshop productions with brief runs and without critical notice. Experimental theatres seldom had resources to record the development of their productions when funding for their season or even the next play was a priority. When available, programs, reviews, and interviews have been consulted to gain a sense of production values and directorial choices. While these are inadequate resources for a comprehensive stage history, the resulting overview will suggest directions for further research.[1]

Kennedy indicates that both *Funnyhouse of A Negro* and *The Owl Answers* were completed manuscripts when she applied to Edward Albee's Circle in the Square workshop,[2] and that the script of *Funnyhouse* produced in the workshop was the original. In an interview, performer Billie Allen (see chapter 18) comments on her sense of Kennedy's writing as "finished": "It is all there, and it is all done." With Kennedy, as with any writer, there are manuscripts that were written and abandoned or not produced,[3] or produced in workshop but not published (e.g., *Diary of Lights*, *Boats*), or performed in workshop and then altered by others (e.g., *The Lennon Play:* or *In His Own Write*). Other works were published initially in a journal or anthology but not republished in the author's collected plays (e.g., *A Beast Story*, *An Evening with Dead Essex*).

Even if manuscripts and variants of Kennedy's plays were available for study, a script alone would not tell us the nature of the production, because dramaturgical improvisation brings the nuances and the suggestive possibility of images and nonlinear structures to life in performance. Music, though seldom designated in the script, is often integral to production values (Sun, She Talks to Beethoven, the adaptation Solo Voyages), and musical forms even generate theatrical shape. Visual effects are visceral evocations of subliminal/emotional realities (the massive sculpture of Queen Victoria in Funnyhouse of a Negro in the Théâtre Odéon production, the rotating stage of The Owl Answers in the 1969 production at the Public Theater, the simultaneous layers of reality expressed by multiple levels of staging in The Owl Answers, the projections of An Evening with Dead Essex, the dominant color in the set of Orestes and Electra).

It is clear from interviews with directors and actors that Kennedy's plays are open to a directorial hand, as indicated in Michael Kahn's comment (see chapter 15) that he did not stage the jungle scene in Funnyhouse, though he would today, and in Gerald Freedman's note that Kennedy's plays require "new techniques and new answers."[4] In some cases the final form of the play varies considerably from the original. Differing slightly in title (A Beast Story), the published version of A Beast's Story is not the same as the one indicated by the prompt books and acting scripts when it was performed as part of Cities in Bezique at the Public Theater (1969); in production the number of beasts multiplied, and the beasts' costumes indicated by the text were dropped in favor of rehearsal clothes (see interview with Gerald Freedman in chapter 17).[5] There are also changes from script to performance that reflect variations in the playing space, conceptualization of a character, or casting; there were differences in the production of An Evening with Dead Essex in the small rehearsal space of the American Place Theatre and the larger stage at Yale, and differences between the original production of Funnyhouse of a Negro and that directed by David Wheeler at the Theater Company, Boston. Complete records of these productions and their variations would be desirable, because they would offer interpretive illuminations of the plays.

The interviews published in this collection are important precisely because of the suggestions that they provide about production values. Of course, memory cannot be as comprehensive as a director's production notes, complete photographs, or a videotape of a production. Reviews do provide a glimpse of staged images, howbeit limited by personal and cultural biases of interpretation.

Kennedy's early writing is largely unpublished. Pale Blue Flowers (1955), a one-act play modeled on Tennessee Williams's The Glass Menagerie, has not been published or performed. In an interview with Kathleen Betsko, Kennedy describes working on it for two years: "I had written the play in a course at the New School taught by Mildred Kunner," who entered it in a play contest in Chapel Hill, North Carolina; it didn't win. She then sent it to Williams's agent, Audrey Wood, "who wrote me a long letter which said she couldn't take me as a client, but that she thought I was very talented. That was a great encouragement to me."[6] Kennedy's first published writing, "Because of the King of France," appeared under the name Adrienne Cornell in *Black Orpheus: A Journal of African and Afro-American Literature*.[7] The short story about the vicissitudes of Sidney Carter as viewed by a middle-class young woman, the writer, prefigures the themes and narrative shifts of the plays that follow it: racial exclusion and punishment for loving across racial barriers, artistic gifts expressed within the Eurocentric traditions, self-hatred and deformity, class discrimination, and imaginary conversations with historical figures.

In *Deadly Triplets*, Kennedy describes submitting *Funnyhouse of a Negro* to Edward Albee's workshop at the Circle in the Square in application to the workshop; Michael Kahn called her later to say "Edward Albee liked your play very much[;] you have been selected to be in the workshop" (DT, 100-101). Although Kennedy indicates (see interview in chapter 1) that the play done in the workshop production was the original version, she felt that her play was too revealing and, at one point, had decided to drop out of the class. She reports Albee's response: "A playwright is someone who lets his guts out on the stage and that's what you've done in this play....It's your decision" (DT, 101).[8] The play was done first at the Circle in the Square and then again at the Actor's Studio (1964), directed by Michael Kahn, with Diana Sands, Fran Bennett, Lynne Hamilton, Yaphet Kotto, and Andre Gregory in the cast.

Kennedy says that she wrote *Funnyhouse of a Negro* in 1960, "when I was exactly twenty-nine," and that the play reflected fourteen months spent in Europe, Ghana, and Nigeria:

> My writing became sharper, more focused and powerful, and less imitative. It was a tremendous turning point....I would say that almost every image in *Funnyhouse* took form while I was in West Africa where I became aware of masks....I discovered a strength in being a black person and a connection to West Africa.[9]

Funnyhouse of a Negro opened at the East End Theatre on January 14, 1964, produced by Theatre 1964 (Richard Barr, Clinton Wilder, and Edward Albee), with performances twice a night (closing February 9, 1964).[10] The play was directed by Michael Kahn; settings and lighting were by William Ritman and costumes were by Willa Kim. The role of Sarah was played by Billie Allen (see interview in chapter 18); other actors were Cynthia Belgrave, Ellen Holly, Gus Williams, Norman Bush, Ruth Volner, Leonard Frey, and Leslie Rivers. In describing the play as "the hallucinated horrors that torment the last hours of a Negro girl," Howard Taubman acknowledged the power of the play, saying that Kennedy "digs unsparingly into Sarah's aching psyche." He also describes the sideshow figures of *Funnyhouse*, positioned on either side of the stage, and the presence of a statue of Queen Victoria, and elaborates: "Her other companions [the Duchess of Hapsburg, Queen Victoria, Jesus, and Patrice Lumumba] are the impalpable figments of her imagination...that become corporeal on the stage. She speaks the brief litany of her fears and hatred and despair and her ghosts often repeat and mock her."[11]

Edith Oliver sketches the elegance of "elaborate period costumes of white" with "white or gray masklike makeups" worn by the figures of Victoria, Hapsburg, and Jesus; she contrasts the image of Lumumba, black and dressed "in tatters"; she notes that the Funnyhouse man and woman are in "clown makeups" and move with "marionette gestures." Although Sarah's monologue supplies the play's narrative, Oliver notes that "she is in no shape to give it" and that Sarah's "obsession with hair" parallels the "obsession with grief and guilt over her treatment of her father, whom she has driven away because of his blackness." She comments that Kahn's expressionist attempt to "reproduce the girl's madness and anguish...seems appropriate" and that *Funnyhouse* is a "strong and original" first play.[12]

Although George Oppenheimer saw the play as bad theater of the absurd and a dismal "charade," a "non-play" with a "non-plot,"[13] Taubman concluded, "If nothing much happens according to conventional theatrical tenets, a relatively unknown territory is explored and exposed."[14] Writing for *Nation*, Harold Clurman underscores the uniqueness of Kennedy's voice:

> The play...embraces far more than plays of similar theme when they are couched in terms of pathetic appeals for "tolerance" and fair play. The torment of the colored girl in Funny House [sic] of a Negro parallels that of all people who suffer the pathology of minorities. Their number extends far beyond the boundaries of race.[15]

Funnyhouse of a Negro was awarded an Obie for "most distinguished play" in May 1964. The play was produced by the Theater Company of Boston beginning March 11, 1965. Directed by David Wheeler, this production conceptualized Sarah, played by Barbara Ann Teer, as a powerful female; Gustav Johnson enacted the role of Lumumba, with settings by Robert Allen and lighting by Neville Powers. Wheeler's production em-

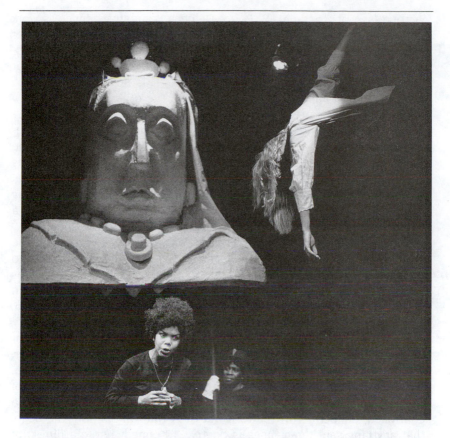

Toto Bissainthe in the Petit Odéon (Paris) production of *Drôle de baraque* (*Funnyhouse of a Negro*), March 1968, Jean-Marie Serreau, director. Photograph courtesy of Agence de Presse Bernand.

phasized the mythic element of the play, building to "an unbearable crescendo"; strips of black muslin were hung at angles, so that props and figures seemed to emerge from the nightmare.[16] Kevin Kelly said that Wheeler "captured the focal fear at the heart of the play and exposed it with an unfaltering sense of drama."[17]

Funnyhouse was presented as *Drôle de baraque* on a double bill with Sam Shepard's *Chicago* at the Petit Odéon in Paris under the direction of Jean-Marie Serreau on March 8, l968 (see DT, 115-16). Adapted by Augy Hayter, the play featured Toto Bissainthe, a Haitian, as Sarah and Douta Seck as Lumumba. "The play expresses [Sarah's] dreams, her fantasies, her nightmares brought on by the horror of her estranged condition in a white world."[18] Central to the production was a huge white bust of Queen

Victoria (see photograph). B. Poirot-Delpech compares Kennedy's work to Genet's *The Blacks* and O'Neill's *Emperor Jones*.[19] Jean-Jacques Gautier emphasized the production's grating music, which underlines the "spasmodic monologue" in which Sarah "kills her father. It is true. It is not true." He finds the production ambiguous—"it is nearly impossible to know who is who and who does what."[20] On the other hand, the review in *Combat* is very appreciative: "Showing a young black [woman] imprisoned in the complexes and conditioning that American society has created in her," Kennedy's theatre has "fantastic life (and so real at the same time)"; it is "theatre that has a power to attack that is, finally, as sure as that of LeRoi Jones." Supported by jazz rhythms and physical movement, "the black American problem is evoked in an excruciating way."[21] The review in the *Journal de Genève* said of the production, "In a dance macabre rhythm and full of a poignant poetry, the spectacle... astonishes with its content and its form, with the ensemble as with the least detail, with its rhythm where the music plays in counterpoint to the role of the broken and cruel world in which we live."[22] And Jacques Lemarchand wrote, "Adrienne Kennedy defines an aspect of the American problem with great simplicity in reverie, without proposing solution, without preaching sufferance or reconciliation."[23]

Funnyhouse of a Negro was presented by the English Stage Society at the Royal Court on Sunday, April 28, 1968, with *A Lesson in Dead Language*; there it was directed by Rob Knights with Sheila Wilkinson as Sarah. Michael Billington wrote, "Unfortunately the phantasmagoric nature of the action...only serves to confuse....Miss Kennedy's language has a controlled, deliberate rhythm to it but even this suffers from the belief that anything said three times is poetry."[24] Kennedy wrote a filmscript of *Funnyhouse of a Negro* with Pablo Feraro in 1971; it was not produced.

Kennedy had written *The Owl Answers* by the time she submitted *Funnyhouse of a Negro* to the Edward Albee playwriting workshop (see interview in chapter 1). The original production by Lucille Lortel was at the White Barn Theater, Westport, Connecticut, on August 29, 1965, as a benefit for the Free Southern Theater; it was also performed at the Theatre de Lys in New York as part of the ANTA Matinee Theater Series on December 14, 1965. Directed by Michael Kahn, the production starred Ellen Holly as "She who is Clara." Like *Funnyhouse of a Negro*, *The Owl Answers* "takes place on different levels of consciousness," said Kahn. "She has several father figures...and several mothers,...and historical figures...who appear as passengers on the subway and as jailors."[25] Kennedy points to personal experience as embedded in the play. Living in Ghana, she would hear owls in the trees, and particularly at night "the owls sounded as if they were in the very center of the room"; memory of the owl sounds mingle with fear, as Kennedy recounts listening to them while confined to bed with a difficult pregnancy. "In a few months I would create a character who would turn into an owl" (*People*, 122).

When produced by the New York Shakespeare Festival (Joseph Papp), *Owl Answers* was paired with Kennedy's *A Beast's Story* under the title, *Cities in Bezique*. Actually, *Cities in Bezique* was the title of a play that Adrienne Kennedy had written in 1967–68; it had been commissioned by Joseph Papp for the New York Shakespeare Festival, but Papp found it "too chaotic and abstract" and instead used this title for the two one-act plays, *Owl Answers* and *A Beast's Story* (see DT, 118). As Kennedy indicates in the interview (chapter 1), Joseph Papp said, "Well, I don't really like the play very much. But I'd like to use the title." Gerald Freedman, who directed the program at the Public Theater, describes the original *Cities in Bezique* in the interview with Paul Bryant-Jackson (chapter 17):

> A lot of it was images....I thought I could do a wonderful piece of it in a darkened room with a slot where one person could look through, and I could change images....[However,] it didn't become practical for the Public Theater to do it. It would have been a wonderful performance piece.... Bezique is a card game...of chance and so her text actually had pictures in it. And cards turned over....I would have loved to do it, but I don't know a theatre company that could afford to do it.[26]

The production of *The Owl Answers* and *A Beast's Story* as *Cities in Bezique* ran for sixty-seven performances at the Public Theater, January 4 to March 2, 1969. Gerald Freedman directed, with settings by Ming Cho Lee, costumes by Theoni V. Aldredge, lighting by Martin Aronstein, and incidental music by John Morris. "She who is Clara Passmore who is the Virgin Mary who is the Bastard who is the Owl" was played by Joan Harris; Cynthia Belgrave played the mother(s); Moses Gunn, the father(s); Henry Baker, the white bird; and Paul Benjamin, the Negro Man in *The Owl Answers*.

Reviewers noted the similarities to *Funnyhouse*: both plays explored a "lightskinned Negro woman's mental anguish and search for a sense of identity."[27] Although beginning in realism, *The Owl Answers* introduced other dimensions of time and space. Lee Silver wrote of Clara as "a nice student in tweed skirt and sweater, calmly reading through the screeching noises of the underground," and Richard P. Cooke describes transmutation into the surreal: "Through the subway aisles parade creatures of [Clara's] imagination—Shakespeare, Chaucer, William the Conqueror, Anne Boleyn, along with some Negroes in modern dress. White people are represented by masks."[28] As Richard Watts observed, "Past and present merge, characters shift from being one person to another, and time is telescoped."[29]

Comparing Kennedy's double bill to "the surrealist school of films of the 30's," George Oppenheimer found "kinship in manner and mood," if not symbolic clarity, with Cocteau.[30] John Simon describes the variety of settings: the Tower of London, St. Paul's Cathedral [Chapel], and a Harlem hotel room, noting that place and time shift continually and characters double; he describes "a large white papier-mâché bird, which flaps its wings at arbitrary intervals," hovering above the stage and "a large black man clad in white feathers who occasionally speaks."[31] Labeling Cities in Bezique as a "happening," Steve Tennen wrote:

> [Freedman] has molded the plays into nightmarish, almost ritualistic forms. Through precisioned movement of his cast, their vocal quality and facial expressions, he has removed them from the human element and left only the shadow of the supernatural.
>   Theoni Aldredge's costumes & masks…add to this strange dimension. Ming Cho Lee's set is dark and forbidding, and, combined with John Morris' music and sound, it becomes rattingly eerie.[32]

In what he calls "the female face of tragedy," J. Lance Ermatinger says that Kennedy "aims a poet's eye along a surgeon's scalpel, and she penetrates layer after layer of the white/black protagonist….The birds represent both the Holy Spirit of Christianity and the *coq blanc* of Voodoo that traces its flight back from Harlem to Haiti to Dahomey in West Africa….[Cities in Bezique] immolates the white consciousness in a vortex of the Black Context." Ermatinger also offers comment on audience response to the plays at the Public Theater:

> The witnesses are completely involved, although there is no physical invasion of the audience. Neither black nor white can deny the power of Adrienne Kennedy's fierce poetry….Yet both react with confused anger.
>   What provokes this anger? I think it is the absence of the doctrinaire in Bezique. The White Liberals are offered none of the clichés that bring cold comfort to our day of confrontation. The Black Militants, on the other hand, hear no sizzling slogans. All witness only the story of one human being in a context as richly personal as it is beautifully black.[33]

A Beast's Story (1965) was commissioned by Herbert Blau and Jules Irving for Lincoln Center but was not produced until its performance as a part of Cities in Bezique, with Amanda Ambrose as the Woman, Moses Gunn as the Man Beast, and Robbie McCauley, Theta Tucker, and Camilie Yarbrough as the Girl Beasts. The published text indicates a single Girl Beast, whereas the production at the Public Theater had three.[34]

Understood by Clive Barnes as a "word image," the play evokes sexual fear and repression as it enacts the rape of a young girl by a man whom she "identifies with her father," a subsequent stillbirth, and "the murder of the young man with an ax."[35] Cooke writes, "[The] young woman's personality is projected by three other women"; they are "painting the colors of the sun, to represent the feelings experienced on the day [the] girl murders the man who violated her."[36]

"Roles seem to be interchangeable between girl beasts, while woman, human woman beast, man beast and other beasts enact an allegory... [with] a haunting quality," wrote George Oppenheimer.[37] Walter Kerr described his impressions:

> All roles blur, blend, divide and recombine while two doves—one white, one black beneath the white—flutter moldy wings overhead and the heavens light up with fingerpainted child's pictures of houses, robins, bloodstains, and ebony suns. Sounds, sights, gestures recur as in a dream that won't move forward...back.[38]

Gerald Freedman discusses (in chapter 17) the evolution of the production he directed, with particular reference to the Beast figures. David Marash indicated that the two plays were "worlds apart," citing *The Owl Answers* as "the best play off-...or for that matter on Broadway this year" but *A Beast's Story* as "beastly, boring and banal."[39] Martin Gottfried called the plays "unjustified indulgence," but Richard Watts said, "If what [Kennedy] is saying is at times difficult to decipher,...she is giving us important and moving insights into the minds and emotions of deeply tormented people."[40] Although Walter Kerr felt that the spectator was left outside of the plays and that in them "nothing is drawn to a center, distilled, condensed to leave a residue," there was "a spare, unsentimental intensity about the work that promises to drive a dagger home some day."[41] On the other hand, despite their expressionism, Edith Oliver noted that the plays "command and hold one's unflagging attention."[42] *Cities in Bezique* was published in 1969;[43] only *The Owl Answers* was republished in *Adrienne Kennedy in One Act*.

A Rat's Mass, written in 1963, was directed by David Wheeler of the Theater Company of Boston (opening April 12, 1966) and was named one of the best plays of the Boston season. The cast included Paul Benedict, Edward Finnegan, Warren Finnerty, Josephine Lane, James Spruill, Nadine Turner, and Blythe Danner. The play was produced by F. Carlton and Ann Colcord at the San Saba Theatre in Rome (opening June 21, 1966) with Ben B. Ardery, Jr., directing it on a program with Ardery's *Beside the Pool* and Sam Shepard's *Icarus*. Joan Sutherland and Nat Bush played Sister and Brother Rat, with Betty Jane Hobbs as Rosemary. Ann Colcord described the theme and action of the play: "They gnaw and nibble surreptitiously at the very standards of life that Americans use to hold themselves together, individually and as a group."[44] Brother and Sister

Rat are unable to expiate their guilt for a childhood incest inspired by playmate Rosemary, a Catholic girl dressed for her first communion, who also refuses to pardon them; the siblings are caught in and alienated by the white/Christian ethos. Kennedy has said that the images of A *Rat's Mass* were based on a dream she had while traveling by train from Paris to Rome: "I had this dream in which I was being pursued by red, bloodied rats. It was [a] very powerful dream, and when I woke up the train had stopped in the Alps. It was at night....I was just haunted by that image for years, about being pursued by these big, red rats."[45]

Italian response to the play was enthusiastic. *L'Unità's* reviewer discussed the "archetypal symbolism" that insists on a "historic reality, almost an existential reality": rather than being characteristics of individuals, the segregation and bestial behavior of the characters are the image of a "degrading collective condition."[46] In *Specchio*, A *Rat's Mass* was described as a "kind of black spiritual," with Kennedy's voice both "lyrical and obsessive"; "instead of the liberation of catharsis...we have a regression to the terrible condition of rats."[47] The conviction of the production impressed the reviewer for *Il Messaggero*: "Even to people who do not understand the English text, the play speaks with the suggestion of a ballet."[48] A *Rat's Mass* played in the repertory of the New American Theater at the Cultural Union in Turin from October 28, 1966.

It was produced in New York by La Mama E.T.C. (August 17, 1969), directed by Seth Allen, with music by Lamar Alford; Mary Alice played Sister Rat; Robert Robinson, Brother Rat; and Marilyn Roberts, Rosemary. Allen staged the play as a "parody mass" and "illuminate[d] its shadows and heighten[ed] its echoes." Barnes continued, "[Kennedy's] plays read like nonsense and yet, when acted, their phrases float accusingly in the mind....Of all our black writers, Miss Kennedy is most concerned with white, with white relationship, with white blood. She thinks black, but she remembers white."[49] La Mama took A *Rat's Mass* to London's Royal Court Theatre; there it was directed by Ching Yeh, with Barbara Montgomery as Sister Rat, Lamar Alford as Brother Rat, and Patricia Gaul as Rosemary. Irving Wardle observes that Kennedy, unlike most black American playwrights, is an experimentalist, and he sees A *Rat's Mass* as a lurid poetic ritual; Rosemary turns into a Medusa head as Brother and Sister Rat become rodents "who infest the beams of the house."[50]

As Kennedy mentions (in her interview in chapter 1), the La Mama production of A *Rat's Mass* enjoyed great success, and Ellen Stewart proposed to do the play as an opera. In 1976, A *Rat's Mass/Procession in Shout* was performed at the La Mama Annex with music by Cecil Taylor, jazz composer and pianist. Taylor used fragments from the original play in dialogue and lyrics and used orchestrated voices as instruments. Played by the Cecil Taylor Unit, "the plangency of the music echoes the doom-filled sentiments of the text," wrote Mel Gussow.[51] A Rat's Mass was published in New Black Playwrights (1968).[52]

A Lesson in Dead Language (1964) was presented by the English Stage Society at the Royal Court (London) on a double bill with Funnyhouse of a Negro (April 28, 1968). Directed by Rob Knights, the production featured Julia McCarthy as the Teacher and Anne Thompson as the Pupil. Michael Billington called it a "playlet of startling brevity and obscure intent" and mentions engaging music by Ginger Johnson and his African Drummers as part of the program.[53] Gaby Rodgers directed a workshop performance of A Lesson in Dead Language, a production of Theatre Genesis, at St. Mark's Church in New York from April 22 to May 2, 1971. In the interview with Howard Stein (chapter 16), Rodgers details the process of discovery that was involved in developing her production. As is suggested by the first line of the play, "Lesson I bleed," sexual maturation is treated as trauma. Rodgers recollects that Kennedy had a nun in mind in creating the figure of the teacher, depicted as a white dog teaching a class of adolescent girls, all in white dresses with red stains. In Rodgers's production, the setting included the stations of the cross, and movement included actors as religious sculptures. She also used gospel music played by Lamar Alford. A Lesson in Dead Language was published in Collision Course (1968).[54]

In the "Theatre Journal" included in Deadly Triplets, Kennedy explains that her son had the nonsense books of John Lennon, A Spaniard in the Works and In His Own Write, and she often "sat among [his] toys" reading them (104). Interested in doing a play from them, and encouraged by Gillian Walker at the Circle in the Square, Kennedy began writing The Lennon Play in a borrowed studio atop the Dakota (ironically, where Lennon later was living at the time he was shot) shortly before she left for England on a Rockefeller Grant. In London she was introduced to Victor Spinetti, who had been in the Beatles movies; he became interested in directing the play and helped Kennedy adapt Lennon's books to the stage (DT, 110, 114). Later, after a single performance of the play (at that time entitled Act I Scene 3) for an invited audience (1967), it was decided that the play should be done, but without Kennedy.[55] She asked Lennon to intervene ("After working on this play for almost a year I hear they want me out of it"), and he did by calling Kenneth Tynan, literary manager at the National Theatre (DT, 115-16). It was announced that Victor Spinetti would direct the "emended production" at the National Theatre in June 1968 and that John Lennon was collaborating with Adrienne Kennedy on the play.[56] Martin Esslin's review notes that the play was "originally devised" by Adrienne Kennedy, but "extensively revised" by Spinetti and Lennon.[57] Under the direction of Victor Spinetti, the play was modified with improvisational work by the cast.

It opened as *The Lennon Play: In His Own Write* as part of *Triple Bill* (with Henry Fielding's *The Covent Garden Tragedy* and a Victorian farce by John Maddison Morton, *A Most Unwarrantable Intrusion*) at the Old Vic of the National Theatre on June 18, 1968. The central figure of the play is "Me" (played by Ronald Pickup), who, as a member of a family of television addicts, invents his own fantasy world out of vignettes of childhood and popular culture. Irving Wardle's review describes "a montage of working-class provincial upbringing" (boys' comics, Sherlock Holmes, "a burlesque *Hamlet*,...nonsense sermons and launching ceremonies, nightmares, and quarrels"); the production "made elaborate use of side screen and back projections," costume changes, and "spirited" group movement. He found it faithful to the Lennon word games and cartoons, but said, "It leaves you with...a soporific flow of mindless punning."[58] In the *New York Times*, Wardle says that Lennon's books consist of "brief pieces directed against every sacred British cow." He adds, "The books are anything but theatrical, but with the aid of an American adapter, Adrienne Kennedy, and the director, Victor Spinetti, they have been assembled into the loose but workable stage form of a boy's struggle between his fantasies and his environment."[59] Clive Barnes called attention to Lennon's obsession with language, notably "strange surrealistic malapropisms," and called the production "fast, furious and fun."[60] *The Lennon Play* was produced in Albany, New York, by the Arena Summer Theatre in August 1969; it was published as *The Lennon Play: In His Own Write* (1968).[61]

Sun: A Poem for Malcolm X Inspired by His Murder was commissioned by the Royal Court Theatre in 1968 and was produced at the Theatre Upstairs, the Royal Court, in August 1969. It was published in *Scripts* (1971).[62] In her interview (chapter 1), Kennedy indicates that she had been commissioned by Jerome Robbins to write something for the Theatre Lab and had begun to write about Malcolm but did not finish it; then, when she was commissioned to write a play by the Royal Court, she was "working on some material from drawings of Leonardo da Vinci." Complemented by sound effects/music, improvisational lighting, and rear-screen projections, movement merges with verbal and visual imagery in a tone poem about a man dismembered among the shattered elements of a cosmos; the only remnant is a "tiny black Sun" (*Sun*, 77). Wilfred Leach directed *Sun: A Poem* at La Mama E.T.C. (Cafe La Mama) January 11 to 13, 1974; Andre Mtumi played "The Man." The production was "conceived by The Present Elements"; visuals were done by Karma Stanley, audio by Ancel O'Garro, and lighting by Charles Embry. Lance Williams calls *Sun* a choreopoem, precursor to Shange's *For Colored Girls Who Have Considered Suicide When the Rainbow Is Enuf*, because it "combines poetry and body movement to create dramatic intensity"; he particularly notes the improvisational "Free Jazz" accompaniment by the Ornett Coleman Double Quartet in the La Mama production.[63] Director Gaby Rodgers indicates that she had developed a production of *Sun* "frame by frame, but it was finally too expensive to mount for Off-Off Broadway."[64]

Kennedy's play, *Boats*, was commissioned for "An Omnibus of Short Works," organized by Gordon Davidson and directed by Ed Parone. It was performed at the Mark Taper Forum in Los Angeles as part of the second "Evening of Plays" on October 11 and 12, 1969. The script of this brief play is not available.

Adrienne Kennedy mentions the way that *An Evening with Dead Essex* evolved from a sniper incident in New Orleans that ended with the slaying of James Essex (see interview in chapter 1).[65] A departure for Kennedy's dramaturgy, the play uses projections of Vietnam news headlines to counterpoint the story of Essex. Its situation is a rehearsal; the director-producer works with black actors to recreate scenes from the life of the dead Essex. Brechtian projections establish media representation of Essex as a presence in the play (the projectionist, who never speaks, is designated as the only white character). Images of religious comfort, such the Twenty-third Psalm, stand in opposition to Essex's story and war headlines from Vietnam, reports of other assassinations (President Kennedy, Malcolm, Robert Kennedy, Martin Luther King, Kent State), black revolutionary slogans, a tape of "When I've Done the Best I Can," and Nixon's banalities intended to gloss military aggression in Viet Nam.

Both at the American Place Theatre (New York), directed by Gaby Rodgers (November 28, 1973), and at the Yale Repertory Company (New Haven, Connecticut), directed by Andre Mtumi (March 1974), the process of producing the play reflected the volatility of racial tensions at that time. In the interview with Howard Stein (chapter 16), Gaby Rodgers elaborates on the improvisations and struggles that took place in rehearsal of this play that is itself a rehearsal—of a life and of a play; its cast included Mary Alice, Bill Cobbs, Sid Morgan, Jr., Andre Mtumi, Fred Seagraves, and Karma Stanley.

When Kennedy was a CBS fellow at the Yale School of Drama (1973–74), *An Evening with Dead Essex* was produced on a program with Sam Shepard's *Geography of a Horse Dreamer* by the Yale Repertory Company (March 1974). Robert Brustein describes the rehearsals and performance of the play in *Making Scenes*: "In her own mind, Adrienne had written not a documentary but an activist piece with revolutionary implications, and the director she selected [Andre Mtumi] wanted to treat *Dead Essex* as a piece of racial propaganda." On the other hand, Brustein had perceived Essex as a "symbol of violence," and he was concerned that the production conferred martyrdom on Essex as "a victim of a repressive white police state." The script has each character leave the theatre for home at the end of the play; however, in rehearsal for the production, Brustein says, "the play ended with everybody passing a gun from hand to hand, the implication that they were preparing to take up Essex's dedication to violence." Brustein asked that the gun be removed from the play, but admits his ambivalence because any act of censorship was troubling and created an impasse for the production.[66] An *Evening with Dead Essex* was published in *Theater* (1978);[67] it was not reprinted in *In One Act*.

Directed by Joseph Chaikin as a work-in-progress in the workshop series of the New York Shakespeare Festival at the Public Theater in New York, A *Movie Star Has to Star in Black and White* was performed in November 1976.[68] Robbie McCauley played Clara, the writer, with Avra Petrides as Bette Davis, Elin Ruskin as Shelley Winters, and Gloria Foster as the mother. Arthur Sainer, in the *Village Voice*, described the play as the vision of a single character, a writer, "whose life is so tied up with the films that...scenes from these films (*Now, Voyager, Viva Zapata!*, and A *Place in the Sun*)...become structures within which the events in her life are replayed." Sainer saw the play in the same "confessional" vein as *Funnyhouse of a Negro*, but reported that knowledge about the character was blocked rather than revealed.[69]

According to Eileen Blumenthal, *Movie Star* was the "only new script" that Chaikin had directed that was "not connected to one of his laboratories"; she also indicates that Chaikin worked closely with Kennedy, "condensing, tightening dialogue, and clarifying."[70] He was drawn to her "depiction of direct experience being redigested and reshaped to conform to popular culture models."[71] The play was first published in *Wordplays* 3 (1984).[72] It was produced at the University of Houston (from February 8, 1985), and directed by Ntozake Shange.

Kennedy was commissioned to write *The Lancashire Lad* by the Empire State Youth Theater Institute, where it was performed in May 1980. The play is a fictionalized account of the childhood of Charles Chaplin, based on Chaplin's biography. Produced by Patricia B. Snyder, the play includes musical numbers and "a full-blown Palladium review, complete with fan dancer and low comics."[73] Frank Rich says that Kennedy "tells her central story with such heart-stopping passion that not even a circus could upstage it or blunt it." The boy, here called William Grimby, contends with an alcoholic father, a mentally disturbed mother, and grinding poverty. Although he succeeds as a performer, Kennedy does not "allow her audience to escape her drama's gravest implications." The play was directed by Joseph Balflor, with music by George Harris; John Thomas McGuire III was William Grimby. Rich concludes that "the real star is Miss Kennedy, whose language achieves powerful emotional effects with the sparest of means."[74] The text of the play is not available.

Black Children's Day, a children's play, was commissioned by Brown University while Kennedy was artist-in-residence; it was directed by George Houston Bass and produced by Rites and Reason at Brown University, Providence, Rhode Island (November 1980). Kennedy discusses the evolution of this play in the chapter 1 interview.

Orestes and Electra, adaptations of Euripides' plays, were commissioned by the Juilliard School, where they were directed by Michael Kahn as a performance project (November 5 to 9, 1980) and in repertory (April 11 to 14, 1981). With music and vocal sounds by Kirk Nurock, sets and lights by Loren Sherman, choreography by Randolyn Zinn, and costumes by Mariann Verheyen, the cast included Linda Kozlowski as Electra and Val Kilmer as Orestes. Ronn Smith commented that the plays were "loosely condensed and finely adapted" by Kennedy.[75] Noting the female-dominated chorus and a robust Electra, Robert Massa called it an "Amazon production"—"an interesting approach, since the plays chronicle the re-establishment of the patriarchal order after the Trojan War."[76] Mythic dimensions, heightened by primitive and feathered costumes combined with movement and color ("performers writhing about the burnt-orange bowl-shaped stage"), created a "visceral production of ancient drama."[77]

Kennedy's Diary of Lights, a musical without songs, was directed by David Willinger at CitiRep, Davis Hall, City College in New York, from June 5 to 14, 1987. The production of this autobiographical play included a jazz continuo by Gib Veconi and abstract dance movements superimposed on the text; Tracy Hendryx designed the choreography.[78] "The play is concerned with the youthful idealism of a young black [married] couple on the inter-racial Upper West Side of New York City."[79] The text is not published.

Solo Voyages, Joseph Chaikin's adaptation of three monologues from the plays of Adrienne Kennedy (The Owl Answers, A Rat's Mass, and A Movie Star Has to Star in Black and White), was performed by Robbie McCauley. Produced by the Interart Theatre in association with the American National Theatre at Kennedy Center, the adaptation was performed in New York (September 11 to October 20, 1985) and Washington (November 25 to December 14, 1985). The production included music composed and performed by Skip LaPlante and Edwina Lee Tyler, set by Jun Maeda, and puppets by Ronnie Asbell. Alisa Solomon's review in the Village Voice describes LaPlante's "wispy strains on various string and wind instruments" that play from the shadows, while Tyler's insistent drums establish "a rich dialogue with McCauley…suggesting a heritage which Clara barely acknowledges."[80] "Poetic language, music, solo performance and design blend and give a theatrical immediacy to an interior monologue," wrote Mel Gussow.[81]

Chaikin chose "excerpts that emphasize the cross-references among Kennedy's works…; the images accrete, referring to and illuminating what came before, eventually converging on the grievous complications of an unfixed black, female identity," wrote Solomon.[82] The voyages are a quest for "ancestry (literary as well as genetic)" through the mind of Clara Passmore, who is both "tourist and refugee" of a Eurocentric/Hollywood culture.[83]

David Willinger, assistant director of *Solo Voyages*, discusses the development of the piece in chapter 19, "Developing a Concert for the Spoken Voice," and includes an interview of Robbie McCauley. The collaboration of music, scene, mask, and puppets enrich the varied and expressive performance of Robbie McCauley "on her mystical pilgrimage toward self recognition" in this chamber piece.[84]

Kennedy's *Deadly Triplets: A Theatre Mystery and Journal* (1990) includes a novella based on her experiences in London in the sixties; it is set in the theatre world. "It concerns confused identities and the [narrator's] own search for a clearer sense of self as she considers what she knows about her estranged (and possibly dead) mother."[85] The "Theatre Journal" includes Kennedy's memoirs from the same period in London; these vignettes suggest the counterpoint between autobiography and the novella and rehearse important backgrounds for Kennedy the playwright.

The Ohio State Murders was given in a workshop production by the Great Lakes Theater Festival (which commissioned the work) in Cleveland, Ohio, on June 16 and 17, 1990 (three performances), at the Eldred Theatre, Case Western Reserve University, and in Yale University's "Winterfest," January 16 to February 9, 1991 (fifteen performances), at the University Theatre. Both productions were directed by Gerald Freedman. At the Great Lakes Theater Festival, Hazel Medina played the central figure, writer Suzanne Alexander, with Bellary Darden as the younger Suzanne; at Yale, the role of the "present Suzanne" was enacted by Olivia Cole and Simi Junior was "Suzanne in 1949, 1950 and 1951."

Kennedy set her play on the Ohio State University campus, "where Suzanne Alexander, a prominent black writer who attended Ohio State, has been asked back to lecture on the roots of the violent imagery in her work. Told mostly in flashback sequences that recount Alexander's student years in Columbus, *The Ohio State Murders* is a shocking portrait of a young black woman's struggle in the racially torn America of the late 1940's and early 1950's."[86] If, as Kennedy says, her "plays are meant to be states of mind," then this work examines the concourse of social violence and hatred in the life and mind of a sensitive student-become-writer. Although given A's for her brilliant analysis of Hardy's *Tess of the D'Urbervilles*, Suzanne is prevented from becoming an English major because of race; seduced by her white professor, Suzanne and her children become the victims of violence and guilt. The narrative structure allows past and present to merge in a timelessness that permits repressed fears to be a presence on the stage.[87]

Kennedy's *She Talks to Beethoven* was published in *Antaeus* (1991); it was given a staged reading at River Arts (Woodstock, New York) in 1989. Kennedy sees the material in this play as an extension of *The Ohio State Murders*.[88] The central character is also the writer, Suzanne Alexander, who writes about and speaks to Beethoven in a meditation that merges time into presence. It is framed and interrupted by radio broadcasts about Suzanne's husband, David, who is missing under mysterious circumstances; he has received threats and has disappeared to protect his wife from whom he is otherwise inseparable. Although the play is set in Legon near Accra, West Africa, Suzanne's writing concerns Beethoven's life in Vienna; the play becomes a dialogue between writer and composer merging distance and time in a bond of mutual understanding, while music sustains a continuum emphasizing the counterpoint of Eurocentric and African-American culture. Having revealed to Suzanne that her wound is not healing, Beethoven confides his deafness and his need for "conversation books" to her. Imagining this loss through reading the "conversation books," Suzanne also discovers poems and encouragement from the absent David, who left them between the leaves of the books. Finally, as Beethoven's death scene is read from Suzanne's manuscript, David returns to her side, his danger abated. Tonally unlike Kennedy's earlier writing, *She Talks to Beethoven* discovers connections that comfort.

The Film Club conveys the anxiety of Suzanne Alexander awaiting the release of her husband, who is detained in West Africa. Images from Bette Davis movies are counterpointed by scenes from *Dracula*; compulsive walks in Windsor Park near London prefigure dread-become-hysteria when Suzanne returns to Washington. *The Film Club* is published with *She Talks to Beethoven* and *The Ohio State Murders* as *The Alexander Plays*.[89]

Adrienne Kennedy continues to write new plays, and so conclusions about the place(s) of her oeuvre in the context of American theatre are necessarily tentative. As their production history suggests, her plays have intrigued producers and directors of the experimental stage. Among the plays on New York stages in 1964 were Samuel Beckett's *Play*, Harold Pinter's *The Lovers*, Edward Albee's *Who's Afraid of Virginia Woolf*, Eugene

Ionesco's *Le Piéton de L'Air*, Pirandello's *Right You Are (If You Think You Are)*. Like Kennedy's *Funnyhouse of a Negro*, these plays expressed the problematic of fragmented selves and self-perception; unlike them, Kennedy's materials and dramaturgy reflected a uniquely Afro-American circumstance. Also on stage in New York in 1964 were Amiri Baraka's *Dutchman*, Athol Fugard's *Blood Knot*, James Baldwin's *Blues for Mr. Charlie*, and Lorraine Hansberry's *The Sign in Sidney Brustein's Window*, each bringing voice to racial and social issues. Among them, Kennedy's material and method was an anomaly. Michael Kahn indicates (in the interview in chapter 15) that Kennedy's early work was ostracized because the plays were "considered neurotic and not supportive of the black movement." When Kennedy turned to a more overtly political event in *An Evening with Dead Essex*, critics saw a new facet in her writing, yet, no matter how deeply they are embedded within the psyche of a character, Kennedy's plays all express cultural conflict and allude to wider events (as in, for example, the Nazis in *A Rat's Mass*, Lumumba in *Funnyhouse*).

The commissioned works of the 1980s (*Black Children's Day, A Lancashire Lad*, and the adaptations of *Orestes* and *Electra*) were based on structures of narrative; perhaps these and the autobiographical writings (*People Who Led to My Plays* and *Deadly Triplets*) have led to the new plays, *The Ohio State Murders* and *She Talks to Beethoven*, which conflate narrator with writer.

Naturally, the reception of Kennedy's works reflected critical expectations and circumstance as much as it did the world and methods of her plays. Audiences have been confused and negative as well as enthusiastic and moved by her writing. European response, particularly in Rome (*A Rat's Mass*, 1966) and in Paris (*Drôle de baraque*, 1968), showed appreciation for Kennedy's plays, recognizing her articulation of racial politics in a personal and intense mythopoetic dramaturgy. Over the thirty years that Kennedy has been writing, American theatre has embraced new forms; the plays that invited excitement because of their challenges seem more accessible.

Notes

1. Thomas Taylor, "Preserving the Text," *American Theatre* (May 1990): 7. Noting that ours "is an age in which football games are more carefully documented than play productions," Taylor issues a call for theatrical documentation. He observes the need to have a record of the text performed, of the playwriting process—especially when it is collaborative, of regional (and one might add workshop) performances.

2. Adrienne Kennedy, *Deadly Triplets* (Minneapolis: University of Minnesota Press, 1990), 100 (hereafter cited in the text as DT); and interview in chapter 1 of this volume.

3. See Adrienne Kennedy, *People Who Led to My Plays* (New York: Knopf, 1987), 37, 84 (hereafter cited in the text as *People*).

4. David Marash, WNEW radio of *Cities in Bezique*, Jan. 14, 1969, quoting Gerald Freedman's program notes for the production at the Public Theatre.

5. Paul Carter Harrison, ed. *Kuntu Drama* (New York: Grove Press, 1974), 191–202.

6. "Adrienne Kennedy," in *Interviews with Contemporary Women Playwrights*, eds. Kathleen Betsko and Rachel Koenig (New York: Morrow, 1987), 247–48.

7. Adrienne Cornell, "Because of the King of France," *Black Orpheus: A Journal of African and Afro-American Literature*, no. 10 (1963): 30–37 (reprint, Nendeln: Kraus Reprint, 1972).

8. Betsko and Koenig, eds., *Interviews*, 250–51.

9. Ibid., 248–49.

10. The play was scheduled to close on January 26 but was extended with the support of Isabel Eberstadt; "*Funnyhouse* Is Reprieved after Receiving $2,400 Gift," *New York Times*, Jan. 28, 1964, 24.

11. Howard Taubman, "The Theater: *Funnyhouse of a Negro*," *New York Times*, Jan. 15, 1964, 25.

12. Edith Oliver, *New Yorker*, Jan. 25, 1964, 79.

13. George Oppenheimer, "*Funnyhouse of a Negro*, at the East End," *Newsday*, Jan. 15, 1964, 2.

14. Taubman, "*Funnyhouse*," 25.

15. Harold Clurman, *Nation*, 198 (Feb. 10, 1964): 154.

16. David Wheeler interviewed by Lois Overbeck, Dec. 1990; Alta Maloney, "Funnyhouse of a Negro," *Boston Traveler*, Mar. 15, 1965.

17. Kevin Kelly, "'Funnyhouse' and 'Charlie' Theater Company Bill," *Boston Globe*, Mar. 12, 1965.

18. C. G., "Jeunes Américains," *Les Nouvelles Literraires*, Mar. 7, 1968; translation mine.

19. B. Poirot-Delpech, "Drôle de baraque, d'Adrienne Kennedy," *Le Monde*, Mar. 19, 1968; translation mine.

20. Jean-Jacques Gautier, "Spectacle Shepard-Kennedy," *Le Figaro*, Mar. 11, 1968; translation mine.

21. Jean Paget, "Spectacle: Shepard-Kennedy," *Combat*, Mar. 19, 1968; translation mine.

22. *Journal de Genève*, Apr. 6, 1968; translation mine.

23. Jacques Lemarchand, "Drôle de baraque d'Adrienne Kennedy au Petit-Odéon," *Figaro Litérraire*, Mar. 25, 1968; translation mine.

24. Michael Billington, "A Racial Dilemma," *Times* (London), Apr. 29, 1968, 13.

25. "New Kennedy Play," *New York Herald Tribune*, Aug. 25, 1965.

26. The promptbook is in the archives of the Public Theater.

27. "Off-Broadway Reviews: *Cities in Bezique*," *Variety*, Jan. 29, 1969.

28. Lee Silver, "*Cities in Bezique* Has Grim Sights and Sounds," *Daily News*, Jan. 13, 1969, 46; Richard P. Cooke, "The Theater: World of Fantasy," *Wall Street Journal*, Jan. 14, 1969.

29. Richard Watts, Jr., "Two on the Aisle," *New York Post*, Jan. 13, 1969, 24.

30. George Oppenheimer, "On Stage: *Cities in Bezique* Is Haunting Though Confusing," *Daily Item* (Port Chester, N.Y.), Jan. 13, 1969, 21.

31. John Simon, "Whirled without End," *New York*, Feb. 3, 1969, 54.

32. Steve Tennen, "Off-b'way Shows," *Show Business*, Jan. 25, 1969.

33. J. Lance Ermatinger, "Of Women and Other Things" and "Best Since Zoo Story," *Off-Off*, no. 5 (April 1969): n.p.

34. Paul Carter Harrison, ed., *Kuntu Drama* (New York: Grove Press, 1974), 191–201.

35. Clive Barnes, "Theater: *Cities in Bezique* Arrives at the Public," *New York Times*, Jan. 13, 1969, 26.

36. Richard P. Cooke, "The Theater: World of Fantasy," *Wall Street Journal*, Jan. 14, 1969; *Long Island Examiner*, Jan. 23, 1969.

37. Oppenheimer, "Cities in Bezique."

38. Walter Kerr, "Some Day Adrienne Kennedy Will...," New York Times, Jan. 19, 1969, sec. 2, 3.

39. David Marash, WNEW radio review of Cities in Bezique, Jan. 14, 1969.

40. Martin Gottfried, "Cities in Bezique," Women's Wear Daily, Jan. 13, 1969, 63; and Richard Watts, Jr., "The Gift of Adrienne Kennedy," New York Post, Jan. 13, 1969, 24.

41. Kerr, "Someday Adrienne Kennedy Will..."

42. Edith Oliver, "Off Broadway," New Yorker, Jan. 25, 1969, 77.

43. Adrienne Kennedy, Cities in Bezique: Two One-Act Plays (New York: Samuel French, 1969).

44. John Francis Lane, "Rome Off-Broadway," Rome Daily American, June 26–27, 1966, n.p.

45. Adrienne Kennedy, "A Growth of Images," Drama Review 21 (Dec. 1977): 44.

46. "Teatro: Atti unici americani," L'Unità, June 23, 1966, n.p.; translation mine.

47. A.P., "Tanto di cappello alla buona volontà," Specchio, July 3, 1966, n.p.; translation mine.

48. Vice, "Le Prime Roman: San Saba: Tre atti unici di autori americani," Il Messaggero, June 23, 1966, n.p.; translation mine.

49. Clive Barnes, "A Rat's Mass Weaves Drama of Poetic Fabric," New York Times, Nov. 1, 1969, 39.

50. Irving Wardle, "Tormented Fury," Times (London), May 27, 1970, 14.

51. Mel Gussow, "Theater: A Rat's Mass: Death Images Dot Play about Prejudice," New York Times, Mar. 11, 1976, 42.

52. William Couch, ed., New Black Playwrights (Baton Rouge: Louisiana State University Press, 1968), 61–70.

53. Michael Billington, "A Racial Dilemma," Times (London), April 29, 1968, 13.

54. Edward Parone, ed., Collision Course (New York: Random House, 1968), 33–40.

55. "Miss Kennedy Adapts Beatle Books," Village Voice, Dec. 21, 1967; the performance was Dec. 3, 1967; DT, 115.

56. "A Beatle at the National Theatre," Times (London), Jan. 19, 1968, 6; Sam Zolotow, "London Will See a Beatle's Play," New York Times, Feb. 27, 1968.

57. Martin Esslin, "Two Trifles and a Failure," New York Times, July 14, 1968, sec. 2, 4.

58. Irving Wardle, "Unknown Plays for New Directors," Times (London), June 19, 1968, 11.

59. "John Lennon Play, In His Own Write, Is Staged in London," New York Times, June 10, 1968, 50.

60. Clive Barnes, "Irreverence on London Stage," New York Times, July 9, 1968, 30.

61. John Lennon, Adrienne Kennedy, and Victor Spinetti, The Lennon Play: In His Own Write (New York: SImon and Schuster, 1968).

62. Adrienne Kennedy, Sun, Scripts 1 (Nov. 1971): 51–56.

63. Lance Williams, Black Theatre in the 1960s and 1970s: A Historical-Critical Analysis of the Movement (Westport, Conn.: Greenwood Press, 1985), 148.

64. Gaby Rodgers interview with Lois Overbeck, Feb. 5, 1990.

65. Time reports that six persons were killed and nine wounded in the sniper attack and police response that ended in the slaying of Mark Essex ("Death in New Orleans," Time, Jan. 22, 1973, 20–21). Although at the time, police believed there were two snipers, one of the wounded said that Essex was not the gunman who had shot him (Time, 21). Initial reports suggested Essex's involvement in a conspiracy against police; New Orleans police had been following Mark Essex (a suspect in a police attack on New Year's Eve and allegedly involved in an auto accident and chase in New Orleans that morning) when he entered the motel and began shooting. After twelve hours of seige, with hundreds of police in

teacher. He enlisted in the navy; a minister claimed that in the navy he had come to hate whites and returned to denounce the church in which he had been raised as "white man's religion" ("New Orleans Sniper Identified; Rifle Linked to Killing of Rookie," *New York Times*, Jan. 10, 1973, 1, 22; "Sniper is Remembered as Quiet Youth Who Grew to Hate in the Navy", *New York Times*, Jan. 10, 1973, 22; "Victim Says Slain Man Was Not His Attacker," *New York Times*, Jan. 10, 1973, 22).

66. Robert Brustein, *Making Scenes: A Personal History of the Turbulent Years at Yale, 1966–1979* (New York: Random House, 1981), 176–77.

67. Adrienne Kennedy, *An Evening with Dead Essex*, Theater, no. 2 (Spring 1978): 66–78.

68. Serge Moglat, archivist at the Public Theater, indicates that there were open rehearsals Nov. 5 and 6 with performances beginning Nov. 9, 1976.

69. Arthur Sainer, "Gavella Orchestrates a Sigh," *Village Voice*, Nov. 29, 1976, 97, 99.

70. Eileen Blumenthal, *Joseph Chaikin: Exploring the Boundaries of Theater* (New York: Cambridge University Press, 1984), 222, 185.

71. Blumenthal, *Joseph Chaikin*, 30.

72. Adrienne Kennedy, *A Movie Star Has to Star in Black and White*, in *Wordplays* 3 (New York: Performing Arts Journal Publications, 1984), pp. 51–68.

73. Frank Rich, "Stage: *Lancashire Lad* for Children," *New York Times*, May 21, 1980, sec. 3, 30.

74. Ibid.

75. "The 1981 Juilliard Season," *Theatre Crafts* 15 (Aug./Sept.1981): 109.

76. Robert Massa, "Bits," *Village Voice*, April 22, 1981, n.p. Kennedy indicated that female casting was incidental to the performance situation (Feb. 24, 1990).

77. Massa, "Bits."

78. David Willinger, interviewed by Lois Overbeck, Jan. 26, 1991.

79. Advertisement in *Black Masks*, May/June 1987, 6 (reprinted in *Contemporary Black Playwrights and Their Plays: A Biographical Dictionary and Dramatic Index*, Bernard L. Peterson, Jr., ed. (Westport,Conn.: Greenwood Press, 1988), 288.

80. Alisa Solomon, "Sojourner's Truths," *Village Voice*, Oct. 1, 1985, 98.

81. Mel Gussow, "Stage: *Solo Voyages*, Play Excerpts," *New York Times*, Sept. 20, 1985.

82. Solomon, "Sojourner's Truths," 97.

83. Gussow, "*Solo Voyages*."

84. Ibid.

85. Jean Keleher, "Deadly Triplets: A Theatre Mystery and Journal," *Library Journal*, 115 (May 1, 1990): 114.

86. News release, Great Lakes Theater Festival, June 1990.

87. Marianne Evett, "*Ohio State Murders* at the GLTF Workshop," *Plain Dealer* (Cleveland), May 31, 1990.

88. Adrienne Kennedy, *She Talks to Beethoven*, Antaeus 66 (Spring 1991): 248–58.

89. Adrienne Kennedy, *The Alexander Plays: She Talks to Beethoven, The Ohio State Murders, The Film Club, The Dramatic Circle* (Minneapolis: University of Minnesota Press, 1992).

PART II

Intersecting Dramatic Traditions

4

Kennedy's Travelers in the American and African Continuum

Paul K. Bryant-Jackson

I have been in dialogue with the plays of Adrienne Kennedy for many years; although words are not to be entirely discounted, images represent the essence of the dialogue. Images form the core of Adrienne Kennedy's theatre. Kennedy achieves her greatest impact in the arresting, though critically resisting, images that surround her major protagonists as they endlessly and restlessly move along a continuum of time, matter, and space. In *Funnyhouse of a Negro*, Sarah's hair continues to fall out as she moves along an African/European/American cultural and historical continuum. In *The Owl Answers*, Clara's metamorphosis into an owl replicates Sarah's movement along a similar continuum. In *She Talks to Beethoven*, Suzanne, who is situated in Ghana soon after independence (1961), converses with Ludwig van Beethoven (1770–1827) about the opening of *Fidelio* (1803). I have been in continual discourse with Kennedy's images and with the images that others around me have used to describe, discern, and distinguish this pivotal figure of American theatre. Kennedy's images resist explicit identification.

Image I: The Transcendentalists

> *Silent and amazed even when a little boy,*
> *I remember I heard the preacher every Sunday put*
>   *God in his statements,*
>
> *As contending against some being or influence.*
>   —Whitman, "A Child's Amaze"

45

OUR MINISTER REV _____: *He was always angry when
he finished preaching, and the congregation seemed angry. I was afraid
of him.*
He had dark eyes and dressed in black robes. He seemed evil.
—Adrienne Kennedy, People Who Led to My Plays

*I think I could turn and live with animals, they are so
placid and self-contained,*
I stand and look at them long and long.
—Whitman, Leaves of Grass

The owls and myself: The owls in the trees outside the Achimota Guest
House were close, and at night, because we slept under gigantic mosquito
nets, I felt enclosed in their sound. In the mornings, I would try to find the
owls in the trees but could never see them. Yet at night in the shuttered
room, under the huge white canopied nets, the owls sounded as if they
were in the very center of the room. I was pregnant again and there were
difficulties. I had to stay in bed for a week as I bled. I listened to the owl
sounds, afraid. In a few months I would create a character who would turn
into an owl.[1]

It would never have occurred to me to look at the European-American
transcendentalists as an origin for Kennedy's images, except that Esther
Jackson would often say, in describing the protagonist in modern American drama, "I tell you, Whitman's boy goes into the wilderness, and in
O'Neill, Williams, and Albee, let me tell you, he gets clobbered."
Kennedy's characters, Sarah, Clara, and Suzanne, appear to exhibit some
kinship with the transcendentalists. They share a restlessness that is reminiscent of Whitman's "boy"; they, too, seek refuge from an empirical
universe and solace in a metaphysical one. This kinship is evident in
Thoreau's passages on the traveler and the sanctity of nature.

The traveller's whole employment is to calculate what cloud will obscure
the moon and what she will triumph over. In the after-midnight hours the
traveller's sole companion is the moon. All his thoughts are centered in
her. She is waging continual war with the clouds on his behalf. What cloud
will enter the lists with her next? This employs his thoughts; and when she
has fought her way through all the squadrons of her foes, and rides
majestic in a clear sky, he cheerfully and confidently pursues his ways and
rejoices in his heart.[2]

Though man's life is trivial...Nature is holy and heroic. With what infinite
faith and promise and moderation begins each new day! It is only 2 o'clock
and already there is evidence of morning in the sky.[3]

For Thoreau, travel and nature provide the means to commune with a profound presence and find a metaphysical peace. Likewise, Kennedy's characters appear to "travel" along a transcendental continuum and often speak of the sanctity of nature. This desire for a transcendental peace is heard in Sarah's plaintive cry as she agonizes over the Christ/father in *Funnyhouse*:

> He pleaded with me to help him find Genesis, search for Genesis in the midst of golden savannas, nim and white frankopenny trees and white stallions roaming under a blue sky, help him search for the white doves. (*Funnyhouse*, 14)[4]

In *The Owl Answers*, Clara substitutes the landscape of London for the "golden savannas."

> We had a lovely morning, we rose in darkness, took a taxi past Hyde Park through the Marble Arch to Buckingham Palace, we had our morning tea at Lyons, then came out to the Tower. We were wandering about the gardens, my father leaning on my arm, speaking of you, William the Conqueror. My father loved you, William....(*Owl*, 27–28)

Kennedy uses Beethoven's *Fidelio* (the transitional work to "Romanticism") as the continuo of *She Talks to Beethoven* to underscore Suzanne's transcendental desire.[5] Although Kennedy's characters are cognizant of the potential of transcendence (Suzanne employs music to transcend time, Clara uses London to transcend the American space, and Sarah looks to nature to transcend the materiality of the past), they do not achieve it.

While Kennedy's "travelers" articulate the American transcendental ideals, they appear unable to "experience" communion with the metaphysical. Sarah does not rejoice in the sanctity of nature, Clara is denied admission into the Tower of London, and despite the comfort that Beethoven offers, Suzanne is sick with an "undisclosed illness." So it would seem that Esther Jackson's caveat about the Whitman "boy" in modern American drama is fulfilled in Kennedy's plays, as it is in O'Neill, Williams, and Albee. In O'Neill's *The Hairy Ape*, Hank, the muscular "individual" who thrives in the uniquely O'Neillian steamroom of a ship, is destroyed in urbanized America. The homosexual poet, Sebastian, in Williams's *Suddenly Last Summer*, is eaten alive by carnivorous birds when he ventures out-of-doors. In Albee's *Zoo Story*, Jerry, realizing that his entire life is a "zoo," attempts to deliver Peter from his "zoo" through a symbolic crucifixion. Clearly Kennedy's Aframerican characters have an affinity with Whitman's "boy" and Thoreau's "traveller," but their sociopolitical realities, namely race, class, gender, and culture, configure a different matrix.

Thus, although Kennedy's images are linked to the transcendentalist continuum, the "through-action" and final tableaus in both *The Owl Answers* and *Beethoven* pose realities that resist identification with this tradition. Clara's transformation into an owl is hardly traditionally or canonically Western, and Suzanne's encounter with Beethoven does not in the least resemble the Emperor Jones's encounter with his phantoms. In order to discern the significance of the closing images of Kennedy's plays, other critical approaches need to be employed.

One approach that can be used to explicate Aframerican experience is autobiographical writing, alongside other conventional critical approaches. Nellie Y. McKay sees autobiography as a central and complex component in the writings of Aframericans:

> [We are forced] to continue to reevaluate the personal and cultural meanings of autobiography....[Although] theories of Western autobiography proliferate and take a prominent place in our understanding of history and literature, it is necessary for readers to maintain flexibility in their reception of texts, especially those by minorities, when they do not fit the models we have come to expect from the genre. For black women, in particular, the ability to name the self autonomously is an important part of their historical identity, a means of reclaiming and affirming selves.[6]

With McKay's injunction in mind, it is evident that Adrienne Kennedy's autobiographical writing, particularly *People Who Led to My Plays*, is essentially a theatrical act of self-ascription. When it is used as an access to Kennedy's "resisting images," many possible interpretations of Kennedy's dramaturgy are opened. For example, Kennedy speaks of her trip to Ghana in terms of a personal renaissance:

> In front of the House of Parliament in Accra was a statue of Nkrumah....To see a man and to see a statue of him in the same space of time broke through boundaries in my mind. (*People*, 122)

> I remember...I had seen Jesus as sweet, docile. I had believed "what a friend we have in Jesus." But that spring, sitting in the Pensione Sabrina, I went on creating a cruel Jesus Christ. (*People*, 123)

Embedded in Kennedy's African renaissance is a discovery of self on an organic, though at times fragmented, cultural continuum. In both *The Owl Answers* and *She Talks to Beethoven*, this continuum allows her to transverse matter, space, and time. Kennedy's travelers shift positions freely. When Kennedy's characters move on the African continuum, everything that composes them travels as well. For example, Sarah brings the Duchess of Hapsburg (who is also Bette Davis in *Juarez*) into the jungle. As a result, the images of the self (or selves) accompanying the central characters are travelers on the continua as well. Thus the images exhibit

African-American, Aframerican, African, European, and European-American features and contribute to the conflict!

To unravel these resisting images is to trace the genealogy of Kennedy's plays to its African sources. Martin Owusu's *Drama of the Gods* offers a framework for this genealogy. Owusu divides West African drama, specifically Nigerian, into sacred and secular. Developing from the sacred drama are myth plays and from the secular, masquerades. Both *The Owl Answers* and *She Talks to Beethoven* have affinities with these traditional dramas. *The Owl Answers* is similar to the Anansegoro, which utilizes the transformation of character from person to animal to achieve its purpose; *Beethoven* is like the Egungun, a ritual that involves worshiping of the dead.[7] Kennedy's autobiographic/personal experiences inform and suggest this similarity.

Adrienne Kennedy, recalling her experience in Ghana, feels "close" with the owls. Dramatized in *The Owl Answers*, this closeness becomes union: "She who is Clara Passmore who is the Virgin Mary who is the Bastard who is the Owl." Kennedy's personal experience with the owls and the later dramatizing of the experience represents a quintessential African theatrical event: a communal sacred ritual, in which the central narrator, as well as other characters, can assume or change identities for religious purposes. Within this African framework, the differences between an African and an American "transcendent event" cannot be minimized: Whitman only desires to be with animals; Kennedy's characters become animals.

Ola Rotimi's "Traditional Nigerian Drama" also discusses a wide range of theatrical practices in Nigeria and provides an intriguing lens through which *Beethoven* can be understood. The action of *Beethoven* takes place in Ghana during the course of one evening and centers on one event, the return of Suzanne Alexander's husband, David. However, the continuum of time and space extends from 1803 to 1961 and from Ghana to Vienna. The characters of the play are Suzanne (a writer), Beethoven, a radio announcer (who is only heard), and Suzanne's husband, David, who makes a brief vocal appearance at the end of the play. If read as an Egungun ritual that involves the worshiping of the dead, *Beethoven* contains at least three possible connections. Kennedy requests that music from the opera *Fidelio* play throughout the drama. It can be argued that Beethoven's music is used to specify the deity (African? European?) that is to be called forth and accompanies the drums that are used during an Egungun.

The second parallel is related to the announcer's statement about Suzanne:

> It is known that Alexander jests with his wife about her continued deep love for European artists such as Sibelius, Chopin and Beethoven and if

anyone in Accra wanted to hear these composers one had only to pass the windows. (*Beethoven*, 249–50)

The music image defines the continuum, Africa to Europe; hints at the possibility of mixed ancestry; and provides solace while Suzanne is alone and her husband is away. Finally the Egungun, as a ceremony of ancestral worship that employs a masquerader, explains the striking similarity between David and Beethoven: Kennedy's stage direction indicates, "DAVID'S VOICE (*Not unlike Beethoven's*)." (*Beethoven*, 258).

Read as an Egungun, *Beethoven* might unravel as follows: waiting, and worried about the disappearance of her husband, who has received death threats, Suzanne plays *Fidelio* and invokes the spirit of the "ancestor," Ludwig van Beethoven. The composer comforts and teaches her, "You mustn't worry. I've foreseen my death many times. It will be in winter. In Vienna. My friends will come from Graz. [He embraces her.]" (*Beethoven*, 255). It is Suzanne's and David's joint belief that brings about David's safe return:

SUZANNE: David you sent Beethoven, until you returned. Didn't you?

DAVID'S VOICE: (*Not unlike Beethoven's*) I knew he would console you while I was absent. (*Beethoven*, 258)

Rotimi also describes a variation on the format of ancestral worship that the Kalabari and Yoruba employ:

It is night-time, and early warnings have imposed a curfew on the community. A member of the secret cult concerned is fully masked. He is supposed to represent the deceased whose memory is being honoured. Accompanied with drumming and chanting by fellow members of the cult, he emerges from the cult house or sacred grove and approaches the home of the deceased. Reaching there, chanting and drumming abate or stop quickly while the cult elder or cult priest calls the name of the deceased loudly, invoking him to return to life and visit with the children he left behind. He intones repeatedly, supported by drum or choral accent. Finally, the masker speaks. His voice is sufficiently disguised to sound like that of the deceased himself or dehumanized to reflect the ethereal eeriness of Spirits' voices. He then addresses his children within, giving words of advice, of reassurance, of blessing, or of harsh reprimand. The children within may respond where need be. Some other ritual may follow, like formally accepting or rejecting the gifts that have been placed on the threshold by the children. This done, he withdraws with his followers to the land of the dead.[8]

In this analogy, by evoking the spirit of Beethoven to comfort the entire community, which is also worried about the missing David, Suzanne emerges as cult priest. African readings illumine the complexity of

Kennedy's resisting images in a way that Eastern readings illumine Strindberg. When we cross-fertilize play and autobiography, Kennedy's resisting images begin to reveal and illumine certain aspects of their complexity and origins.

Image II: The Absurdists

GEORGE: All right, love…whatever love wants (*Stops*). Just don't start on the bit, that's all.

MARTHA: The bit? The bit? What kind of language is that? What are you talking about?

GEORGE: The bit. Just don't start on the bit.

MARTHA: You imitating one of your students for God's sake? What are you trying to do? What bit?

GEORGE: Just don't start in on the bit about the kid, that's all.

—Edward Albee, *Who's Afraid of Virginia Woolf?*

MAN. It begins with the disaster of my hair. I awaken. My hair has fallen out, not all of it, but a mass from the crown of my head that lies on the center of my white pillow.

—Adrienne Kennedy, *Funnyhouse of a Negro*

ROSEMARY. I will never atone you. Perhaps you can put a bullet in your head with your father's shotgun, then your holy battle will be done.

—Adrienne Kennedy, A *Rat's Mass*

Early critical response argued that Kennedy's plays reflected certain components of the theatre of the absurd.[9] One sees this comparison in Kennedy's use of burlesque and the grotesque, and in Eugene Ionesco's ideas about how these elements establish an effective theatre.

> So if the essence of the theatre lay in magnifying its effects, they had to be magnified still further underlined and stressed to the maximum. To push drama out of that intermediate zone where it is neither theatre nor literature is to restore it to its domain, to its natural frontiers. It was not for me to conceal the devices of the theatre, but rather make them still more evident deliberately obvious go all out for caricature and the grotesque, way beyond the pale irony of witty exaggeration of parody. Humor, yes, but using the methods of burlesques. Comic effects that are firm, broad and outrageous. No dramatic comedies either. But back to the endurable. Everything to raised paroxysm, where the source of tragedy lies. A theatre of violence: violently comic, violently dramatic.[10]

It is in this "violent theatre" that one finds the plays of Adrienne Kennedy. (I vividly remember the Great Lakes Workshop production of *The Ohio*

State Murders, and the image of Suzanne walking slowly on the stage and stating that she would explain why her plays were so violent.) Violence is to be found in both image and text and has been in Kennedy's dramaturgy from the beginning.

Kennedy's autobiographical essay "Becoming a Playwright" documents her personal struggle with the effectiveness and violence in the word "nigger" in *Funnyhouse*. Originally Kennedy had used the word throughout to illustrate and "define" Sarah's self-hatred, but then she took all instances of the word "nigger" out of the script. Edward Albee chided her for this action: "Well, do you know what a playwright is? A playwright is someone who lets his guts out on the stage and that's what you've done in this play."[11] In the area of language, Kennedy follows in an absurdist tradition that includes Albee, Kopit, and Baraka.

Another component to this aspect of violence in the theatre of the absurd is the fear of the "absent presence." John Killinger in *Worlds in Collapse* describes the following characteristics of the absurd movement.

> But most Theatre of the Absurd derives its basic absurdity, its awryness, from this discovery of metaphysical emptiness, of the vacuum where for centuries it had been believed there was a presence. God is the linchpin suddenly discovered missing from the machinery of living; and the moment the absence is noticed, everything flies apart, nothing coheres, the world collapses into anarchy and madness.[12]

In *A Rat's Mass*, a Kennedyesque description of this worldview, a world without a presence, is spoken in the words of Rosemary through Brother Rat:

> Where are you going Rosemary? we say. And she says, "I have to go to Catechism." Why do you always go to Catechism? "Because I am Catholic"; then thinking, she says, "Colored people are not Catholics, are they?"
> (*Rats*, 58)

In an absurd context, "colored" Brother and Sister Rat are without benefit of a religion and therefore, a presence, and this absence gnaws at the base of their existence. We see the same desire for presence in *The Owl Answers* when Clara says, "I want what everyone wants....Love or something" (*Owl*, 36), and in *Movie Star*, when Clara says, "I belong to God and the owls" (*Movie Star*, 101).

In addition to "violence" and a longing for "presence," the absurd playwrights often placed their plays in a stylized, symbolic, subjective universe. Kennedy's relationship to the absurd derives in part from her emphasis on a nonempirical reality, primarily represented as myth, history, and the significance of a "voyage." Kennedy documents how she shifted styles:

After I read and saw *Blood Wedding*, I changed my ideas about what a play was. Ibsen, Chekhov, O'Neill and even Williams fell away. Never again would I try to set a play in a living room, never again would I be afraid to have my characters talk in a non-realistic way, and I would abandon the realistic set for a greater dream setting. It was a turning point. (*People*, 108)

Although not a member of the absurd movement, Lorca, the poetic, polemic, imagistic, revolutionary playwright, would form a central structure within Kennedy's dramaturgic architecture. Both Lorca and Kennedy frame political questions within a subjective, poetic, "inner" universe, and they both share the absurdist's obsession with the theme of individual struggle within pre- and overdetermined realities.

The "dream setting" within the Kennedy theatre often represents the unraveling of one or several intertwined myths at the crisis of racial, sexual, and cultural intersection. Kennedy's preoccupation with myth forces her to abandon mimetic representation on the physical stage and substitute an altar upon which she stages an ontological argument in which nothing is certain except the mutable resisting image before us. Kennedy employs this technique to illustrate her concern with the absent presence. Kennedy's characters could be said to represent a crisis of spirit(s). At some point, the process of individuation has become either fragmented or stripped away, leaving the character in desperation and longing for a presence (or presences). Kennedy's universe for A *Rat's Mass* is the absurd picturization of a philosophical/psychological/personal/cultural angst and includes past, present, and future history, often occurring simultaneously:

Kay within our room I see our dying baby, Nazis, screaming girls and cursing boys, empty swings, a dark sun. There are worms in the attic beams. (*Stands*.) They scream and say we are damned. I see dying and grey cats walking. Rosemary is atop the slide. Exalted! (*Kneels again*.) Kay within our room I see a dying baby, Nazis, again they scream. (*Stands again*.) and say we are damned. Within our once Capitol I see us dying. Rosemary is atop the slide exalted. [Give that one to your set designer!] (*Rats*, 56)

Within a violent universe, Sarah (*Funnyhouse*) is haunted by several figures, her "selves," all of whom represent archetypes within her collective unconscious: Queen Victoria, the Duchess of Hapsburg, Patrice Lumumba, and Jesus Christ. Sarah needs to order these figures, represented as myths, or perhaps image, in order to define self. Sarah states:

When I am the Duchess of Hapsburg I sit opposite Victoria in my headpiece and we talk. The other time I wear the dress of a student, dark clothes and dark stockings. Victoria always wants me to tell her of whiteness. She wants me to tell her of a royal world where everything and everyone is white and there are no unfortunate black ones. For as we of royal blood know, black is evil and has been from the beginning. Even before my mother's hair started to fall out. Before she was raped by a wild black beast. Black was evil.

   As for myself I long to become even a more pallid Negro than I am now; pallid like Negroes on the covers of American Negro magazines; soulless, educated and irreligious. I *want to possess no moral value, particularly value as to my being.* I *want not to be.* I ask nothing except anonymity.
(*Funnyhouse*, 5–6; italics added)

It is when Sarah views her "selves" in relation to one of the historic figures that she is most comfortable. For Sarah, however, the action of the play occurs when the myths are "resisting" each other. It is at this existential nucleus of "selves," with its multiple vertices of race, gender, class, and culture continuously represented as resisting, maddening, metamorphosizing images, that Sarah has glimpses of *all and none* of her realities, and with that, knowledge of an absent presence.

Many African peoples believe that every person has a male and female side; one of Sarah's "selves" is Patrice Lumumba (the assassinated, quintessential African hero). When Lumumba speaks, we witness the disintegration of Sarah's personal histories and consequently of her universe as well:

Too then, there is no theme. No statements. I might borrow a statement, struggle to fabricate a theme, borrow one from my contemporaries, renew one from the master, hawkishly scan other stories searching for statements, consider the theme then deceive myself that I held such a statement within me, refusing to accept the fact that a statement has to come from an ordered force. I might try to join horizontal elements such as dots on a horizontal line, or create a centrifugal force, or create causes and effects so that they would equal a quantity but it would be a lie. For the statement is the characters and the characters are myself.[13]

Sarah's inability to exist at the intersection of resisting realities and images, to unravel their meaning within an Aframerican context, marks her as a person without reality (or within madness). External forces that shape character have the potential to destroy the inner spirit. As a result of conflicting external forces, a battle is waged in Sarah between projected image(s) of self/selves and a real self. Kennedy treats and elaborates this theme repeatedly in her next work, *The Owl Answers*, and later in *A Movie Star Has to Star in Black and White*.

   It is tempting to situate Kennedy as a modern American absurdist, one whose origins could be traced to the fall of the American transcendentalists' idealism. However, this approach succeeds only partially; such a discussion illumines aspects of Kennedy's theatre but leaves us groping for more. For me, this discussion of the absurd minimizes the struggles of Kennedy's characters and limits them within traditional gazes. Kennedy's characters ultimately rise above their individual struggles, and this is due in part to their Aframerican composition and Kennedy's "materialist gaze."

Image III: The Diaspora

Chinosole's essay, "Audre Lorde and Matrilineal Diaspora" is one of the most stimulating articles I have read on Aframerican writing because it develops an Afracentric framework that acknowledges the impact of a diasporic aesthetic. Chinosole centers her discussion on the assumption that the forced displacement of African-Americans (as a result of the slave trade), economic underdevelopment, and colonization aesthetically impacted Aframerican culture. However, miraculously and over time, the positive concept of matrilineal diaspora developed:

> [It is] the capacity to survive and aspire, to be contrary and self-affirming across continents and generations. It names the strength and beauty we pass on as friends and lovers from foremothers to mothers and daughters allowing us to survive radical cultural changes and be empowered through differences. Matrilineal diaspora defines the links among Black women worldwide enabling us to experience distinct but related cultures while retaining a special sense of home as the locus of self-definition and power.[14]

Chinosole derives her concept of matrilineal diaspora from the autobiographical writings of Audre Lorde and later links this concept to Paule Marshall, Toni Morrison, Alice Walker, and others. I would like to extend the concept to Kennedy.

As we have seen, Kennedy's trip to Africa is pivotal for many reasons: her connection with African theatrical practices, her personal renaissance, and her reevaluation of "presence." A final product of that "voyage" is related to the concept of matrilineal diaspora in its broadest sense. While in Africa, upon notification of her first formal publication, Kennedy rejoices in her connection with

> Chinua Achebe, Amos Tutola, Wole Soyinka, Efua Sutherland, Lawrence Durrell (poems, especially one called "Christ in Brazil"). I bought these books at the bookstore at the University of Legon. Now that I was going to be published in Black Orpheus, I was joined to these writers and I wanted to read their work. (People, 121)

In Ghana, Kennedy feels joined to other black writers of the diaspora. Within a diasporic cultural context of displacement, the difficulty I have encountered in placing Kennedy's images and character might be explained. Chinosole argues that

> the forced displacement of Blacks resulted in a sense of self that was often culturally contradictory and fragmented in a hostile, dominant society. The Black diaspora experience required an acceptance of fragmentation and adaptation as critical to survival.[15]

When viewed under Chinosole's lens, Kennedy's characters can be said to possess an inner/inter cultural, an inner/inter textual, and an inner dramaturgically fragmented and culturally contradictory restlessness. Echoes of restlessness are heard in the chorale finale of *Funnyhouse* in which all the "selves" speak:

> He never tires of the journey, he who is...the darkest one of them all. My mother looked like a white woman, hair as straight as any white woman's. I am yellow but he is black, the darkest one of us all. How I hoped he was dead, yet he never tires of the journey. It was because of him that my mother died because she let a black man put his hands on her. Why does he keep returning? He keeps returning forever, keeps returning and returning....
> But he is dead
> And he keeps returning. Then he is not dead.
> Then he is not dead.
> Yet, he is dead, but dead he comes knocking at my door.
> (*Funnyhouse*, 20-21)

Fragmentation and restlessness might account for the extensive use of metamorphosis in Kennedy's dramaturgy. Kennedy's characters assume image as part of their fragmentation and alienation, and they are in the restless process of survival: Clara, from woman to animal; Sarah, in reincarnation of "selves"; and Suzanne, in time omnipresent.

In conclusion, I am tempted to develop the poetic-historical context of the diaspora and an African and American continuum to say that Kennedy's travelers are existentially suspended in the historic middle passage and are headed homeward. As Efua Sutherland has said:

> You don't always have to have a message when you communicate. You are thinking *through a problem* or something. If this is a problem which forms the theme of your play you ought to be able to communicate it.[16]

Whatever the final words, I do feel comfortable in saying that Kennedy's characters, a true product of multiculturalism *and* cultural pluralism, are created to resist and that the characters, the images, *and* Kennedy are continually joined matrilineally.

Notes

I would personally like to thank the following people for their assistance in the development of this essay: Lois More Overbeck, Alma Jean Billingslea-Brown, Chinosole, and Rosemary Curb.

1. Adrienne Kennedy, *People Who Led to My Plays* (New York: Knopf, 1987), 122; hereafter cited in the text.

2. Henry David Thoreau, "Hymn to the August Moon," from *Journal*, in *The American Transcendentalists*, ed. Perry Miller (New York: Doubleday, 1957), 80.

3. Thoreau, in *The American Transcendentalists*, 70.

4. All text citations to *Funnyhouse of a Negro, The Owl Answers*, A Rat's Mass, and A Movie Star Has to Star in Black and White are from *Adrienne Kennedy in One Act* (Minneapolis: University of Minnesota Press, 1988), and are cited in the text.

5. Adrienne Kennedy, *She Talks to Beethoven*, in *Antaeus*, ed. Daniel Halpern (New York: Ecco Press, 1991), 248–58.

6. Nellie Y. McKay, "The Autobiographies of Zora Neale Hurston and Gwendolyn Brooks: Alternate Versions of the Black Female Self," in *Wild Women in the Whirlwind: Afra-American Culture and the Contemporary Literary Renaissance*, ed. Joanne Braxton and Andree Nicola-McLaughlin (New Brunswick, N.J.: Rutgers University Press, 1990), 280.

7. Three sources were consulted to develop the section on Kennedy's connection to African drama. Often conflicting information was given. For example, following Rotimi, Owusu places the Egungun within a secular tradition. Soyinka, however, talks about religious aspects of the Egungun. I would assume that different peoples might attach different importance to the ritual. (Martin Owusu, *Drama of the Gods: A Study of Seven African Plays*, [Roxbury, Mass.: Omenana, 1983], 1–12; Ola Rotimi, "Traditional Nigerian Drama," in *Introduction to Nigerian Literature*, ed. Bruce King [London: Africana, 1971], 36–49; Efua Sutherland with Maxine Lautre, interview in *African Writers Talking*, ed. Cosmo Pieterse and Dennis Duerden [New York: African Publishing, 1972], 184–95.

8. Rotimi, "Traditional Nigerian Drama," 38.

9. Doris Abramson, *Negro Playwrights in the American Theatre, 1925–1969* (New York: Columbia University Press, 1969), 281.

10. Eugene Ionesco, *Notes and Counternotes*, trans. Donald Watson (New York: Grove Press, 1964), 72.

11. Adrienne Kennedy, "Becoming a Playwright," *American Theatre* 4 (Feb. 1988): 27.

12. John Killinger, *World In Collapse: The Vision of Absurd Drama* (New York: Delta, 1971), 25.

13. Adrienne Kennedy, *Funnyhouse of a Negro*, in *Black Drama: An Anthology*, ed. William Brasmer and Dominick Consolo (Columbus, Ohio: Merrill, 1970), 238. This passage is not included in *Funnyhouse of a Negro* as published in *Adrienne Kennedy in One Act*.

14. Chinosole, "Audre Lorde and Matrilineal Diaspora," in *Wild Women*, ed. Braxton and Nicola-McLaughlin, 379.

15. Ibid., 392.

16. Sutherland, *African Writers*, 187.

5

Diverse Angles of Vision: Two Black Women Playwrights

Margaret B. *Wilkerson*

One can never know fully the intricacies and complexities of the creative mind. For the mind not only records the events of one's life, but projects itself into a fictive, imaginative realm capable of clarifying the deeper truths of existence. The minds of black women have been bombarded by the cruelties and absurdities of racism and sexism, which, when added to the normal assaults from the external world, become forces strong enough to destroy the creative spirit or to make withdrawal from the world tempting, if not necessary. Yet from black American women have come some of the most incisive and socially conscious literary works of our time. A recent article on feminist fiction published in the New York Times observed that the work of black women writers, while reflecting interior and intensely personal perspectives, retains a strong consciousness of social involvement.[1] These writers seldom pursue the inner world to the exclusion of external realities, but create a literature that ultimately reveals the personal self as it engages the social and political world.

The plays of Lorraine Hansberry and Adrienne Kennedy offer interesting variations on this choice. Their approaches represent distinctly diverse angles of vision that illuminate not only black experience but aspects of the human condition as well. This essay reflects some of my current biographical and critical research on these playwrights and offers an opportunity for preliminary exploration of each writer's approach to the act of playwriting and her manipulation of experience in the creation of drama.

Hansberry and Kennedy are fascinating because of the power and distinctiveness of their work. Both use the social and political conditions facing blacks as well as their own personal experience as singular reference points for their reflections on important human issues. Yet each is unique in her approach. The difference in their handling of source material is indicative of a difference both in sensibility and theatrical style.

Lorraine Hansberry

Lorraine Hansberry wrote A *Raisin in the Sun*, the first play by a black writer to win, in 1959, the New York Drama Critics Circle Award. She was also the first woman and youngest playwright to win that award. Born in 1930, she lived a brief, intense, socially committed life, dying in 1965 at the age of 34. Her short span of years yielded five published plays (one of which was completed by her former husband and literary executor, the late Robert Nemiroff) and more than sixty magazine and newspaper articles, poems, and speeches. Among her unpublished works are several playscripts, filmscripts, and adaptations, including a treatment and preliminary notes for a play on Mary Wollstonecraft, the nineteenth-century feminist. Her stunning opening scene for a play on the great Haitian liberator Toussaint L'Ouverture was published in 1986. She wrote the text for *The Movement*, a photographic essay on the civil rights movement. *To Be Young, Gifted and Black*, a dramatic compilation of her writings prepared by Nemiroff, toured the country after her death, playing to thousands on campuses and in communities and adding a new and vital phrase to the American idiom. An activist artist, she spoke at civil rights rallies and writers' conferences and confronted then–U.S. Attorney General Robert Kennedy in a controversial meeting with black leaders about the role of the FBI in the Deep South.

Hansberry was a fiercely independent thinker who trusted the intellect instinctively. The roots of her philosophical views lie in Chicago, the place of her birth. Her childhood there held curious contradictions. On the one hand, she grew up in an upper-middle-class family; her father was a powerful realtor who built his fortune on the sale and rental of kitchenettes to relieve the crowded housing conditions of blacks. He won a Supreme Court case against housing discrimination. Her mother, at one point a ward committeewoman, helped to manage the buildings and tenants, but had plenty of time for the leisure-time activities typical of the bourgeoisie. The parents taught their four children pride in themselves and in the race, and nurtured in them the belief that their possibilities were (or should be in a fair society) limitless. On the other hand, she lived in Chicago, a city of racial and ethnic barriers and boundaries. The burgeoning population of blacks, increased periodically by waves of immigrants from the South, was literally confined by restrictive covenants to a sixty-block-long area with a few small neighborhoods nearby into which blacks had moved. Despite her family's financial resources, they could not purchase any home they could afford, nor could they eat in certain restaurants, nor even try on shoes in some of the city's major department stores. Wealth may have freed her mind and spirit, but it could not free her colored body. It should not be surprising, then, that these conditions began to cultivate in the young Lorraine an utter abhorrence of racial discrimination and oppression, and the stereotyping and labeling that come with them. Seeing the absurdities of color prejudice, sometimes played out in her own race, helped her to recognize that racism and other isms were artificial devices used by some peoples to conquer others. In a now-famous statement, she charted her spiritual journey from Chicago to the world community:

> I was born on the South Side of Chicago. I was born black female. I was born in a depression after one world war, and came into my adolescence during another. While I was still in my teens the first atom bombs were dropped on human beings at Nagasaki and Hiroshima. And by the time I was twenty-three years old, my government and that of the Soviet Union had entered actively into the worst conflict of nerves in human history—the Cold War....
>
> I have, like all of you, on a thousand occasions seen indescribable displays of man's very real inhumanity to man, and I have come to maturity, as we all must, knowing that greed and malice and indifference to human misery and bigotry and corruption, brutality, and perhaps above all else, ignorance—the prime ancient and persistent enemy of man—abound in this world.
>
> I say all of this to say that one cannot live with sighted eyes and feeling heart and not know and react to the miseries which afflict this world.[2]

Her abhorrence of narrowness and parochialism later led her to an awareness of the hidden alliance between racism and sexism long before it was popular to do so, and to shape a vision cognizant of the many dimensions of colonialism and oppression. Anticipating the women's movement of the 1970s, Hansberry was aware of the peculiar oppression under which women lived and the particular devastation visited upon women of color. Recognizing its devious forms, she argued forcefully that antihomosexual attitudes were linked to the oppression of women and man's predilection to gain mastery over other men. In an unpublished letter written in 1961, she wrote:

> I have suspected for a good while now that the homosexual in America would ultimately pay a price for the intellectual impoverishment of women

and, in this instance, of homosexual women. It is true that all human questions overlap and while our understanding of a trial in Israel or an execution in Viet Nam may not momentarily be rapid-fire, life has a way of showing up why we should have cared all along. Men continue to misinterpret the second-rate status of women as implying a privileged status for themselves: heterosexuals think the same way about homosexuals; gentiles about Jews; whites about blacks; haves about have-nots....And men, as a sex, find themselves socially strapped and trapped into incredible patterns of conformity that dictate what and how their "manliness" should be in order to hold the place over the lessers....

The relationship of anti-homosexual sentiment to the oppression of women has a special and deep implication. That is to say...that the reason for the double standard of social valuation is rooted in the societal contempt for the estate of womanhood in the first place....Women are not held as responsible for themselves as men are because they are not held as definitely human. There is nothing fine in it; it is, indeed, a reprehensible situation. And it confounds many, including women, of course, and heterosexual and homosexual males. Some homosexual males actually seem to envy a mistaken notion of the "favored" place of women in our culture. They are, as yet, unaware that the pedastal [sic] is really an iron-shoe.[3]

For Hansberry, nothing was "more universal in the world than man's oppression of man." This issue is what "most great dramas have been about, no matter what the device of telling it is.[4] Blacks, women, homosexuals, and any others whose oppression is profitable will be victimized. Within her highly political and humanistic worldview, all art was social—whether intentionally so or not. And it was her role as artist to expose the myths and illusions of her time and culture so that the human race could achieve its true stature.

In a telling response to a young man's query, Hansberry reveals a key element in her approach to playwriting and her handling of raw material. "Why," the young man said to her, "are you so sure the human race *should* go on? You do not believe in a prior arrangement of life on this planet. You know perfectly well that the *reason* for survival does not exist in nature!" Hansberry recounted her response: "I answered him the only way I could: that man is unique in the universe, the only creature who has in fact the power to transform the universe. Therefore, it did not seem unthinkable to me that man might just do what the apes never will—impose the reason for life on life."[5] Impose the reason for life on life. Like a sculptor molding clay, she could create characters and structure a world in which beauties and absurdities of human action could be exposed or treasured, as the case might be.

In the early 1950s Hansberry worked as a journalist and associate editor for *Freedom*, a black progressive newspaper in New York City founded by Paul Robeson. During this time, undercurrents of social protest were quietly growing, despite the Red Scare, McCarthyism, and hearings by the House Un-American Activities Committee. Numerous violations of human rights, brutality of the Deep Southern variety, and labor protests filled the pages of *Freedom* as Hansberry gained an education in politics, culture, and economics unparalleled in any university curriculum. While she treasured this work, she found journalism ultimately too restrictive— for one had to stick with facts, even if they obscured deeper truths. Among her unpublished papers are two versions of a news story about a young black man on trial, falsely accused of draft evasion: one is the article of Hansberry, the journalist, reporting the daily events of the trial; the other is an attempt by Hansberry, the novice playwright, to fictionalize the events by restructuring the incidents and language in order to emphasize the injustice of the situation.

In *A Raisin in the Sun* (1959), we see her first successful attempt to transform the experience of her early years in Chicago into a drama that captures the deferred dreams of a race of people, while exposing the materialistic dangers of the society that evokes, then frustrates those dreams. While aspects of the play obviously illustrate her detailed knowledge of South Side Chicago, the development of the major theme reveals how Hansberry used and then transformed her personal experience into something quite different.

A Raisin in the Sun dramatizes the seductiveness of American materialistic values by depicting the aspirations of a black family, the Youngers, who live in South Side Chicago in the 1950s. The title and theme are taken from a Langston Hughes poem, "Harlem," which asks, "What happens to a dream deferred?" Three generations of Youngers live in a cramped kitchenette apartment. When ten thousand dollars in insurance money is paid to Lena Younger (Mama), the elder of the household, she places a down payment on a house (in a white neighborhood), to the dismay and anger of her son, Walter, who dreams of capitalizing the windfall by investing in a liquor store. Moved by Walter's frustration, Mama gives him a portion of the money—which he promptly loses in a dubious business deal. The financial crisis that he precipitates becomes a critical test of Walter's personal values. The Clybourne Park Improvement Society, historically a familiar fixture in Chicago's housing business, offers to buy out the Youngers at a handsome profit in order to maintain the racial purity of the neighborhood. Sorely tempted to sacrifice his pride and integrity for mercenary values, Walter decides, at first, to accept the offer even if he must degrade himself before these white bigots. "There ain't no causes," says Walter, "there ain't nothing but taking in this world and he who takes most is smartest—and it don't make a damn bit of difference how."

It is indeed a moment of truth for a black man who seeks enough material resources to improve his family's economic situation and to provide his son with a future. Those aims seem acceptable enough. However, Walter's dream is dangerously flawed: he also seeks the kind of material wealth that comes at the price of deceit and oppression. The extent of Walter's dream is revealed in his statement to his son, Travis, about the future that he envisions for him.

> You wouldn't understand yet, son, but your daddy's gonna make a transaction...a business transaction that's going to change our lives.... That's how come one day when you 'bout seventeen years old I'll come home and I'll be pretty tired, you know what I mean, after a day of conferences and secretaries getting things wrong the way they do...'cause an executive's life is hell, man—....And I'll pull the car up on the driveway...just a plain black Chrysler, I think, with white walls—no—black tires. More elegant. Rich people don't have to be flashy...though I'll have to get something a little sportier for Ruth—maybe a Cadillac convertible to do her shopping in....And I'll come up the steps to the house and the gardener will be clipping away at the hedges and he'll say, "Good evening, Mr. Younger." And I'll say, "Hello, Jefferson, how are you this evening?" And I'll go inside and Ruth will come downstairs and meet me at the door and we'll kiss each other and she'll take my arm and we'll go up to your room to see you sitting on the floor with the catalogues of all the great schools in America round you....All the great schools in the world! And—and I'll say, all right son—it's your seventeenth birthday, what is it you've decided?...Just tell me where you want to go to school and you'll go. Just tell me, what it is you want to be—and you'll be it....Whatever you want to be—Yes sir!...You just name it, son...and I hand you the world![6]

House, secretaries, cars are all emblems of the success he seeks. But the dreams of Mama and Walter differ dramatically. Mama wants the family to advance materially without becoming materialistic, while Walter embraces materialism and power—of the kind that has already limited his opportunities. He seeks merely a transfer of power, not a change in the systems of power. If he accepts Lindner's offer to purchase the house, he will take the first step down the self-destructive path of materialism toward a manhood devoid of integrity, compassion, and dignity.

Hansberry had seen the dangers of such confusion in her own brothers, who upon their father's death inherited his business, but little of his philanthropic vision, social commitment, and business acumen. Eventually, through a series of mishaps (some of which were not of their own making), they lost their property in Chicago and moved West. Despite

Hansberry's comfortable life, she rejected the fruits of capitalism and the conspicuous consumption of the bourgeoisie, dressing simply even as a high-school student and ignoring her mother's urging to buy expensive clothes so that she would be in style. In a 1961 interview, Hansberry explained the difference between material need and materialism.

> We have confused acquisition of...trivia, of the paraphernalia of life with a good life...in the United States and we have gotten to a place where...you have the intellectuals turning a very long nose towards what they think is materialism. They have confused trivia with the material good base of life which all human beings need in order to live....Before they can even discuss happiness philosophically, they at least have to have everything that it requires just to bring up....children without rickets or without tuberculosis, and this confusion results in people saying "Well, we've got too many automobiles in America, we've got too many Cadillacs and television sets and all of this...."
>
> The fact of the matter is that there are thousands, millions of people in the United States who don't have too much of anything. They don't have enough and there's a fine and important distinction between that kind of material base of life which simply provides what people need to live a decent life and the middle-class preoccupation with acquisition, with affluence, with these things that they can demonstrate to their neighbors to show that they are keeping up with the fashions.

The Youngers, Hansberry continues, are "between the two":

> They really don't have enough yet. The fact of the family that I was writing about not having a home where a child can have his own bedroom in a country quite as wealthy as this, shouldn't be confused with the fact that some American children drive to school every day in their own private automobiles. Those are two different questions. They are people who are still trying to guarantee just the basic things of life.

Hansberry, however, was not satisfied simply portraying the economic disparity between the poor and the wealthy. She proceeded to attack materialism even when it appeared in the midst of poverty, as she explains in the following excerpt from the same interview:

> At the same time, if I may say so, the complication of the play is that I don't want the hero of the play to get lost....[He] thinks that he wants yachts and pearls because this is what he sees all around him...the people who seem to command his world, to be in charge of it are full of yachts and pearls in their lives. I don't want him to get confused about the reality of the one thing he really does need for his family with the other. One is paraphernalia, one is fluff and the other is a real base of good life and good living—and he is confused. He is representative of those people in

our culture who are [confused]....The play makes the statement at the end that when money intrudes on those things which we know that we have to have for any kind of moral health as a people, and I mean all Americans, by Heavens, let us choose for the other thing, not for the money.

The focal moment of that play very much hangs on the denunciation of money values when the mother confronts the son who is considering this betrayal of his heritage of a great people and says: "I want what the bourgeois has." The Mother says to him from her resources as a daughter of the Negro peasantry, of Negro slave classes: "I come from five generations of slaves and sharecroppers and ain't nobody in my family never taken no kind of money that was a way of telling us we wasn't fit to walk the earth."[7]

This is Hansberry—engaged in life but at once also observing it, and refusing to be a prisoner of middle-class upbringing.

The Sign in Sidney Brustein's Window (1964), the second and the last of her plays to be produced during her lifetime, offers even more striking examples of Hansberry's objectivity toward her material. The play, which shocked some critics because it was not about black people specifically, focused on Sidney Brustein, a Greenwich Village intellectual, who, through his new and struggling newspaper, supports a local politician's campaign for office. The play charts Sidney's personal odyssey toward self-realization and affirmation of his responsibility to engage and act in this world. Some early notes on this play indicate that Hansberry originally intended the title to be *The Sign in Jenny Reed's Window*, with a female character as the central figure. However, over a period of time she decided that it would not suit her purposes. While speculation continues as to why she made this change, her choice demonstrated her ability to write authentic, convincing male characters, if she had not already proven that talent in *A Raisin in the Sun*. One suspects that the final structure of the play with its male protagonist served her social statement as well as if not better than a Jenny Reed would have. For while Sidney is the central figure, he is educated to his own chauvinism, intolerance, and self-indulgence by three sisters who collectively present a tapestry of women victimized by this society.

The primary woman in Sidney's life is Iris, his wife, who tolerates the "Pygmalion-like" relationship that initially attracted and continues to hold her husband. Despite his progressive outlook on society, Sidney's views on women are nearly Neanderthal. He demeans Iris's attempts at intellectual discourse and reinforces a girl-child image, complete with flowing hair and idyllic ignorance. When Iris begins to rebel against this image (she eventually cuts off her long hair), Sidney is shocked. In an attempt to gain some independent status and to compensate for her failures as an actress, she settles for television commercials whose products make unjustifiable claims, participating knowingly and willingly in this deception. However, Iris's desire for the tinsel of stardom does not blind her to the truth about the "progressive" politician whom Sidney is supporting. She realizes that he is a stooge of the political bosses who have always fostered dope traffic and other criminal activities in the area. Sidney, with all his erudite intellectuality, has not seen through a cheap politician.

Mavis, his sister-in-law, is portrayed as a bourgeois matron—the stereotype of the uptight Gentile whose racial prejudice and provincialism come through in the simplest of conversations. Sidney and his friends enjoy many laughs at her expense. Yet it is Mavis who teaches him about courage—she who has lived with the secret that her straitlaced husband has supported a young mistress and illegitimate son for years, and who has made peace with that knowledge. Noting Sidney's shock, Mavis comments on his naiveté:

> Sometimes I think you kids down here [Greenwich Village] believe your own notions of what the rest of the human race is like. There are no squares, Sidney. Believe me when I tell you, everybody is his own hipster.[8]

Sidney can only salute this woman whose humanity and intellect he has ridiculed.

Finally, Gloria deals the deathblow to his smugness—Gloria, the high-priced prostitute who had the fantasy that she could leave her mink-lined, sordid profession, with its dope addiction and violent repercussions, by marrying Alton, a young black man. Sidney's last illusions are shattered when Alton breaks the engagement and Gloria commits suicide, while Sidney lies in a drunken stupor, wrapped in his own disappointments. Gloria is the most tragic victim, symbolizing the ultimate, perhaps in the oppression of women. Mavis has reconciled her disappointment and made life, such as it is, with her husband. And by the end of the play, Iris has asserted herself and forced Sidney to view her and himself in a different way. The possibilities for their relationship begin at the end of the play. But for Gloria there is no new beginning—at least not in this life. She had become trapped in a role that her world made attractive, a role that she continued to accept and to which she became addicted. Her end is inevitable self-destruction. Hansberry places in the hands of this "Greek chorus," the Parodus sisters, the true "education" of Sidney and reveals the varied permutations of women's victimization.

Her handling of the only homosexual character in the play exemplifies her ability to use material without regard to her personal experience or preference but to expose ignorance and pretentiousness wherever she found it. By the time this play was written, Hansberry had already written some plays, short stories, and essays exploring the theme of homosexuality and denouncing homophobia. By this time she had also become comfortable with her own lesbianism and was involved with a circle of intimate women friends. Yet David, a playwright in *The Sign in Sidney Brustein's Window* who is a homosexual, embodies many of the characteristics personally detested by Hansberry. He is a whining, self-indulgent character who wears his sexual preference like a chip on his shoulder, daring anyone to knock it off. He writes absurdist plays—such as one for which he has won a prize, about two men who are married. The entire action takes place in a refrigerator. (Some say that he is an intentional parody of Edward Albee, but Hansberry denied it.) When David accuses Alton, the only black character in the play, of persecuting him and suggests that he might be a closet homosexual, Hansberry puts these words in Sidney's mouth:

> Oh no...Come on, David! Don't start that jazz with me tonight. Is that the best you can do? I mean it! Is that really it? Anybody who attacks one—is one? Can it, boy!

David reacts:

> It seems to have conveniently escaped your attention that *I* am the insulted party here.

Sidney retorts:

> If somebody insults you—sock 'em in the jaw. If you don't like the sex laws, attack 'em, I think they're silly. You wanna get up a petition? I'll sign one. Love little fishes if you want. But David, please get over the notion that your particular "thing" is something that only the deepest, saddest, the most nobly tortured can know about. It ain't—...it's just one kind of sex—that's all. And, in my opinion—...the universe turns regardless.[9]

Even so, Hansberry later grants David his humanity and complexity by exposing his painful sojourn through his life as a homosexual.

Again, here is Hansberry the intellectual, controlling her characters (and her own emotions) and insisting on distance between herself and her subject matter while utilizing the knowledge and memory of passionate encounters. Only in this way, can she command her universe to yield the truths that she seeks for her audience.

This imposition of will suggests a "dark" side to Hansberry that is as much aware of the brutal, selfish, irrational side of humankind as of its transcendent potential. A *Raisin in the Sun*, in fact, whose upbeat ending sometimes obscures the danger into which the family is moving, had a different ending in an earlier version. This earlier ending showed the family seated in the darkened living room of their new home, shades drawn, family armed, awaiting the inevitable attack by their hostile white neighbors. Probably no other line dramatizes this idea more effectively than Sidney's speech near the end of *The Sign in Sidney Brustein's Window*. Now having faced the abyss of human corruption and suffering, he acknowledges his pain—but pushes through it to action. The line is written as one sentence with practically no punctuation so that the words tumble out of Sidney in an emotional outpouring. But even as he is swept up in this passionate response, he imposes his own will and intellect on that rush of words—directing them toward action when they could just as easily lead him to withdrawal from the world.

> |I am| a fool who believes that death is waste and love is sweet and that the earth turns and men change every day and that rivers run and that people wanna be better than they are and that flowers smell good and that I hurt terribly today, and the hurt is desperation and desperation is— energy and energy can move things.[10]

Adrienne Kennedy

Adrienne Kennedy is quite opposite in her approach to and structuring of material, for hers is not a journalistic or dialectical style, but rather imagistic.[11] Her plays are short and intense, with the dense language of symbolic poetry. Working in a surrealistic theatrical style, Kennedy acknowledges the violence that is just beneath the surface in most human beings. Her characters walk the line between dream and consciousness, between reality and the surreal fantasies of the subconscious.

Adrienne Kennedy is one of the few accomplished black playwrights who employs the surrealistic mode of theatre. *Funnyhouse of a Negro*, her first produced work, earned an Obie Award in 1964 and established hers as a unique voice in the avant-garde theatre of the 1960s. "While almost every black playwright in the country is fundamentally concerned with realism—LeRoi Jones and Ed Bullins at times have something different going but even their symbolism is straightforward stuff—Miss Kennedy is weaving some kind of dramatic fabric of poetry," observed *New York Times* critic Clive Barnes in a 1969 review.[12] Kennedy's plays have been produced in major theatres in the United States and Europe, including the Royal Court Theatre and the National Theatre in London, the Petit Odéon in Paris, the Yale Repertory, La Mama Experimental Theatre Company, and Joseph Papp's New York Public Theater. Several of her scripts have been translated into Spanish, French, Danish, German, and Portuguese and have been broadcast by Radio Denmark and the BBC. Kennedy's audience amounts to a cult following and includes many of the leading theatre artists in the world. Her plotless, richly symbolic plays are evocative and appeal to a racially diverse audience. Employing images from her dreams and memory as well as figures from the mythical and historical past, she brings unusual impressionistic insights to the human and particularly the American experience. Of the more than fourteen plays that she has authored, most have been produced professionally and published.

When growing up in the comfortable, middle-class community of Cleveland, Ohio, Adrienne Kennedy gave little indication of the intense, violent images that would later characterize her plays. She was an imaginative and gifted child who learned to read at the age of three. Adrienne grew up in an integrated neighborhood rich with the ethnic cultures of Italians, blacks, Jews, Poles, and others. She enjoyed activities such as social clubs and Latin clubs characteristic of middle-class families of the time. Both parents were college graduates and had high expectations for their daughter. They urged Adrienne to be competitive and to aspire to professional work. The supportive atmosphere gave Adrienne confidence in herself and nurtured her belief that people of diverse cultural backgrounds could live together harmoniously. An avid reader, she encountered the classics early and devoured new books in her local library as quickly as they arrived on the shelf. Reveling in the many stories that she read and her own active imagination, she began writing fiction at an early age.

The culturally diverse and receptive community of Cleveland did not prepare her for the hostile atmosphere of Ohio State University, where she matriculated. There she found overt racism and discrimination more characteristic of southern cities of the 1950s. Many of the restaurants were segregated and the white students on campus did not socialize or interact in any fashion with black students. This experience made an indelible mark on her sensibility and engendered an anger and hatred for prejudice and racism that would later find compelling expression in her plays.

Kennedy graduated from Ohio State University with a degree in education and, two weeks later, married Joseph C. Kennedy on May 15, 1953. In six months, she found herself pregnant and back home with her parents, waiting for her husband to return from Korea where he had been sent by the U.S. Army. Lonely and with time on her hands, she turned to creative pursuits, and made her initial attempts at writing: a piece based on Elmer Rice's *Street Scene*, and *Pale Blue Flowers*, based on Tennessee Williams's *Glass Menagerie*. In 1961, she found her own voice as she began *Funnyhouse of a Negro*, her best-known and longest dramatic play.

Adrienne Kennedy's plays are an expression of her self. She views writing as "an outlet for inner, psychological confusion and questions stemming from childhood" and a creative way to figure out "the 'why' of things."[13] Because of her experiences as a black woman, her knowledge of the classics, and her extensive travels in Europe and Africa, the material lodged in her memory is rich with the stuff of cultural as well as personal conflict. The individual's struggle with self and internalized social and cultural forces is the focal point of most of her plays. Writing from the inside out, as it were, Kennedy's works are autobiographical and surrealistic, and project onto the stage an interior reality. She uses her family and personal experiences as metaphors rather than literal examples. The name of a family member, for example, may be assigned to a character who is in fact a composite of historical and mythical as well as living figures.

The shocking nature of her images emanates from her insistence on honestly portraying material from the subconscious. "Your intellect is always working against you to censor....One must always fight against that imitation of oneself."[14] Thus, her plays are controversial, intense, and force unrelenting encounters with myriad selves. She will create a character like Sarah in *Funnyhouse of a Negro*, in whose confused mind Patrice Lumumba, a hero of African liberation movements, becomes a raping father and husband. Kennedy's characters reveal the dysfunction between public and private selves, as well as the terrifying world of the subconscious. The multiple levels of consciousness make her plays both personally and politically significant.

A poet of the theatre, Kennedy's language is condensed, imagistic, and rhythmic. The repetition and seeming irrationality of the dream world is characteristic of her dialogue. They are the theatrical counterpart of the short story, both in length (her longest dramatic work has a forty-five-minute playing time) and in power. Plot, event, and character in the traditional realistic sense are absent from her plays. A character may represent the several selves of the central figure or may be multiple, having several names to designate the various parts of his or her personality. Metaphor, image, and symbol are the major elements in her work.

In 1960–61, Kennedy took an extended trip through Europe and Africa; it would become a turning point in her life. Because her husband was away much of the time conducting a research project and her son was very young, Kennedy had a lot of time to reflect and to write. For several years, she had tried to capture in dramatic form the theme closest to her heart, the individual at war with inner forces and struggling with conflicting sides of the personality. She had used the works of favorite playwrights Tennessee Williams and Garcia Lorca as models, but the results had lacked power and the confidence of her own style. However, new images from the strange yet familiar places that she visited crowded into her consciousness and combined with memories from her earlier life to create the material for *Funnyhouse of a Negro* and several subsequent plays. She saw, for example, the mammoth statue of Queen Victoria in front of Buckingham Palace in London, and later used it prominently in this play. In an unpublished interview, she describes her impressions of Africa.

> This was a thirteen-month trip that started in London to Paris to Madrid to Africa—one month in Liberia, five months in Ghana, and eight months in Rome. [It] changed my whole life, changed my writing....I started it in Ghana. We lived in this white house...with a black fence in Accra. My husband was gone all day. He was on this research grant and so my son and I were in this house and they had this person who was a gardener. I really respond to heat, I don't know what the temperature was. That's when I started to write *Funnyhouse*—because this heat, there was something frightening about this heat. There were lizards all around....There were a lot of rats in the underbrush—and the sun. This is how I felt it—the sun was just like right here [close].

The sights, sounds, and smells of Africa were palpable to Kennedy as the physicality of the landscape permeated her consciousness. She continues:

> And the moon—I could go out at night—it was like the moon was that close because you're near the equator. Right? The heat, the moment you got up, you were in the heat again....When you walked outside there was the overpowering smell of...flowers—sick, sweet smell. The air was filled with that. There were owls in the trees. At night, rats were in the underbrush. To me it was the most intense thing I had ever experienced. We went for these drives—on the savannah—we went for these drives. And to me that was the most beautiful part. Saw all the trees—the white frankopenny trees.

Ghana had gained its freedom from colonial rule only seven years earlier and was still in the throes of establishing its political and economic independence. Kennedy observed the people's response to their new government and also felt the repercussions of unrest in neighboring Zaire (formerly the Belgian Congo).

> One thing that was important was the whole psychological thing....
> Nkrumah was president, so we used to go to the airport and would watch Nkrumah when he'd fly in—this is what people did on Sunday afternoon. Just to do something. They'd go and watch Nkrumah come in from

somewhere. But the people were so beautiful. All that cloth from Belgium. Most of it had Nkrumah's face on it and, of course, Patrice Lumumba [the first president of Zaire] was murdered while we were there. So that's all that people talked about, that Patrice Lumumba was murdered and we were on the beaches and the beaches were just white beaches with wild horses running on them. It was exactly twenty-one years ago, but it's so clear to me as if it were right this moment because to come out of New York City into that was to me the most indelible, it was indelible....I've never seen colors like that. I've just never seen colors like that.

As Kennedy describes her visit to Liberia, she sharpens her political focus without sacrificing the poetic metaphors characteristic of her language and thought patterns.

Then we took a trip in this tiny plane to Liberia. Someplace on the coast. I really was shocked and this played a big part in *Funnyhouse* because I didn't know, it just never occurred to me that Goodyear owned almost all of Liberia. Remember now, it was just like a learning experience. We got off in Liberia and drove for miles and miles and miles and miles in this taxi. And the driver says, "This all belongs to Goodyear." All the rubber plantations. I was shocked when we arrived at this dingy little town, Monrovia, and stayed in this place. They had only two hotels. One was the Hilton and we didn't want to stay there; and the other was owned by this man from Lebanon. We stayed there, and there were bugs all over the room. But we didn't want to stay at the Hilton. And this guy on the street said, "Hilton owns this; Goodyear owns the rest," and that was Liberia.[15]

Notice that the words *colonialism* and *oppression* are not used here. But the *images* of that historical condition are unmistakable.

She began writing *Funnyhouse of a Negro* in West Africa and completed it in Rome, while carrying her second son, Adam. In this play she found her own potent voice. The title derives from an amusement park in Cleveland that featured a "funnyhouse" with two huge white figures perched on either side, bobbing back and forth and laughing hysterically at the confused patrons within. The play, set in a nightmare world, features Sarah, a young Negro woman, who is tormented by personifications of her various selves: a balding Queen Victoria and Duchess of Hapsburg, mother figures dressed in cheap satin, who fear the return of the black father/husband; Patrice Lumumba/father/husband who surrounds himself with white friends in order to forget his calling to save his people; and an impotent Jesus Christ who is haunted by his inability to escape his blackness. Unable to bear the ambiguities and burdens of being black, Sarah commits suicide at the end of the play. Her landlady and Raymond, her Jewish boyfriend, who parallel the laughing figures of the Cleveland funnyhouse, deliver the eulogy: "The poor bitch has hung herself....She was a funny little liar." While "truth" is utterly subjective in this play, the violence and power of the images lend a stark reality to the destructive confusion in Sarah's mind.

The contrapuntal, repetitious dialogue of the characters combine with the myriad symbols (e.g., white doves, black ravens, falling hair) to reinforce Sarah's struggle with identity, love, and God. There is no plot in the traditional sense. As one character explains in the first pages of the text:

> There is no theme. No statements, I might borrow a statement, struggle to fabricate a theme, borrow one from my contemporaries, renew one from the master, hawkishly scan other stories searching for statements, consider the theme then deceive myself that I held such a statement within me, refusing to accept the fact that a statement has to come from an ordered force. I might try to join horizontal elements such as dots on a horizontal line, or create a centrifugal force, or create causes and effects so that they would equal a quantity but it would be a lie. For the statement is the characters and the characters are myself.[16]

Despite this seeming disclaimer, Kennedy creates a highly coherent, evocative piece.

While Kennedy drew on close relatives and family stories in shaping this play, she does not treat them literally, but uses them as metaphors for particular forces at work in Sarah's life. Thus while Sarah's conflict is intensely personal and emanates from Kennedy's own explorations of her consciousness, it is also metaphorical and symptomatic of the ambiguous state of a people who were created out of the clash of African and European cultures. On one level, the play dramatizes the anguish of a Negro woman—wracked with self-hatred—whose father is black and whose mother is fair-skinned. But on a more profound level, Sarah is the progeny of Europe and Africa, two mighty continents engaged in mortal combat. The Duchess of Hapsburg and Queen Victoria between them represent the royal line beginning with the Holy Roman Empire, which solidified the power of Europe and thrust England into preeminence as a colonial power. Jesus Christ suggests the religion that became the rationale for conquest. Patrice Lumumba, the martyred leader, represents the emerging African nations. In the play, these figures constantly clash—the Duchess's and Queen's claim of rape being the metaphor for every contact between Sarah's father and mother. Thus Sarah's "personal identity crisis" is at once a crisis with political and social resonance—a legacy of the historical confrontation between white Europeans and black Africans.

In her second play, *The Owl Answers*, Kennedy continues to draw from her memorable trip. This work, however, probes the cultural and mythical dimensions of the encounter between Africa and Europe. As in *Funnyhouse of a Negro*, the central figure is a young Negro woman, She, who desperately seeks to resolve her love/hatred for black/white and to reconcile her conflicting impulses toward carnality and purity so that she can formulate a coherent identity. Instead of multiple selves personified by different characters/actors as in the first play, the female protagonist in *The Owl Answers* assumes several personifications: in the cast list, "She" is designated as "She who is Clara Passmore who is the Virgin Mary who is the Bastard who is the Owl." The identity conflict is internalized and potently realized in rich symbolism: the pagan and deathly images of the owl, the fecund tribal mythology of the fig tree, and the spirituality and carnal denial of the Virgin Mary. The cultural past and present are symbolized in three characters (Shakespeare, Chaucer, and William the Conqueror) and in the protagonist's parents: Bastard's Black Mother who is the Reverend's Wife who is Anne Boleyn, and the Goddam Father who is the Richest White Man in the Town who is the Dead Father who is Reverend Passmore. The intellectual rape of this black woman and the impossibility of coping with the multilayered historical, mythical, and cultural contradictions is dramatized by her complaint: "I call God and the Owl answers."[17] The play ends with the image of She turning into an owl, lifting her bowed head, staring into space and crying, "Ow...oww."[18]

Kennedy's characters suggest a terrifying relationship between the private self and public history, between African and European mythology. Although her black female protagonists, in particular, feel the awful weight of an antithetical Western civilization, the destructive conflict within them depicts the dilemma of all who live in the New World.

Lorraine Hansberry was, in retrospect, the intellectual, consciously imposing order on the chaos of experience and generally working within the framework of theatrical realism. She insisted on meaning, on affirmation, willing it into being, even though she was deeply aware of the absurdity and irrationality of human beings. Her efforts to affirm life while recognizing its negative aspects suggest a desperate desire to prevent the "dark side" from taking over. Thus her plays focus on individuals as they struggle to act responsibly and humanely in this world. The implications for social action are strong in the plays. She draws from personal experience as well as from historical material, and so transforms that material within the dialectical structure of her plays that she successfully masks the reality of her own life. Adrienne Kennedy, on the other hand, is comfortable with the violence in people and works against the censoring intellect. Her characters walk the thin line between fantasy and consciousness, between dreams and reality. Approaching her theatrical material as poet, she writes plays pregnant with symbolism and language dense with multiple meanings. Kennedy stares into the abyss and grants it a metaphor. Thus her characters are not necessarily affirming beings, but rather explicate the mysterious and primeval fears of humans. Peering at her characters from a different angle, Kennedy studies the psychological effect of historical forces on her characters. Their personal fantasy world becomes the battleground for cultural identity and soul. Her intensely personal images combine with political and social symbols to evoke disturbing thoughts about the cultural being in the New World. Hansberry's and Kennedy's diverse angles of vision bespeak creative minds that offer their own unique perspectives on what it means to be a black woman and what it means to be human.

NOTES

1. Elinor Langer, "Whatever Happened to Feminist Fiction?" New York Times Book Review, March 4, 1984, 1, 35.

2. Lorraine Hansberry, To Be Young, Gifted and Black (Englewood Cliffs, N.J.: Prentice-Hall, 1969), 11–12.

3. Unpublished letter written by Lorraine Hansberry, dated April 18, 1961.

4. Lorraine Hansberry, interview by Eleanor Fisher for Columbia Broadcasting Company, June 7, 1961.

5. Hansberry, To Be Young, Gifted and Black, 40.

6. Lorraine Hansberry, A Raisin in the Sun and The Sign in Sidney Brustein's Window (New York: New American Library, 1987), 108–9.

7. Hansberry interview.

8. Hansberry, A Raisin in the Sun and The Sign in Sidney Brustein's Window, 308.

9. Ibid., 247–48.

10. Ibid., 317–18.

11. Portions of the literary and biographical material on Kennedy are excerpted from Margaret B. Wilkerson, "Adrienne Kennedy," in Afro-American Writers after 1955: Dramatists and Prose Writers, ed. Thadious M. Davis and Trudier Harris, vol. 38 of Dictionary of Literary Biography) (Detroit, Mich.: Gale Research, 1985), 162–69.

12. Clive Barnes, "A Rat's Mass," New York Times, Nov. 1, 1969, 39, col. 1.

13. Adrienne Kennedy, "A Growth of Images," Drama Review 21 (Dec. 1977): 42.

14. Ibid.

15. Unpublished interview with Adrienne Kennedy conducted by Margaret B. Wilkerson, May 30, 1982.

16. Adrienne Kennedy, Funnyhouse of a Negro, in Contemporary Black Drama, ed. Clinton F. Oliver and Stephanie Sills (New York: Scribner, 1971), 195.

17. Adrienne Kennedy, The Owl Answers, in Black Theater U.S.A., ed. James V. Hatch (New York: Free Press, 1974), 763.

18. Kennedy, The Owl Answers, 764.

6

Adrienne Kennedy and the First Avant-Garde

Elinor Fuchs

There are some writers in the theatre, not many, whose works read as if they were scooped up by radiotelescope. One finds the widest range of previous sources, entire traditions, reflected in their intensely concentrated fields. This is the experience of reading Adrienne Kennedy. Whatever angle I engage her from, Kennedy, like Kilroy, has been there. Her echoes and intimations of the European avant-garde alone span nearly a century of that tradition in both theatre and criticism, from the symbolists to (among others) the surrealists, Lorca, Artaud, Genet, and Roland Barthes. This essay will suggest my own sense of Kennedy's strong connection to what John Henderson has called the "first avant-garde," the international symbolist movement inaugurated in theatre with Van Lerberghe's *Les Flaireurs* and Maeterlinck's short plays of the early 1890s.[1]

The early Kennedy plays of the 1960s, *Funnyhouse of a Negro*, *The Owl Answers*, and *A Rat's Mass*, are mystery or passion plays. They take the form of ritual reenactments, enclose ceremonies and processions, and culminate in dark sacrificial events. Kennedy wrote them in a period when ritual theatre, via Artaud and Genet, was coming into vogue. Yet much of this work (Grotowski, Brook, Serban) became known or was created well after Kennedy found her own way to what I have elsewhere called the modern *mysterium*, a lineage that can be traced to those brief, often terrifying plays written by the symbolists just before the turn of

76

the twentieth century and to Strindberg's post-*Inferno* pilgrimage/dream plays.[2]

Without being religious drama, these plays were steeped in the sense that human beings are exposed without mediation to vast, mysterious forces in the universe. In them, proximate concerns of the social order give way to questions of ultimate destiny—sin, death, and redemption. Playwrights found a dramatic vocabulary, derived in part from allegory, from the moralities, from the passion play, and from the atmospherics of mysticism, to signal the audience that the stage represented not merely a particular time and place, but the universe; and that characters were not only individuals, and sometimes not even individuals, but emblematic figures embodying transcendental human destiny. The *mysterium* evolved past the symbolists to include many expressionists, Artaud (whose *Le Jet de sang* is a fractured mystery out of the Book of Revelation), and eventually Beckett. In America the flamboyant symbolist Sadakichi Hartmann, as well as Eugene O'Neill and Percy MacKaye, experimented with mystery plays.

Kennedy's plays of the sixties belong in a general sense to this tradition of the modernist mystery. However, her work has many specific, sometimes uncanny, points of contact with the turn-of-the-century avant-garde.[3]

In the night worlds of Van Lerberghe's *Les Flaireurs*, Maeterlinck's *The Intruder* and *The Death of Tintagiles*, and many other early symbolist plays, the reigning sign is death. The first wave of symbolist plays projected a closed and fatal universe inhabited by abstract, doomed figures. The characters stalked by death are frequently the young, like Hofmannsthal's adolescent aesthete in *Death and the Fool*, the Daughter in *The Intruder*, the child Tintagiles, and a host of others. "The entire corpus of symbolist writing for the theater...is haunted by mortality," writes Daniel Gerould, "yet filled with a perverse animism—hence the dualistic vision of life in death and death in life that is the central paradox of drama in the symbolist mode."[4] The first generation of symbolists, it is worth noting here, had been inspired by Villiers, whose ideal of death became something of a fashion. Axel's cry, "Live? Our servants will do that for us,"[5] resonates with Kennedy's generation of white fifties intellectuals in *Funnyhouse*: "My white friends, like myself, will be shrewd, intellectual and anxious for death" (*Funnyhouse*, 6).[6]

Kennedy's mystery plays, like Maeterlinck's early plays, take place in a hermetic night world, the time of dreams, madness, and darkness of the soul. In *Funnyhouse*, the playing area is surrounded by "unnatural Blackness" (*Funnyhouse*, 2);[7] it is crepuscular and candle-lit in *A Rat's Mass*, and sealed in the prisonlike steel of a subway car in *The Owl Answers*. All three project stifling and fatalistic universes whose central characters are doomed by their own guilt, the crimes of earlier generations, and a sense of extrusion from the normative world. As the doomed center of *Funnyhouse*, Sarah, the generic educated "Negro" with the noose around her neck, is dead even before she hangs herself. Death pervades the setting, whose white curtain resembles "the interior of a cheap casket." Black ravens out of Poe circle the mausoleum room, dominated by a monumental bed "resembling an ebony tomb" (*Funnyhouse*, 2). Death is not merely atmospheric in *Funnyhouse*, however, but finds a structural equivalent in the paralytic stasis that is at the core of Kennedy's early dramaturgy, reminiscent of the sense of stasis at the heart of Maeterlinckian theatre.

In 1896, Maeterlinck published a seminal essay, "The Tragical in Daily Life," that rejected external action in drama as a noisy distraction. A static theatre, he believed, could be used to put the spectator in touch with the invisible, the unknown, "the ominous silence of the soul and of God."[8] In his early one-act plays, plot and character recede and the sense of dramatic change or dynamism is carried by mood and tone. The rustling of leaves, the groaning of a door, the rising wind, the rising of a cold moon, the gliding of swans, and other effects provide the sense of an alive universe and become a substitute for the gross conflicts of an articulated narrative.

For all their intensity, Kennedy's plays are in this tradition of a static theatre. Something has happened in the past—one is not sure what—that hangs like a shroud over the fraught, yet actionless, stage. To seek to know whether Sarah killed her "black beast" of a father, or Clara (the "Bastard") Passmore's father was actually her mother's white employer, or the Rat children actually committed the crime of incest is to seek a realism that Kennedy does not intend. The guilt of crime and sin, real or imagined, and the torment of unresolvable racial antinomies create a charged environment in which Kennedy's essentially stationary characters obsessively repeat their titanic conflicts. Though Kennedy's conditions of stasis differ from Maeterlinck's, once they are created she, too, rejects progressive narrative for a dramatic texture created through variations in repeating patterns of language and effects. These effects revolve feverishly, yet nothing happens, and nothing *can* happen, except death (suicide in *Funnyhouse*, machine-gun fire in *Rat's Mass*) or the overwrought immolation of *Owl*, hinting of Wagner, whose own techniques of stasis and repetition were a direct influence on symbolist playwriting.

Accordingly, Kennedy's texts do not so much progress as recircle, proceeding through accreting motifs, not unlike the Wagnerian leitmotiv. "My mother looked like a white woman"; "It begins with the disaster of my hair"; "white stallions roaming under a blue sky"; "photographs of Roman ruins, pianos and oriental carpets" are among the many recurring themes that inhabit Kennedy's *Funnyhouse* text almost like characters. These repetitions, as other commentators on Kennedy's work have noted, endow Kennedy's language with the quality of litany or incantation, repetition in the service of a ritual event.[9]

A consequence of creating a closed and static dramatic world, and the most obvious link between Kennedy and the symbolists, is the necessity of finding a concentrated dramatic form. A dramaturgy that eschews plot and character development tends to reveal itself through sheer density or saturation. Kennedy follows the same dramatic logic that led the symbolists to the one-act form. Maeterlinck was never more successful than in this form, and as symbolism spread outward from Belgium and France, Yeats, Miciński, Briusov, and others discovered its virtues. In *Waiting for Godot* Beckett made a cosmic joke of the static aesthetic by in effect repeating the one-act form twice.

The symbolists swept away the concerns and conflicts of family and society so that the mysterious could penetrate the spectator directly. But Kennedy appears to differ from them definitively in her relationship to culture and history. The death net that traps the figures in symbolist plays is metaphysical and timeless, beyond the social and political order. Kennedy's plays revolve about just those explosions of violence the symbolists detested, festering family crimes like patricide, rape, and incest; political crimes like assassination or tyranny; and most of all the deep cultural crime of racism. And yet in Kennedy's mystery plays, the social/political itself is raised to the power of metaphysics. The signs may be historical, but their power is eternal. Whatever is always was and cannot be altered. The Rat children are forever trapped in crime and guilt, and the Nazis will always punish them. Clara is racially torn on a rack that is built into her flesh. (Her name Passmore is a pun on racial "passing"—will she pass more, or less? Does she believe in the white Virgin, or the African Owl?) And Sarah of *Funnyhouse* is forever ground between the millstones of Europe and Africa, between the hideously white English queen and the black African leader with the mask in his hand.[10] The Negro's white personae cannot for all eternity rid themselves of their black father.

VICTORIA: Why does he keep returning? He keeps returning forever, coming back ever and keeps coming back forever. He is my father....

DUCHESS: We are tied to him unless, of course, he should die.

VICTORIA: But he is dead.

DUCHESS: And he keeps returning. (*Funnyhouse*, 3–4)

Maeterlinck depicted his characters as estranged in a cold, echoing universe. His shivering, puppetlike figures are defenseless against a manipulative fate. Maeterlinck's early plays were, in fact, written to be performed by puppets, an expression of a widely shared symbolist aesthetic of distancing from the human figure. Kennedy's characters are more likely to die of fever than of cold. Her masks and animal costumes are related to the symbolist interest in puppets, marionettes, and maskwork, but she uses them to intensify rather than distance. Similarly, Kennedy's characters are not so much estranged as trapped. Her female protagonists are condemned to retell their stories from the penitentiary of airless distorted funnyhouses, rathouses, and screeching subway cars. Her plays implode. Her stasis has the quality not of the void, but of an impacted wound that can never heal. The pain expressed in them is far more violent and tragic—in the conventional sense that Maeterlinck wanted to avoid—than Maeterlinck's own metaphysical ache. There is, in short, a sharp difference in "feeling tone" between the abstract, universalized cruelty of the symbolist universe and the cruelty concentrated on the dismembered black and female psyche of the Kennedy universe. But even as Kennedy places her characters in a thicket of cultural and historical contradictions and boiling subjectivity, she still continues a fundamental link to the symbolists, for her focus is never social interaction but, like theirs, the mystery of the isolated soul.

Strindberg acknowledged that his later dream and chamber plays owed an immense debt to Maeterlinck, whose work struck him with the force of a "newly discovered country."[11] In a startling shift of focus in the late 1890s, Strindberg took up the symbolist commitment to depicting "structures of the soul."[12] However, Strindberg extended the theatrical viability of symbolist spirituality with two dramatic strategies: the pilgrimage form, taken from medieval station drama, and a transformational dream dramaturgy. The resulting dramatic form has frequently been acknowledged as proto-expressionist, but in the effect that Peter Szondi has described as the "static, futureless quality of the scenes," it is strongly linked to symbolist aesthetics.[13]

Kennedy attributes her own discovery of the "greater dream setting" to her reading of Lorca, but her way of writing the dream/nightmare/hallucination feels closer to Strindberg.[14] Her funnyhouse is a descendent of Strindberg's ghost house. Her burning altar as the final image of *Owl* is reminiscent of his burning castle in A *Dream Play*. Her lightning scenic transformation from the Duchess of Hapsburg's palace to the African jungle is as extreme and bizarre as Strindberg's leap from the Lawyer's Office to Foulstrand. The very disappearance of linear time into spatial

transformation in Kennedy can be traced to Strindberg's discoveries in
A *Dream Play*.

Still, it is the quasi-allegorical Strindberg nearer to the symbolists,
the Strindberg of *To Damascus, Part I*, with whom I particularly connect
Kennedy. It was there that Strindberg first emerged with his new bilevel
drama of correspondence. Where older dramatic forms were dialogic and
interactional, this drama of correspondence was almost totally subjective,
organized around a central character whose interior states are the spectator's principal focus.[15] These internal states assume transcendental
importance, however, because all events on the individual plane are
mysteriously linked with the operations of cosmic forces. In Strindberg
this open horn to the universe both inflates and ironically diminishes
his central character's every move. Each quite ordinary event that befalls
his Stranger is lit up with supernatural significance. While waiting for a
check, the Stranger can become Adam, Cain, Paul, the accursed of Deu-
teronomy, and Christ. But the same motion undercuts the flight of myth
and allegory above his head, for the heroic seeker on the road to Damascus is still merely a down-on-his-luck writer.

This is Strindberg's interchangeable I—now naturalistic and autobiographical, now historical, mythic, and biblical; now many texts within a
single character, now broken into separate individuals. Kennedy's prismatic characters, as well as her daring placement of myth and life on
the same ontological footing, can be traced to this Strindbergian inno-
vation.[16] Thus Clara Passmore of *Owl* and Sarah of *Funnyhouse* are simultaneously autobiographical and generic figures. While Clara passes
through multiple aspects as "the Virgin Mary who is the Bastard who is
the Owl," Sarah-Negro of *Funnyhouse* is fragmented into freestanding
separate bodies sharing a single if divided mind.

The almost casual combination of the painfully autobiographical and
the mythic, the quotidian and the typological, invented by Strindberg,
was not to my knowledge recreated until Kennedy, but Kennedy extended
the Strindbergian drama of correspondence by adding to it a dialectical
tension. Kennedy's worlds are not only aligned vertically—between the
intimate and the mythic—they are also in dialectical relation horizontally.
Sarah's "selves" are black, white, and "high yellow," male and female,
and riven by opposed ideologies. Sarah's search for a place to stand or
to hide is more complex than Strindberg's Stranger's. She passes through
roles the way the Stranger passes through "stations." But all that is
required for the Stranger to pass through the Stations of the Cross is a
change of heart, whereas Sarah can never resolve the tension between
roles. She faces not only spiritual necessity, to which she might rise, but
historical necessity, which she is powerless to control. Strindberg's

Stranger is willing to walk to the door of the church at the end of his journey through the Dantean inferno, but Kennedy's Negro cannot make the Stranger's leap from Saul to Paul; she can find no religious, cultural, or ideological identity on which to rest. Her tragedy is that "she" can find no cohesive "she" outside the historical contradictions that dismember her. This is the deepest meaning of the multiplicity of Sarah's selves.

The "mysterium" in the modernist sense may not be religious drama, but its chief interests are eschatological, and it frequently avails itself of the vocabulary and imagery traditionally associated with such questions. Religion can function in contradictory ways, often in the same play, as warning or scourge, as model, haven, or trap, but it is never without significance. Without conveying a sense of doctrinal resolution or commitment, Strindberg fills his late plays with the emblems of religion, and with characters who stagger toward and away from those emblems in terrible struggles to come to terms with an oppressive sense of sin. Kennedy similarly creates characters who are tormented by guilt, and this guilt is elevated to the level of metaphysical problem by her inclusion of religious figures and/or ceremonies in all three of the mysteries. At the same time these emblems of religion are often used blankly or ambiguously, and sometimes with hostility.

In *Funnyhouse*, Jesus is one of Sarah's selves, but this Jesus is a hunchbacked, yellow-skinned dwarf, the Jesus that was left after Sarah discovered that her loving relationship with him was a lie (*Funnyhouse*, 7). In *The Owl Answers* the High Altar seems the antipode to the harsh subway, but it is also a place of brutal blood sacrifice and agony. The central images of A Rat's Mass are a communion mass and religious procession. The procession, with its Holy Family, Wise Men, and Shepherd, seems at first a comforting image from childhood; by the end of the play the procession has turned into brutal Nazis with shotguns. "God is hanging and shooting us," the Rat children cry (A Rat's Mass, 64). Religion waits patiently for Strindberg's Stranger while he rages at it, flirts with it, then backs away again. Kennedy's view of the religious sign is more complex. It can turn punishing and vengeful, or its affirmative power may be exactly balanced by a sign from another culture—the Virgin Mary by the Owl, the pale Jesus by the black Lumumba—leading to spiritual doubt and paralysis.

Modernism in theatre can be traced to the first avant-garde at the turn of the century. It was the symbolists who first rejected realism in both its classical and "romantic" variants, and attempted to create a theater uncompromisingly of the inner world and of the cosmos.[17] The early Kennedy of the mystery plays shares the symbolists' and the late Strindberg's attraction to the absolute. Though history is always recognizable in Kennedy, from the assassination of Patrice Lumumba to the withering depiction of her generation of fifties intellectuals, Kennedy emerges in the early mystery plays as one who asks not, "How can I change the social order?" but "Where do I stand in the universe? What is my destiny? Is there redemption for me?"

After 1970, these questions recede in Kennedy's work in favor of more direct issues of gender and sexuality (A *Lesson in Dead Language*), of race and class (A *Movie Star Has to Star in Black and White* and *An Evening with Dead Essex*). In these plays Kennedy continues to use the transformational dream setting and the technique of corresponding levels, but her theatrical worlds are lighter, more open, more humorous, and more grounded in the immediacy of life. Her symbolist moment had passed.

Notes

1. John A. Henderson, *The First Avant-Garde, 1887–1894* (London: Harrap, 1971).

2. Elinor Fuchs, "The Mysterium: A Modern Dramatic Genre," *Theater Three*, no. 1 (Fall 1986): 73–86.

3. Many theoretical statements made by symbolist authors located the creation of the "mystery" as the central project of symbolism. Relating specifically to theatre, one of the clearest statements was F. Sologub's "The Theater of One Will" (1908), published in *The Russian Symbolists: An Anthology of Critical and Theoretical Writings*, ed. and trans. Ronald E. Peterson (Ann Arbor, Mich.: Ardis, 1986), 107–21. "[T]he task of the theatre worker," says Sologub, "...consists of bringing [theatre] nearer to ecumenical activity, to mystery play and liturgy" (109). Particularly interesting in relation to Kennedy is Sologub's idea that in the mystery form, unlike conventional realistic drama, "there are no different people, there is only one person, only one I in the whole universe, willing, acting, suffering, burning in an unquenchable fire" (111).

4. Daniel Gerould, ed., *Doubles, Demons, and Dreamers: An International Collection of Symbolist Drama* (New York: Performing Arts Journal Publications, 1985), 8.

5. Philippe August Villiers de l'Isle-Adam, *Axek*, trans. June Guicharnaud (Englewood Cliffs, N.J.: Prentice-Hall, 1970), 183.

6. Citations to *Funnyhouse of a Negro* and *A Rat's Mass* are from *Adrienne Kennedy in One Act* (Minneapolis: University of Minnesota Press, 1988), and are hereafter given in the text.

7. In *Funnyhouse*, black and white must be read racially and politically, but Kennedy intends the metaphysical association, if only ironically.

8. Maurice Maeterlinck, "The Tragical in Daily Life," in *The Treasure of the Humble*, trans. Alfred Sutro (London: George Allen, 1908), 98.

9. Herbert Blau describes Kennedy's language as being "like litany and prayer" ("The American Dream in Amerian Gothic," in *The Eye of Prey* [Bloomington and Indianapolis: Indiana University Press, 1987], 42–64, at 45). Rosemary K. Curb contrasts Kennedy's repetitions with Gertrude Stein's, finding in Kennedy "magic spells and incantations" spiraling toward an "infernal pit filled with unspeakable horrors." See "*Funnyhouse of a Negro* and *The Owl Answers*," in *Theatre Journal* 32, no. 2 (May 1980): 180–95, at 194.

10. The manichaean struggle between opposing forces was a distinctive feature of Polish and Russian symbolist theatre. A symbolist mystery visually built around a struggle between dark and light is Andrei Bely's *Jaws of Night*, in *Doubles, Demons, and Dreamers*, ed. Gerould.

11. August Strindberg, *Letters to the Intimate Theatre*, trans. Walter Johnson (London: Peter Owen, 1967), 300.

12. Gerould, ed. *Doubles, Demons, and Dreamers*, 13.

13. Peter Szondi, *Theory of the Modern Drama*, ed. and trans. Michael Hays (Minneapolis: University of Minnesota Press, 1987), 26.

14. Adrienne Kennedy, *People Who Led to My Plays* (New York: Knopf, 1987), 108. Helene Keyssar has also noted the similarity between Strindberg's and Kennedy's dream worlds (see Helene Keyssar, *Feminist Theatre: An Introduction to Plays of Contemporary British and American Women* [New York: Grove Press, 1984], 110).

15. The Swedenborgian idea of correspondences turned up in the early symbolist experiments in theatrical synaesthesia well before Strindberg took up the idea in *To Damascus, Part I*. However, Strindberg went beyond other symbolists by sustaining an entire dramatic world on corresponding levels.

16. This is not to say that Kennedy did not also have nearer examples of such experimentation, themselves traceable to Strindberg, like Williams's *Camino Real*.

17. I use the word *romantic* here in the sense in which it was put forward by Friedrich Schlegel, who more than any other theorist turned it from a descriptive into a critical concept. Raymond Immerwahr has written that Schlegel "used the words 'Roman' and 'romantisch'…each in reference to the other, and each as an ideal realization of cultural and aesthetic tendencies of the Middle Ages and the Renaissance." In this sense, Shakespeare is the preeminent romantic author (see Raymond Immerwahr, "The Word *romantisch* and Its History," in *The Romantic Period in Germany*, ed. Siegbert Prawer (New York: Schocken Books, 1970), 51.

7

Adrienne Kennedy through the Lens of German Expressionism

William R. Elwood

Adrienne Kennedy was born approximately eleven years after German expressionism had yielded to the more rational *neue Sachlichkeit* or neo-realism in the history of German theatre. Kennedy's first produced work, *Funnyhouse of a Negro* (1962), places her canon forty-two years after the German movement had ceased to exist as a discrete aesthetic for the theatre. It would not seem plausible that expressionism could exert an influence on an American playwright so many years later, especially with other important movements of the theatre intervening. Yet the influence is there; the more formalist European aesthetic has found its way into the richly textured sensual work of Kennedy.

It is even more remarkable that influence can be cited given the vastly different perceptions of reality upon which the expressionist and the Kennedy canons are based. Paul Carter Harrison, in his introduction to the anthology *Kuntu Drama*, articulates the difference when he compares the rhythms of the African and European cultures. He refers to the European sensibility as the "agonized pursuit of emotions that erects steel bridges and concrete walls, the episodic cataloguing of human failing and success protracted over a long duration of excavations of the mind/heart."[1] Harrison, placing Kennedy in the African context, would distinguish the rhythm of the African culture by summarizing it as a phenomenon composed of tone and rhythm emerging into light and sustaining the spirit as animated form.

Despite the disparity of cultural backgrounds, expressionism is present in rather significant ways in the works of Kennedy. It is, as some would argue, because the essential meaning of expressionism transcends cultural and geographical determinants. In many ways both phenomena were reacting to a constricted artistic ambience, seeking to redefine a functional reality from the perspective of antimaterialism or the nonrational methodology of internal values.

As we shall see, Kennedy's works appear to take the seemingly fragmented quest for emotional truth to a new level of rhythmic presentation. Where the German expressionists disassemble the materialist reality, Kennedy transmutes it through rhythm.

German expressionism is dated roughly from 1907 to 1925. It was a movement spawned by a deep frustration with the reigning Weltanschauung (worldview or perception of reality), which consisted of a militaristic/capitalistic ordering of national events informed by the philosophies of materialism and logical positivism. Germany's socioeconomic outlook was due to a heavy-handed capitalism attendant upon Germany's bid for world dominance following its victory in the Franco-Prussian War in 1871. In belles lettres and in the theatre, expressionism was a radical departure from the dominant styles of realism and naturalism.

The expressionists were anxious to reestablish contact with more transcendental values that, in their opinion, realism and naturalism had obfuscated with the need to create truth on stage through empirical verification and the inevitable determinism of that aesthetic. Expressionism represented the attempt to find a "safer" level of meaning whereby humankind could reassemble the broken pieces of a failed material reality and forge a faculty of perception more consistent with transcendence and the human spirit or soul. With Kokoschka's *Mörder, Hoffnung der Frauen* (*Murderer, the Hope of Women*, 1907), a new perception of reality was proposed in which the soul of humanity became the center for truthful appraisal of reality. We see in that piece, not the causal elements of hostility between the sexes, but violent emotion as event in and of itself.

The core of meaning for the expressionist was the *ich*,[2] and it was transcendental of such dramatic elements as the faithful reproduction of reality through text and the elements of staging. More important than the mise-en-scène was an attention to the emotional apparatuses that were deemed by the expressionists to be far more accurate where truthful perception of reality was concerned. Expressionism was the drama of internal, psychic, and emotional truth rather than the external materialist truth. To the establishment, the slanting walls and grotesque makeup of the expressionist production was a distortion of truth. However, to the expressionist theatre practitioners, the mise-en-scène of the production was a faithful representation of the torment of the age, of the cry against the materialist perception of reality.

German expressionism can be defined as the attempt to express an inner reality by creating the essence rather than the appearance of reality through the use of nonrealistic symbols and the juxtaposition of ordinarily nonrelated realistic symbols.[3]

Through a complex arrangement of the Aristotelian elements of drama, the playwright was able to create a powerful abstraction of human existence, which was in need of a new kind of psychic freedom. In many ways the expressionist playwright and the theatre practitioner were producing on stage what Freud and Jung were proposing in psychology. Through therapy, Freud and Jung probed the unconscious mind for deeper levels of truth and meaning. The expressionist was producing such inquiry through the medium of the theatre.

At first glance it is not easy to see how so abstract a movement on the European continent could manifest itself in any form in the works of Kennedy. The African/American consciousness seems quite disparate from that which created expressionism. Yet there are clear examples of the constituents of expressionism in selected works of Kennedy. Several elements of her plays emerge that bear striking resemblances to the constituents of German expressionism: the spirit as primary locus for the dramatic action; mutability of forms; event as subject of articulation, rather than narrative form; the creation of a perception of reality through the orchestration of words, sounds, and images in modal relationships not limited to the scientific laws of cause and effect; manipulation of time.

The works are crafted in the context of a spiritual rather than physical universe. Matter exists in the plays, but the soul or spirit informs matter. This parallels closely the concept of the *ich*, where the physical universe is manipulated to the ends of the soul. Kennedy's works locate either conflict, as in *The Owl Answers*, or quasi-religious experience, as in *A Rat's Mass*. Indeed the same level of torment appears to be present in these and other works as in such expressionist pieces as Hasenclever's *Die Menschen* (*Humanity*, 1918) or Toller's *Masse Mensch* (*Man and the Masses*, 1919).

The mutability of forms is perhaps the most frequently occurring constituent of Kennedy's work. Because of its omnipresence in the plays, it will be discussed in greater detail later. There are three levels of change of form: physical, psychic, and linguistic. In each instance the playwright is undermining reliance on physical form as a means of communicating the message of the play. In the expressionist canon, the often-used staging device of the slanting walls is an example of mutability of form.

Event as dramatic phenomenon rather than narrative form is consistent with the expressionist canon. Compare brief scenes from *Funnyhouse of a Negro* with Goering's *Seeschlacht* (*Sea Battle*, 1917) as examples of this device. In *Seeschlacht* the sailors are preparing for battle. Their voices articulate the conflict between courage in the face of death and the affirmation of life:

> Listen to it roar. Does it roar?
> Listen to it rumble. Does it rumble?
> Feel it tremble. Does it tremble?
> Feel it shake. Does it shake?
> What happens, what will become of us, what is going on?
> Life! Life!

The environment itself seems to be created out of the fear each sailor experiences:

> There are things that lie in the air. When their time comes, they penetrate each open window regardless of who lives therein. They penetrate even the closed window.[4]

In *Funnyhouse of a Negro* the following stage direction is almost the event in and of itself:

> Scene: In the jungle, RED SUN, FLYING THINGS, wild black grass. The effect of the jungle is that it, unlike the other scenes, is over the entire stage. In time this is the longest scene in the play and is played the slowest, as the slow, almost standstill stages of a dream. By lighting the desired effect would be—suddenly the jungle has overgrown the chambers and all the other places with a violence and a dark brightness, a grim yellowness. (*Funnyhouse*, 20).[5]

In *Seeschlacht*, "it," the battle, becomes an event; in *Funnyhouse of a Negro*, the jungle itself is what we experience. Event is dialogue, not action or idea in Goering's piece. In Kennedy's work, stage setting is event.

Not mutually exclusive from the constituent cited above is Kennedy's skill at the orchestration of images into modal relationships. Clearly such a constituent contributes to the mutability of form, for plays written with modal relationships in mind aim to articulate dramatic energy units to achieve the desired effect.

Eschewing the laws of cause and effect is consistent with expressionism's intent to reveal the soul as a vehicle for knitting together an altered perception of reality. In *A Rat's Mass*, the playwright tells us that prayer voices turn to gnawing voices. In *A Movie Star Has to Star in Black and White*, the so-called real characters of the play are replaced and exchanged with figures from the cinema, such as Bette Davis and Montgomery Clift.

Parallels can be found in such works as Werfel's *Der Spiegelmensch* (*Mirror Man*, 1920), in which a figure comes out of a mirror and assumes a life of its own. In Kokoschka's *Mörder, Hoffnung der Frauen*, the man in the cage grows in size.

Concurrent with the writing technique of modal relationships is the manipulation of time. Time is manipulated, as, for example, in the stage setting for the jungle scene in *Funnyhouse of a Negro*, where it is slowed down; it could even be said that in her works, Kennedy ignores time. Such is the case with *Sun*, in which movement replaces time.[6]

It is in the mutability of forms that Kennedy most closely resembles the expressionist playwrights. Where Kennedy's work is concerned, she adds to the European aesthetic what could be called the fluidity of transition in the transmutation of form. The expressionist tended to categorize the transitions, almost announcing them in advance; Kennedy's treatment of the physical aspects of the environment, such as the African climate, physical violence, and jungle settings, distinguish her work from that of the Germans. When her particular brand of transmogrification occurs, it appears to be devoid of the concreteness of expressionism. For example, in *Funnyhouse of a Negro* the change of physical form is signaled in the opening stage direction: "Before the closed curtain a woman dressed in a white nightgown walks across a stage carrying before her a bald head" (*Funnyhouse*, 2).[7] Kennedy has proposed in this scene a mutilation of physical form as symbol of the perversion of the human condition. Later in the opening stage direction, physical form is juxtaposed: "If the characters do not wear a mask then the face must be highly powdered and possess a hard expressionless quality and a stillness as in the face of death" (*Funnyhouse*, 3). In A *Beast Story*, the cast of characters consists of four characters, three of whom are mutant forms: Beast Girl, Beast Woman, and Beast Man.[8] The fourth character is Dead Human, a speaking role. The stage directions indicate that the beasts are real people but that their speech and movements may suggest an unreal and bestial quality. In this piece the concept of humans as beasts appears to manifest itself in creating primal forces seeking transcendental form. The Beast Girl says:

> My father comes toward me, saying something I do not comprehend. His face exudes a yellow light. The sky turns black. He catches my hand. He begins to sing, no particular melody yet the tone is unwavering and free. No words are distinct. Silence. He goes to the window, looks out, continues to sing. He sings a beast song. Our hair grown, our eyes turned yellow. We are trapped in this beast house singing beast songs. (*Beast Story*, 199)

Later after a sacrificial murder, Beast Man and Beast Woman have effected what they perceive to be spiritual growth:

> Our daughter fled to the hallway and into the attic. She pulled down the ax. She swung the ax upon him. He tried to kiss her but fell dead in his blood. Now the sky above our house is blue, three robins with red chests appear on the horizon. All is warm and sunlit. (*Beast Story*, 201)

In *A Movie Star Has to Star in Black and White*, Kennedy's use of mutation of form more closely resembles the expressionists' mode of articulating an internal consciousness. It could be said that the dialogue is an elaborate and extended manifestation of the *ich* constituent. The characters are interchanged with movie actors: "Instead of Clara, Bette Davis replies" (*Movie Star*, 88). Throughout the play Clara reacts to the characters of mother, father, and husband, but Kennedy interjects and commingles the dialogue between Clara and movie characters, as the following indicates:

> JEAN PETERS: My brother Wally's still alive.
>
> CLARA (*To her diary.*): Wally was in an accident.
> (*Movie Star*, 93)

Kennedy is also concerned with the efficacy of language in her works. Like the expressionists, she attempts a higher level of meaning by devaluing language. Linguistic mutation usually occurs in two ways: disruption of conventional grammar and disruption of syntax.

In *A Rat's Mass*, there are prayer voices that later turn to gnawing voices, indicating a change of sound and a change of meaning as the human voice becomes a rat voice. The implication is that of a progression from a higher to a lower consciousness. In this instance grammar is correct, but the syntax does not follow. Kennedy is articulating a meaning outside conventional linguistic form.

Brother Rat says to Rosemary: "How can I ever reach last spring again if I come with you, Rosemary? I must forget how every day this winter gray cats swing with sunflowers in their mouths" (*Rat's Mass*, 61). The formalism of a Catholic Mass has been changed to animal-like voices and a juxtaposition of linguistic symbols: cats swinging with sunflowers in their mouths. When one considers the title of the play, prayer voices that change into gnawing voices do not translate to meaning based on logic.

In *A Lesson in Dead Language*, similar juxtapositions occur. White Dog orders his pupils to write on the blackboard one hundred times, "Who killed the White Dog and why do I bleed? I killed the White Dog and that is why I must bleed. And the lemons and the grass and the sun"

(*Lesson*, 49). The juxtaposition of complete sentences that produces non-sense devalues language in deference to nonrational meaning. In *The Owl Answers*, the cast of characters indicates multiple personae to enable Kennedy to articulate the search for form in chaos. Four of the characters have multiple forms. For example, "She" is listed as "She who is Clara Passmore who is the Virgin Mary who is the Bastard who is the Owl" (*Owl*, 25). In the play the language is consistent with character delineation. She is on a subway ostensibly to pick up men. She confronts Dead Father and the Mother, who say they don't know her. She says "Call me Mary." Dead Father replies, "If you are Mary what are you doing in the Tower of London?" (*Owl*, 37). The juxtaposition of a visitation from the dead to a subway prostitute to Mary and the Tower of London is a clear example of mutability of linguistic form. Kennedy is undermining the attachment to fixed forms. The solution appears to be transcendence and transformation.

Expressionist techniques in Adrienne Kennedy's plays pose interesting problems for the director. Inherent in the style is the choice of production elements that would have one common denominator: an apparent obliqueness. Scene design, lighting, costume design, plot incidents, and other components of the mise-en-scène are only initially real according to an established norm. Then, when other elements are perceived or enacted, the effect is unreal: it speaks to the audience through their nonrational faculties rather than through what they observe.

Though the changes of forms are physical, psychic, and linguistic, as was stated earlier, there remains a fluidity between each type of form. In each of the works cited, change of form is actually a combination of physical, psychic, and linguistic components. The progression from prayer voices to gnawing voices also creates a psychic effect. Juxtaposing characters from the movies creates an interesting linguistic effect: who is speaking which meaning? In A *Movie Star Has to Star in Black and White*, the mutation of forms creates four levels of reality: movie stars and their stories; characters' stories; movie stars taking Clara and Eddie's story; the entire story as seen by the spectators.

Paul Carter Harrison asserts that Kennedy's plays are marked by a tonality and rhythm that is consistent with African drama. When the "excavation of the mind/heart"[9] is seen through the lens of expressionism, the form of Kennedy's works appears at first to be almost evanescent. In fact, she has redefined form through the tonality of transmutation. It is Kennedy's vision defined as feelings in motion that makes her work unique. Where the Expressionists catalogued internal emotions, they remained as excavations, despite the emotional appeal of the works. The African texture of Kennedy's presentation of the motion of feelings transforms the matrix that is inherent in the German expressionist play into a personal idiom.

Notes

1. Paul Carter Harrison, ed., *Kuntu Drama* (New York: Grove Press, 1974), 23.

2. The constituents are as follows: *ich*, duality of reality, abstraction and empathy, *unio-mystica*, *sie erleben direkt*, flung into space, *der Schrei*, and *Stationen*. For a full description of the constituents of expressionism, see William R. Elwood, *Early Manifestations of German Expressionism in New York Productions of American Drama* (Ph.D. diss., University of Oregon, 1966).

3. See also William R. Elwood, "Expressionism and Deconstructionism: A Critical Comparison," *Text and Presentation*, Comparative Drama Conference Papers, vol. 10 (1990): 1–7.

4. Reinhard Goering, *Prosa, Dramen, Verse* (Munich: Albert Langen, 1961), 316, 286; translation mine.

5. All citations to *Funnyhouse of a Negro*, *A Movie Star Has to Star in Black and White*, *A Rat's Mass*, and *The Owl Answers* are from *Adrienne Kennedy in One Act* (Minneapolis: University of Minnesota Press, 1988), and are hereafter given in the text.

6. *Sun* is one of Kennedy's most hymnic works, articulating an alienated view of the human condition. The core of meaning of the play is that humanity is an integral part of the transitional nature of the cosmos. That cosmos consists of physical and psychic forms in traumatic and violent transition. See William R. Elwood, "*Mankind* and *Sun*: German-American Expressionism," *Text and Presentation*, Comparative Drama Conference Papers, vol. 11 (1991): 9–13. Further, I would recommend subsequent work in which the concepts of surrealism and theatre of cruelty are examined in Kennedy's work. For example, an assessment of *Sun* and *Jet of Blood* would be important for Kennedy studies.

7. This plot incident was used by Walter Hasenclever (1890–1940) in his quintessential piece, *Die Menschen* (New York: Anchor Books, 1963). In that work, the Murderer emerges from the grave carrying a head in the sack.

8. *A Beast Story*, in *Kuntu Drama*, ed. Harrison, 199; subsequent citations to this play will be included in the text.

9. Harrison, ed., *Kuntu Drama*, 23.

8

Surrealism as Mimesis
A Director's Guide to Adrienne Kennedy's
Funnyhouse of a Negro

Robert Scanlan

Preliminaries

> *Today it goes without saying that nothing concerning art goes without saying.*
>
> —Theodor Adorno

Postmodernism is the aesthetic fashion of these times, and a revival of interest in Adrienne Kennedy's work has occurred under its rubric. What follows is a structural, formal analysis of *Funnyhouse of a Negro*, a work praised in its time (it won an Obie Award for Michael Kahn's production in 1964) but infrequently mentioned since, and a notorious example of "nonlinear" playmaking: antirealistic, phantasmagoric, and surrealistic. Its apparent collage of image, text, idea, and disrupted fragments of story looks now like an early example of the postmodernist style. While "postmodern" may be a more accurate label for a later play of Kennedy's, *A Movie Star Has to Star in Black and White* (1976), *Funnyhouse of a Negro* follows a pattern of accumulating sense that is highly traditional, and in fact, from a purely formal point of view, can be seen as a straightforward act of mimesis.

Although Adrienne Kennedy's dream plays of the early and middle sixties are prime examples of "nonlinear" experimental (in its time) writing, ironically enough it is the strict line of the plot of these plays that produces their clarity and power. Adrienne Kennedy has clearly not written in the stage convention of "realism," but she has composed a performance sequence that can only be understood (and can certainly only be staged) *as a sequence.* The unfolding of discrete events and images in time, with a clear order—a beginning, a middle, and an end—is properly called a "plot." And as the following analysis will show, the plot is properly understood as imitating an action. These Aristotelian terms are frequently equated with realism, but they are not intrinsic to that convention. They are formal terms applicable to any performance that unfolds in time: in other words, there is an inevitable linearity to all performance, and any artist composing in the medium of the Stage is composing linearly. The underlying intention in using the term *nonlinear* is usually to describe the relation of *plot* to *story.* In what follows, it will be important to keep a strict distinction between these two terms.

The story material of Adrienne Kennedy's work is highly autobiographical, full of important thematic matter: racial heritage, racial discrimination, social justice, the psychological consequences of oppression, personal experiences of integration, and psychological dis-integration. The material is so potent—especially in the overall historical context in which it emerged—that it is often difficult to keep a strict attention on form alone. In Adrienne Kennedy's case, and especially in her first two plays, *Funnyhouse of a Negro* and *The Owl Answers*, her themes are embedded in a "background" story, and a theatrical plot is created as a formal structure rising out of this matrix of story and theme.

Theodor Adorno, a powerful aesthetician and, to my mind, a theorist of art far more useful than any of the French critics of recent fame, expressed in purely theoretical terms a proposition about art that is particularly relevant to Adrienne Kennedy's plays:

> Control over artistic forms and over how they are related to materials exposes the arbitrariness of real domination which is otherwise hidden by an illusion of inevitability.[1]

The action of *exposing* a disposition of the real world through a counteracting *control of artistic form* seems precisely to be the task Adrienne Kennedy set herself as an artist. The apparent "surrealism" of her work is a strategy for a "grip" on something intractable in the black experience. Her art is perfectly anticipated by another theoretical conclusion of Adorno's:

> In art the difference between purely logical forms and empirically oriented ones does not exist. Space, time and causality, to which Schopenhauer had given the status of principles of individuation, crop up again in art, but in a refracted shape.... [T]his refraction imparts to art the aspect of freedom governing the unity and sequence of events.[2]

These dicta are all the more powerful for my purposes for their having been derived chiefly from the study of modern music. The "aspect of freedom governing the unity and sequence of events" is understandable as the artistic authority that shapes a plot, and a successful plot has an *esemplastic* power (to use Coleridge's useful term),[3] a power to gather disparate elements into a unity. It is this power that animates an artist, for it stands up against a perceived fatality in the real world, apparently out of our control. In other words, one man's "surrealism" may be a lone black woman's faithful act of mimesis.

The Plot of *Funnyhouse of a Negro*

The background story "behind" *Funnyhouse of a Negro* goes something like this:[4] a black woman (Sarah, the "Negro" of the title), who is a student living on and off with a Jewish boyfriend named Raymond in a rented room on the Upper West Side of Manhattan, broods on her troubled ancestry. Her mother, who was a light-colored Negro woman with beautiful straight hair, married a darker black man, whom eventually she ceased to love. This dark father had been raised in Georgia by a devoutly religious mother who, because she wanted her son to become a savior of the black race, urged him to travel to Africa and build a Christian mission in the jungle. She disapproved of his marriage to Sarah's mother. It was in Africa that his estranged wife withdrew emotionally from him, and one night while drunk, he raped her. Negro Sarah, who is the protagonist of the play, was born of this rape. Soon after, the mother began to lose her hair and then, gradually, to lose her mind, ending up in an asylum. Losing his sense of a mission, the father returned to New York, where he lived alone in a hotel in Harlem. Wracked with guilt over the fate of his mad wife, hated by his daughter, feeling he had betrayed his mother's dream, the black father visited his daughter to beg her forgiveness. When she spurned him, he killed himself. Later, haunted by his memory, her guilt, and her resentment, unable to shake off the black identity that is his legacy and that prevents her from attaining her desires in a white world, she, too, takes her own life.

Although that story, as I have roughly summarized it, is made quite explicit by various passages of spoken text in the play, it is never enacted in theatrical time. In other words, it is never *dramatized* in *Funnyhouse of a Negro*. The play that an audience experiences in a live performance is structured on an action differing substantially from the "background" story. What is dramatized in the performance is something that is done as *a result of the story*. The imitated action of the play is a heroic attempt at psychic survival; it is the story of Negro Sarah's struggle to escape from the unbearable psychological stress of her condition. This action ends where the story ends, in the suicide of the protagonist, but it begins only moments before (in story time), at the verge of the act of self-destruction.

The whole play is composed of three different types of segments, or parts. There are first of all pure stage effects: tableaux, stage gimmicks, pantomimes, pop-up horror "visuals." Second, there are a few interspersed "scenes" or traditionally "dramatic" groupings of characters exchanging dialogue in location settings. And lastly there are passages of what the French critics call *"écriture,"* or pure writing: the generation of text in monologue form. The alternation of these three styles in the unfolding of the plot does not alter the fact that a single action line underlies them all.

The potent sexual, racial, and political content of *Funnyhouse of a Negro* obscures the fact that its form is very simple, echoing ancient and traditional dramatic units: the perennial elements of rituals, the simplest elements of a primitive tale. It is also fairly obvious that *Funnyhouse of a Negro* follows the form of a classical Freudian dream. These multiple associations come clear of themselves when the plot structure is read as a succession of "action" segments.[5] The linear arrangement of such segments makes up what is properly called a "plot," and in *Funnyhouse of a Negro* there are ten sequential plot segments. The following outline and analysis of the play is purely formal, based on relations of the parts to each other and to the whole.

Segment 1

Funnyhouse of a Negro opens with a prelude: a crossover before the curtain. A woman in a white nightgown walks across the stage carrying a bald head. This somnambulating figure (readers are told it is the Mother, but audiences are not) suggests a dream is commencing, and the curtain opens on the first tableau of this dream. The opening of any play is highly significant because the beginning is the edge of the formal frame. In this case, the "frame" is a scene of ritualized waiting, expectation, the anticipation of an arrival. We can confirm the importance of the opening action by jumping to the end: the play indeed ends precisely at the other edge of this waiting, when the Expected One arrives in this same setting. In between, there are various transformations that express and elaborate the dread behind the waiting, in part by explaining the meaning of the expected character and partly, too, by revealing why his coming presages a catastrophe.

The opening scene is set in a queen's bedchamber. It is a scene out of Gothic romances, steeped in the familiar atmospherics of Edgar Allan Poe: a dark monumental bed, a heavy chandelier, ravens in flight, candlelight, and an ominous knocking. The queen, holding a mirror, is attended by the Duchess of Hapsburg, who stands at the foot of her bed. It suggests a "lady-in-waiting" scene, a *couchée*: the lady is going to bed, her lady-in-waiting is attending her, both expect the arrival of a dread figure, knocking continues. The sexual atmosphere is dense from these circumstances alone. It is a page taken out of the sexual history of Western women: awaiting the arrival of the male who, for whatever reasons, is entitled to conjugal rights. It might be the husband or the lover or, in this setting, the overlord exercising the time-honored "droit du seigneur"; the women have no choice but to prepare to "receive" him, to prepare to be taken sexually. It must indeed have been, on thousands of occasions throughout history, a scene of recurrent dread and frequent nightmare, one in which desire and anguish are strangely mixed. In any case it has become throughout Gothic romance and horror stories a classic moment of psychosexual stress.

The play is dominated by a threat of rape by a figure identified immediately (in the first spoken line of the play) as the Black Father. The protagonist of the play suffers the continual reappearance of the dread dead father in an unending ritual suggesting incest and violence. My purpose is less to trace the development of this Freudian image through the play than it is to see the underlying armature of succeeding actions the dreamlike work concatenates from scene to scene. The first action in this structure is the tense waiting before sexual assault, made more dreadful and horrible by the fact that it is the protagonist's father who is expected.

The first scene of waiting is formally closed by the reappearance of the somnambulating figure who opened the play, crossing the stage again with her bald head in her hands. We, who know her to be an image of the mad Mother, can make the thematic connection: the anxiety produced by the incipient and recurrent rape is clearly tied to the bald head, the loss of hair (Freudian analysis ties loss-of-hair and baldness anxieties to castration fantasies).[6] But once again, the *action* of the nightgowned figure is more accessible than are the thematic or biographical allusions. The action we witness as framing the first scene of the play, coming before it and repeated after, is the same action we recognize from all the classic sleepwalking scenes, from Lady Macbeth to Lucia di Lammermoor: to escape unbearable anguish, to escape one's Self, to walk away from a tormented psyche. The opening scene of *Funnyhouse of a Negro* is framed by the enactment of the impossible wish to leave oneself behind.

Segment 2

The opening sequence is succeeded by the arrival of the protagonist of the play: the Negro of the title. She makes a truly horrible entrance: a bloodied face; a hangman's rope around her neck; a patch of hair, missing from her crown, that she carries in her hands. This is our first view of the title character. She appears like a sudden horror in an old-fashioned funnyhouse. This is Negro-Sarah, the central consciousness around which the succeeding images and actions of the plot are grouped. Clearly, Sarah is also the source of the dream, the center of the story that links all these episodes together. Negro-Sarah delivers a long self-explanatory monologue that is full of explicit descriptions of what has been going on. This monologue, and others like it, are our source for the story, but to follow the action plot we need only discern what she is accomplishing by narrating. Plot units are usually hardest to discern in a stage play when characters within the work are trying to explain themselves. If they are clever and highly verbal (as Sarah is here), their point of view can convincingly persuade a tractable listener and distract his or her attention from the underlying action, which is "to explain herself." Sarah is trying to "situate" herself in a narrative. She is composing her life with words, and we witness her as a character fully engaged in the declamation of a self-defining "text."

Thus the second major segment of the play is shaped by a character giving a full and precise account of herself. We need not believe her, but we see unmistakably *what* she is doing. Furthermore, that is all she is doing: her narration commands all her faculties. The staging makes this clear by offering a vision reminiscent of a traumatized victim walking out of a bomb blast. A human figure in such a plight is, in action terms, trying to save herself. She is attempting to reintegrate by simple assertion a shattered sense of self. To heighten one's histrionic "feel" for such an action, imagine an injured person scrambling to get up, obsessively repeating, as trauma victims frequently do, "I'm all right, I'm all right." Only from this action vantage point do the words spoken by Negro-Sarah make "sense" in the evolving structure of the play: "I want not to be," or "I want to possess no moral value, particularly value as to my being," or "I find it necessary to maintain a stark fortress against recognition of myself" (*Funnyhouse*, 5, 6).

These are the sorts of things one says to an analyst. They are also action statements, statements of intent. The figure, from what we see, has already committed suicide, or is prefiguring the act. Thematically, we are dealing with suicidal stresses, but dramatically, we are experiencing a cycle of interrelated actions: expectation, the suffering of a recurrent dread and horror, fear of rape and violation, the effort to escape, attempts to *assert* the self.

Sarah's first long monologue culminates in a parade of the characters in the play, all of whom are other "selves" of the protagonist, the players in her dream. Freud was the first to discover that in a dream, all characters are versions of the dreaming self. As the dream selves cross the stage (the Duchess of Hapsburg, Queen Victoria, Jesus as a hunchbacked dwarf, and Patrice Lumumba), Sarah enumerates the "places" they inhabit in her nightmare: a Victorian bedchamber in a castle, a chandeliered ballroom in a Hapsburg palace (presumably the Chapultepec Castle in Mexico City), a hotel room in Harlem, and the jungle (presumably in Africa).

Again, the multiple thematic ramifications of these characters and settings are so numerous, so potent, that they can easily distract our attention from the simple action that has brought them before us: to display the full resources of the play, or the dream. The action here is like that of a magician carefully laying out the specific props she will employ on a particular illusion; it is like a surgeon's assistant preparing the tools of a surgery—*ostentation*, in its original meaning: a setting forth, what the Greeks would have called an epiphany is the action. There seems to be, behind Sarah's show-and-tell parade, an urge to "come clean," a need for orderly procedure, for meticulous control of the play. The parade can also be construed as calculated to gain our credulity and our confidence: the audience is being shown the means of the coming illusion. In this light, it also resembles the classical *parodos* of a Greek tragedy.

Kennedy makes full structural use of the fact that funnyhouses, as we used to find them in amusement parks, are set up very much like the plots of plays. At Euclid Beach, for instance, not far from where Adrienne Kennedy grew up in Cleveland, you were meant to get into a little car, which then led you passively from one "situation" to another, from one "scene" to another, and as you passed, little horror episodes played themselves out. The sequence in which you experienced the episodes of the ride formed an exact analogue to the way in which an audience experiences a play in the theatre.

Segment 3

The third segment or episode of the play is the first landlady scene. The landlady is identified in the stage directions as the Funnyhouse Lady.

She is an outsider looking in on the vision. Her scenes (there are three in the play) mark important structural divisions of the plot. She appears toward the beginning and at the end, and she appears at the precise moment the play reaches its climax, as we will see later. The landlady in her first scene seems to be debunking the versions of what has been going on, what we have seen, and what Sarah has told us. She behaves like a corroborating witness, like an innocent bystander responding to an official investigation of the events. By bearing witness, the landlady helps us structurally in our search for the central event, the heart of the play—what Freud would have called the nucleus of the dream. What she says is less important than her function in the plot.

Segment 4

The play continues with an intimate domestic scene, set in "Raymond's place." Raymond is Negro-Sarah's white lover, and his place (the stage direction tells us) is "above" the Negro's room. Whether or not it can actually be staged that way is an open question. No other scene of the play calls for this setting, and building a separate level on the stage for this scene alone would be possible only in large-budget productions. But the stage direction is a clue that has profound ramifications for the thematics of the play. We may not see this scene enacted "above" Sarah's room, but we can understand her action in the scene as an effort to rise "above" the situation that is driving her to despair.

We discover Sarah clinging to Raymond's leg and begging him to hide her from her black father: "Hide me here so the nigger will not find me" (9-10). Sarah's pleading for protection, her attempted escape from her terrifying and lonely room, are perfectly understandable. Raymond resists Sarah's pleas, reproaching her instead and provoking guilt in her. His unsympathetic response to her desperation creates, in the most time-honored way, a basic structural sympathy for the heroine of the play. The Raymond scene is the most traditional of the play. And Raymond is just a cipher. He speaks fatuously, and he is callous and flip. His sole function is to add to a distress tnat is already acute, and he does this by siding with Sarah's oppressor, the Black Beast who is stalking her. The scene ends in a wild embrace, which one can only imagine as a last effort to hide in the arms of the lover.

Segment 5

Now a new figure emerges, and again we have a "funnyhouse" apparition, one that echoes the apparition of Sarah. A large, dark, faceless man holding an African mask appears in the center of the stage. Strangely, this ominous figure (which we might well take for the dreaded father) starts to recite Sarah's own earlier text, retelling the mother's story, "the disaster of my hair." As he tells this in the same haunted words Sarah had used to tell it, the Duchess of Hapsburg and Queen Victoria reenact in pantomime the horrible discovery of the lost hank of hair on the pillow. Then the apparition identifies himself with Patrice Lumumba, and the mad mother's own black father, the "black shadow" that haunted the mother's conception. This male figure, who speaks as though he were Sarah, using the first person as he repeats her tale in her exact words, gradually emerges as the ghost of the play, the essential Black Male Spirit who is oppressing her and who nucleates the dream.

Lumumba appears here, immediately after we have witnessed the trivial indifference of Sarah's white Jewish boyfriend, to take on the responsibility for the blackness in her blood. He literally "figures" that blackness that so torments her. He stands as the progenitor of the racial strain that made her and her mother black. It is he who separates Sarah from her white ancestry and the white European royalty she so admires. The Duchess of Hapsburg and Queen Victoria are figures of white and female power she would like to identify with, were it not for her Negro hair (which gives away her negritude). We can better understand the preceding scene with the white boyfriend when we see the structural contrast it creates to this apparition of the black man in Sarah's life.

The figure of this faceless black man, who goes so far as to call himself Patrice Lumumba (thereby making at least one of the things he represents unambiguous: the heroic and martyred emerging black political leader— there were to be several more heroic martyrs like him in the years immediately surrounding this play) can help us measure the distance between Kennedy's work and the other emerging black-consciousness literature of the sixties. Kennedy was certainly not jumping on any contemporary bandwagons when she painted such a dreadful portrait of this black progenitor.[7] "I am a nigger of two generations," says the faceless figure, meaning he infected the mother with blackness and engendered a second degree of blackness in her daughter, our protagonist Sarah (*Funnyhouse*, 12).

There are passages in *The Autobiography of Malcolm* X (a book that came out in the same year as this play) that express a similar psychosis, the same obsessive self-hatred, including a similar obsession with kinky black hair.[8] But there, such painful and humiliating confessions were preludes to a political and racial conversion, an awakening to enlightened self-acceptance, and an understanding of the personal psychopathology that is the result of oppression and discrimination. *Funnyhouse of a Negro* took a different tack and focused exclusively on the psychopathology of racism: the experience of feeling "infected" and "diseased" by one's racial heritage. The play makes it clear by the suicide at the end that this is an unendurable state, and the artwork is circumscribed by this view. It never transcends or overcomes the nightmare. This is unfortunate, historically, because *overcoming* was gathering profound and multivalent meaning in the accelerating momentum of the civil rights movement, and Kennedy's play struck some as being out of step with the political rise of black activism.[9]

The horrible nightmare pantomime of the two female figures, Queen Victoria and the Duchess of Hapsburg, discovering their fallen black hair on the white pillow of the bed, as already mentioned, plays in counterpoint to the faceless black progenitor's haunted monologue. The action of the play at this stage is controlled by the Black Father's assumption of responsibility for the nightmare. This figure is the center of the play for the simple reason that he is the source of the problem. His importance is underscored by a sudden "coup de théâtre": a bald head drops on a wire and someone screams. It is pure funnyhouse theatrics, and it plainly images a hanging.

Segment 6

The dropped head launches Negro-Sarah on her second long monologue, and in it she tells in great detail the story of her father: his mother, his mission, his marriage to Sarah's mother, their trip to Africa, the collapse of the marriage, the rape that engendered Sarah, and finally the mother's baldness and madness. This tale is so compelling, and so central, that it can distract from the underlying action of telling it. Why would Sarah tell it? What is she accomplishing by delivering this monologue? What drives her to deliver it?

The passage reads once again like the torrent of narrative a patient would release to a psychoanalyst, and the parallels come from similar motives. When patients "tell all" to their therapist, they are trying to assist a cure, they are trying to understand a past, and to situate themselves in some understandable way within that past. They are driven by anxiety, stress, distress, anguish—all the painful symptoms of inner disorientation, of dis-integration of the sense of self. The action of this monologue is exactly the same, and it forms the pivotal center of the play. It is framed at its end by an exact replication of the theatrical device that marked its beginning: the dropping of a bald head on a wire, a figuration of a hanging. This second time, instead of a scream we get a horrible funnyhouse laugh, and this punctuation propels us into the seventh major segment of the play, a third "scene" of essentially conventional "enactment between characters in a specified setting."

Segment 7

The first scene in a conventionally theatrical style was the opening waiting sequence in the Queen's bedchamber, the second was Sarah's scene in Raymond's place, pleading for his protection, and encountering only his reproaches and his disdain. Now the scene is in the Duchess's place: a chandeliered ballroom with a black and white marble floor.[10]

This seventh episode of the play is a scene between the Duchess of Hapsburg and the grotesque Dwarf-Jesus figure. One can assume this harsh portrayal of Jesus—employing as it does a reprehensible exploitation of dwarfism, which is a medical condition, not a metaphor—is meant to convey a deep disillusion with the conventionally compassionate and just Jesus we learn about in church. The scene is in three parts, with the second and third separated by a long and important monologue by the landlady (her second narrative interlude). Part 1 of this scene shows Jesus and the Duchess revealing to each other that they are in the same plight: their hair has fallen out. After a perfunctory blackout, they reappear and start grooming each other's hair, coping with their mutual plight, helping each other. Snow falls as their hair falls (the play is a constant series of analogical black and white images), and the two characters identify completely with each other in saying aloud together, "Our father isn't going to let us alone" (Funnyhouse, 17).

The double echo of the Lord's Prayer and Christ's last words on the cross makes it clear that the scene is built around a parallel between God the Father and the black father of Sarah. The action of the scene is to suffer the torment of the father: it is a Passion, what the Greeks called a *pathos*, or scene of suffering. The joint lamentation of Jesus and the Duchess is reminiscent of a *kommos*, or choral threnody in a Greek tragedy. The scene is also highly reminiscent of passages in James Baldwin's extraordinary "Down at the Cross," a fiery piece of writing first published in the New Yorker in 1962, which he subtitled "A Letter from a Region in my Mind." This brilliant analysis of the black man's situation could serve over and over again as a key to Funnyhouse of a Negro. Baldwin's description of his early religious crisis, for instance, hinges on the problem of "God the Father" being very evidently white and therefore a cruel deception for blacks who will never be allowed to forget that their forefathers are black. God cannot be "our" Father for the black man.[11]

The Jesus-Duchess scene in Funnyhouse of a Negro creates a literal identification between Jesus and Sarah: both suffer the inexplicable horror of losing a large patch of hair, both are tormented by their father in analogous but ironically incompatible ways, and finally they speak the identical text in unison, each meaning something antithetical. Jesus' biblical cry "Why hast thou forsaken me?" might well provoke Negro Sarah's "Why will you not let me alone?" James Baldwin put this dilemma very clearly in his report from a region in *his* mind:

> If one despairs—and who has not?—of human love, God's love alone is left. But God...is white.[12]

Segment 8 (Interrupts Unfinished Segment 7)

Frozen by a scream in an arresting tableau (they are by this time totally bald), Jesus and the Duchess are interrupted by a second monologue by the landlady. This passage is a straight narrative "fill." It simply tells one version of "what happened." Like Sarah's own monologues, it is a principal source of the story material behind the performance. But nothing it describes is dramatized, and for performance purposes, to understand the structure of the play, we are concerned, as always, only with the action of this telling. Why should the *kommos* be interrupted (suspended in a freeze, for it will continue and play itself out as a scene) to accommodate a gabby, explanatory text interlude? In a play made of theatrical gimmicks (the funnyhouse effects), a few conventionally dramatic scenes, and extended passages of *écriture*, the landlady's speech is the largest single example of "pure (antidramatic) writing."

The landlady's text summarizes the whole story behind the play, with particular emphasis on the final and most dramatic scene between father and daughter: his last attempt to reach her and win her forgiveness, her final inability to embrace him and the race she inherited from him. After this scene (which begs to be dramatized—so much so that the landlady starts quoting dialogue directly in her narrative of the climax of the story) there is nothing left of the tale but the catastrophe, first the father's suicide and then Sarah's. Adrienne Kennedy's writing is at its best in the purely written passages like this one. The dramatic scenes are hallucinatory collages, highly dependent for their effect and coherence on the collaborative work of a powerful director and imaginative designers.

Segment 7 (Concluded)

The Duchess-Jesus scene resumes after the last spurt of blatant textualizing (or "what-happened," *porte-parole* reportage) from the landlady. The concluding portion of the seventh segment is a garbled rehash of already stated thematic material. But in terms of a driving action, we see an important outcome, a reaction to what we were told happened. The Dwarf-Jesus character plays out an interesting recognition and reversal, a "conversion" of sorts, a classical peripeteia. It forms the most potentially political moment of the play. He wakes to the recognition that he has tried "to escape being black" (19). This is the dominant action of the entire play, and the character who brings it to consciousness is necessarily marking the crisis and turning point of the entire piece. From the moment this is uttered, we are on a straight path to an ending. All the miasmal formless anxieties and terrors, dream images and fragments of story coalesce around this statement, and it is a classic "action" statement, in traditional infinitive form.

This *anagnorisis*, to use the classical Greek term for a recognition, is followed by the discovery of its consequences: the Duchess has hanged herself. The juxtaposition follows the compressed form of a dream: the hanged Duchess is discovered already hanged, a classic use (Freud would tell us) of compression and the displacement mechanism in dreams. Although she is one of the "selves" of Negro-Sarah, the Duchess is not yet Sarah in her primary form. The Jesus character's response to discovering the hanged Duchess, however, is the fascinating part of this climax and reversal in the play:

> I am going to Africa and kill this black man named Patrice Lumumba. Why? Because all my life I believed my Holy Father to be God, but now I know that my father is a black man. I have no fear for whatever I do, I will do in the name of God, I will do in the name of Albert Saxe Coburg, in the name of Victoria, Queen Victoria Regina, the monarch of England, I will.
>
> (Blackout)
>
> (*Funnyhouse*, 19–20)

This short and powerful "I will do..." tirade marks a psychological revolution, a peripeteia or reversal of the suffering action of the play. At this moment an impulse toward willful, ethical action is born, and it contrasts markedly with the purely pathetic action of the rest of the play. Hortatory masterpieces like *The Fire Next Time* and *The Autobiography of Malcolm X* might be sources for the proud rhetoric echoing in this moment of the play. But the structure of the play undercuts and isolates this short moment in performance. The formal architecture of *Funnyhouse of a Negro* does not give this passage much weight, and critics have tended to miss it, focusing instead on the far more dominant overall tone of a Lament for Being Black, which does correctly characterize *Funnyhouse of a Negro*. But the militant passage is there, and that should give us pause.

It is perhaps exactly here that a feminist critique of *Funnyhouse of a Negro* could help explore the distinctly feminine aspect of its imaginative patterns. It is clear that conventional dramatic structure (perhaps deeply expressive of the masculine imagination) orchestrates all its craft around just such moments as these. A conventional instinct for the form of theatrics would cash in here, exploiting the full dramatic potential of this moment of "breakthrough." In purely structural action terms, the abrupt termination of this "will-to-do" speech is a wasted opportunity. It is so because the stage has just succeeded in creating, before our very eyes, a powerful "will-to-act." We witness suffering converted into outward-directed (and therefore politically potent) will. It is not lost on me just how "male" such a reading of the play is. All that is clear is that Adrienne Kennedy touched on this possibility only to leave it behind. *Funnyhouse of a Negro* has a different ending from the one so briefly hinted at in Dwarf-Jesus' momentary impulse to rebel.

Segment 9

The ending we *do* have starts with a magnificent opportunity for a director-orchestrated choral finale. The big Jungle Scene assembles all the players and puts them through a ritual of expiation that is a textbook example of the group-improv style that epitomized avant-garde New York performance art in the sixties. The Jungle Scene could have been created by Joe Chaikin's Open Theater, then in its second year of operation. Trust circles and transformations come to mind as plausible forms of staging. The choral delivery, the ritualized repetition of a stylized text, the gradual creation of a stagewide mood or atmosphere not focused on any one player—these were state-of-the-art Off-Broadway in 1964.[13]

In ritualized form, the Jungle Scene recapitulates the entire action of Kennedy's play. It is a rite of expiation, almost an exorcism of the black father's pollution of the almost white child. Forgiveness is sought for the "sin" of injecting blackness into the race-line. An agony of rejection plays itself out. The impossible wish to undo the blackness in Negro-Sarah takes on haunting and primitive shape. It is a ritual of deepest darkest African extraction, appropriately set in a jungle, both for historical and for emotional reasons. It ends in a plea for forgiveness juxtaposed with a wild Dionysiac celebration. The Eternal Return of the Dead Black Father is juxtaposed with a chorus of Saviors in the Jungle.

The selves are all potential saviors (they are destined to fail), for they are strategies of escape; each is a possibility of being other than Negro-Sarah. In the end, neither the individual alteregos nor their collective ritual can save Sarah from her nightmare. The Jungle Scene is, in the dream sequence of the play, the last-ditch effort to keep dreaming. It was Freud who pointed out that the ultimate motive of any dream is to allow the dreamer to dream—in other words, to "resolve" the crisis that would otherwise require that the dreamer wake and deal consciously with the pressures generating the dream.[14] After the Jungle Chorus, Negro-Sarah's nightmare comes to a swift and violent resolution.

Segment 10

Sarah is seen one last time, now as herself, in the situation "enacted" for her by two alternate selves at the opening of the play. She is alone in her room awaiting the horrible return of the Dead Black Father. Rape or murder are equally suggested. At the very least it will be unendurable torment. The knocking that has continued throughout the play pounds away. Finally, just as in a nightmare, the dreaded force breaks through, the horror happens: the black figure, now with bloody mangled hands, breaks in and rushes upon the defenseless Sarah. A blackout blots out the moment of contact between them, and she appears in jump-cut fashion hanged and dead. The final action is, exactly as in a dream, to end the tension, to capitulate to the crisis. It is a classic catastrophe, quite literally, a downturn in the action: Sarah takes the "out" offered by hanging herself. All other alternatives have failed. All the various "actions" of her multiplied "selves"—all of whom tried to save her from her black father—have failed.

The epilogue to the play is brief and predictable. The landlady reappears to wrap up the narrative. She delivers a callous "bottom line" to the play, one devoid of sympathy or understanding: "The poor bitch has hung herself" (Funnyhouse, 22). The utterly marginal character of Raymond (who has been made too much of by other commentators) makes his second and last appearance to demonstrate just how thoroughly out of it he has really been. His own nonsequitur version of things suggests he either never knew or never cared much about what was going on in Sarah's life. He certainly never paid attention. It creates an ending very much like the cynical throwaway tags in Euripides' more bitter plays. The play is over.

Funnyhouse of a Negro divides structurally into ten major passages,[15] a suite of concatenated actions that add up very clearly to the imitation of a single-minded action: to escape the ever-recurring return of the Black Father. This central action is more significant than the suicide's story that accompanies it—in "rationalized time" the whole play may well take place in the last second of life, just before or just after the leap of the hanging victim. But such rationalization is unimportant. What is far more important is the fundamental mass of the play itself, its shape and weight as a made object. Neither the bold and surreal images nor the background "story" should obscure the formal pattern of an artifact consisting of ten distinct, graspable pieces. Adrienne Kennedy has governed "the unity and sequence of events" precisely by her control of the plot, and any good production of the play should make this architecture bold and clear.

Notes

1. Theodor Adorno, *Aesthetic Theory*, trans. C. Lenhardt (London: Routledge and Kegan Paul, 1984), 200.

2. Ibid., 199.

3. Coleridge's own definition of this term is given in his *Biographica Literaria*. See, for example, among many editions, *Coleridge: Poems and Prose*, ed. Kathleen Raine, the Penguin Poets (Harmondsworth, Middlesex: Penguin Books, 1957), 184.

4. All text citations to *Funnyhouse of a Negro* are from *Adrienne Kennedy in One Act* (Minneapolis: University of Minnesota Press, 1988).

5. The concept of "action" pervades the published works of Francis Fergusson, as it did his teaching. This idea derives equally from Aristotle and from Stanislavski. The "action" of a scene is the motive drive within the play that gives each scene, each passage (often called "beats" as a shorthand in the rehearsal hall) its form. It is sensed "histrionically," as Fergusson used to say. It can be seen, once discerned, to bind the parts of a play together, to dictate when a "passage" begins and when it ends. Action so defined is the principle of coherence of dramatic form. Fergusson's essay on histrionic sensibility appears in Fergusson, *The Idea of a Theater* (Princeton, N.J.: Princeton University Press, 1949), 236–40.

6. Sigmund Freud, *The Interpretation of Dreams*, trans. A. A. Brill (New York: Random House, 1950), 244–45. Freudian "interpretation" is tempered by Adrienne Kennedy's own explanations of the hair anxiety: "Often when I was depressed, my hair fell out, as my mother's hair fell out when I was born because of the ether she had to take during a difficult labor" (*People Who Led to My Plays* [New York: Theatre Communications Group, 1987], 117).

7. The idea of accepting and embracing one's blackness, of celebrating it and elevating it to a place of pride and respect, might well suggest itself as a cure for the "state of mind" expressed in Kennedy's play, but she was not the one to suggest it. "Black is beautiful" was the new slogan emerging in the mid-sixties, and Kennedy's brutally frank expression of a black heroine's resentment of her black bloodlines in *Funnyhouse of a Negro* was out of sync with the emerging black politics of the time.

8. Alex Haley, the author of the "autobiography," eloquently transcribed Malcolm X's description of the painful and degrading process of "conking" his hair with a dangerous mixture of lye, starch, and beaten eggs in an effort to rid himself of the "Negroid" feature of kinky hair (see Alex Haley, *The Autobiography of Malcolm X* [New York: Random House, 1965], 52–55).

9. See Loften Mitchell, *Black Drama: The Story of the American Negro in the Theatre* (New York: Hawthorn Books, 1967), 198–99, for a defense of Kennedy's right to her own personal vision.

10. The checkered floor is a difficult effect to save until this point. If there is such a floor in the theatre, the play has probably taken place on it from the start. It shows Kennedy's fundamentally cinematic imagination at work, and presents a problem for a stage director. But in any case, it is a plot progression comprehensible in either medium as a progression to another imitated action.

11. James Baldwin, *The Fire Next Time* (New York: Dell, 1964), 44–80.

12. Ibid., 47.

13. It is perhaps the moment to mention Gene Frankel's watershed production of Genet's *The Blacks* in relation to *Funnyhouse of a Negro*. This production had an enormous influence on the New York theatre scene. Frankel's staging of the play opened in 1961 at the St. Mark's Playhouse and enjoyed a long and influential run in the three years preceding the opening of *Funnyhouse of a Negro*. Genet's ritual enactment of deep-lying fantasies, his repetitive performance of suppressed fears and suppressed hatreds, the fearsome play of masks and racial posing—all these are suggestively echoed in Kennedy's play.

14. Freud, *The Interpretation of Dreams*, 133.

15. The usual markers in a play, incidentally, are more than a little misleading in the case of *Funnyhouse of a Negro*. Anyone who uses Kennedy's "Blackout" markings (which customarily are structural signals for the ends of scenes) will be frustrated and confused. The scene or episode units have a hit-or-miss relation to the blackouts, which are correctly marked for stage business that is frequently within (and not between) scenes. Here in final summary, and for the benefit of anyone who cares to stage the play, are the ten parts of the plot:

1. Waiting scene in the Queen's Chamber (bookended by the two Mad Mother cross-overs) (2–4).
2. Sarah's first monologue (5–7).
3. The landlady's first monologue (8).
4. The pleading scene in Raymond's place (9–11).
5. The emergence of the Shadowy Black Man: the assumption of responsibility for the "problem" (11–13).
6. Sarah's second monologue (bookended by dropping heads and screams/laughter (14–15).
7. The joint lamentation of Jesus and the Duchess (16–17). It is interrupted by
8. The landlady's second monologue (17–19, contains undramatized climax of the *story*).
7. (Concluded.) Turning point and climax of the *play*: birth of will-to-act (19–20).
9. Jungle scene: rite of expiation (20–22).
10. Catastrophe (and epilogue) (22–23).

PART III

Changing Boundaries
Interpretive Approaches

9

Locating Adrienne Kennedy
Prefacing the Subject

Kimberly W. Benston

Preface: 1

Writing about Adrienne Kennedy is not unlike being written by her: one feels always already estranged from any clear point of departure, though a plethora of intellectual, psychic, and political themes suggest themselves as equally plausible centering concerns. Self-narration as crisis and quenchless need, the crossings of race and gender in the construction of identity, arresting but enigmatic juxtapositions of spectacle and verbal image, echoing ruptures between various historical and cultural formations—these are among the more encompassing issues that lend Kennedy's work its characteristic aura of irresolvable disturbance.[1] The ensuing temptation for the reader trapped in this funnyhouse of textual effects is to seize upon a specific representational category or structure in order to thematize Kennedy's project from some consistent conceptual position.

Nevertheless, the highly self-reflexive nature of Kennedy's writing forces any interpretive stance into immediate unease, opening questions about strategies of reading that are at once cognate with her characters' explorations and limitations upon whatever comprehensive account we might offer of them. The very conventions of narrative intelligibility and logical design by which we habitually organize critical response are often indeed themselves the object of Kennedy's distorting critique. Nor, in yet another turn of the critical screw, is it quite sufficient to posit this rich polysemous elusivity as the very hallmark of Kennedy's confounding self-referentiality, thus mastering its uncanny deflection of our sense-making apparatuses in an encompassing gesture of complexity's acceptance. It is not that we cannot produce a sufficient number of thematic, politicized, or contextualized readings to match the work's abundantly intricate figurations; rather, such a compendium of styles and effects can help only if we confront the way Kennedy's writing exceeds our formulations by putting the question of meaning itself into question.

This essay began as an effort to achieve one instrumental norm of reading through some controlled understanding of Kennedy's "language." After suffering the topic's dispersal into a variety of substructures and classifications (language as image, as discourse, as narrative, as spectacle, and so on), attempting to organize my discussion around points of conflict between various discursive and symbolic expressions, I encountered the further bafflement of a discontinuity between assessment of a given work's "linguistic" or paralinguistic means and the uncontainable effects and unaccountable intentions for which those means would conventionally serve as vehicle. Seeking to control this crisis of incommensurate interpretive tasks by establishing its limit through thematized configurations of specific conflictual linguistic performances—in particular, undertaking to establish the contrast in *Funnyhouse of a Negro* between the Jungle and the Room (emblems of reified stasis—statuary, walls, repetition—versus signs of wildness—hair, screams, movement) as synecdochic enactment of a larger defining tension between classicism (such as colonialism, the unified bourgeois subject, modernism) and its disruption or interruption by the Uncanny (such as revolutionary resistance, the subject-in-process, the Imaginary)—I experienced instead the frustration of any sure conceptual grasp as Kennedy's play continuously displaced my schema by its own ceaseless self-interrogations.

In further retreat, questing still for some authenticating source or design at the core of Kennedy's work by which to effect my own mimetic response, I began to pay closer attention to the author's own self-explanations, particularly those offered in the prefatorial statements appended in striking profusion to three recently published books: *People Who Led to My Plays, Adrienne Kennedy in One Act,* and *Deadly Triplets.*[2] The present essay "takes place" at this juncture, taking as its subject Kennedy's "own" taking of herself as subject in writing that stands structurally before but logically outside of the main works they introduce. Not that any "solution" to the critical dilemma here posed can be imagined in advance, for what the prefaces offer, in themselves and taken together, is an interminable series of inscriptions upon the act of self-representation itself, a dazzling and dizzying layering of text upon text, such that any particular touchstone or origin of intention is unlikely to present itself. But as a meditation on the problems of repetition, quest, dissimulation, and self-origination that so haunt her plays' protagonists, the prefaces do at least embody a striking record of the author's entanglement in her works' extravagant perplexity, and so warrant our best powers of engagement.

People Who Led to My Plays: The Self as Supplement

The "subject" of Adrienne Kennedy, in its many figurations and apparent embodiments, seems to us ever elusive, always beyond the traces imprinted before us. Often understood as an effect of her self-confessed penchant for "nonlinear," discontinuous, and expressionistic form,[3] the uncertain notice cast by Kennedy's work might equally be felt as an obsessional evocation of the strangeness of writing itself, a disruptive preoccupation with consciousness conceived at once as uncanny and domesticated, mobile and paralyzed, lyrical and banal.

And yet there exists no lack of tracks and signs for the ardent pursuer of this evasive subject to follow, not least of which remain Kennedy's own recorded searches for self-origin. Autobiography, of the flesh and its inscriptions, is the very signature of Adrienne Kennedy's impossible though endless quest for a clarifying and stabilizing source. Much like her heroines, Kennedy's work seems driven by a search for an incandescent touchstone of self-reference, some primal image, story, or scene, that would heal the self's constitution as wound or lack, its entrapment in dramas scripted from elsewhere. And thus every Kennedy work appears as its own simulacrum or double, juxtaposing the phantasmatic with the empirical, setting fabulous interiorizations against the banalities of public display, casting an aura of compulsive self-exploration while leaving deepest concerns somehow excessive to representation, the subject neither quite present nor absent: familiar, veiled—spectral.

Among the most fascinating of these records of self-search, these charming spectacles of self-exposition, are the various "prefaces" appended, like a delusory afterimage, to several of the theatrical and fictional works. Their typical inaugurating gesture is the submission to a demand for self-explication, as exemplified by the opening paragraph of *People Who Led to My Plays* (the chronicle's de facto preface):

> More and more often as my plays are performed in colleges and taught in universities, people ask me why I write as I do, who influenced me....[T]hey continue to ask. Who influenced you to write in such a nonlinear way? Who are your favorite playwrights?

>   After I attempt to answer, naming this playwright or that one, as time
>   progresses I realize I never go back far enough to the beginning. So I
>   decided to. (*People*, 3)

As Stephen Greenblatt has remarked in his penetrating analyses of theatrical improvisation and discursive power in Shakespeare, the impulse
to self-narration is, paradoxically, the response to a call for public unfolding.[4] But if private rumination is potentially already social property,
Kennedy implies a more complex dynamic by which the energy of persistent public inquiry may itself be turned to serve an inward quest for
origins, the demand of self-performance yielding a "decision" to inter-
rogate the founding stages of that histrionic unveiling. The probing effort
to define the author as an effect or echo is insistent, but no less so is
the equivocating failure to name the self as the past's shadow and so
tame the potential of self-origination.

That equivocation is perhaps the most compelling, if subtle, motivating
impulse behind the subversively antinarrative strategy of *People Who Led
to My Plays*. In a sense, *People* is a collection of such introductory events,
a chain of signifiers of the will-to-begin the process of self-location.
Composed of lists of favored objects, compendia of memories both trivial
and pivotal (the degree of importance must be inferred or imposed),
visual fragments and labels (possibly parodic gestures to the school
yearbook or celebrity scrapbook, with their cavalier commodification of
the knowable subject), *People* makes the possibility of its meaning its
most meaningful issue. So exhaustively banal are some of these cata-
logues, so paratactic are their juxtapositions, that we are left to wonder
whether the life's meaning resides in some residue of silence, in what
still remains to be said about and by an I that is consistent merely in
its relentlessly prosaic quest for the source of careeristic renown.

Put differently, the autobiography's interest lies in what the narrative's
dependence on discrete scenic representation cannot yield, and we must,
if we desire it, supply some explanatory narrative perspective or significance, in short, a story. Because the life's data are given no hierarchical
arrangement or relational balance (Jesus, Mrs. Minever, Leslie Howard,
Little House on the Prairie, favorite childhood belongings, childhood aver-
sions, father, mother, Snow White, among others, compete for space in
the text's and the author's imaginative order), the book frustrates the
interrogative impulse of the opening query, refusing any clear reference
to a conceptual design beyond the text's borders. Despite, if not because
of, the persistence of the first-person pronoun in juxtaposition to these
sketches and anecdotes, no comprehensive thematic structure coalesces

around a perceptual center; no controlling consciousness focuses and justifies the details that would give it referential validity.

In this way, *People Who Led to My Plays* refuses the normative circular logic by which autobiographical narrative establishes an I through tautological pronouncement of that I's confirming incarnations. And yet *People* would be an entirely chaotic jumble of entries, equally devoid of and replete with significant events, were there not operating some principle of emphasis and subordination. And, in turn, any such hermeneutic principle implies behind it a phenomenological entity. But whether we find that centering notion in the unseemly thrust for fame, in the eventual material production of the plays that produce that fame, or in some more occult metaphoric apparatus,[5] the principle is never visible as part of the narrative's own appeal, remaining, like the central subject, like the I's perduring voice, suppressed or deflected. Rather, the subject of *People* is that voice's floating, fragmented inflections, which never cohere into the sort of continuity of belief or crisis or concern through which we normally infer a reflective subjectivity.[6] The very hermetic enclosure of each entry, the seeming finality of each catalogue, means that no overt thematizing of the entries can reduce them to the kind of consistent significance we associate with ontological wholeness. In short, what we're led to in these reflections is not a *person*, but only the author's own textual constitution as a locus of "people." Offering a theoretically infinite stock of self-revelations, Kennedy in effect tells no story of herself at all.

Even so, the reader, unguided by the spurious logic of narrative authority, becomes in some sense a version of the heroine, asking at every turn, "Where am I?," grasping at every moment for some preliminary outline or map. Its organizing voice perpetually decentering the very consciousness it claims to be re-presenting, *People* suggests how the subject responding to the opening injunction to tell is constantly reinvented. The obligation to self-representation hollows the identity it makes possible, nullifying any specific claim to a fullness of truth by the very proliferation of truthful data it engenders. The text is so relentless and nonsyntactically detailed that what might appear as total disclosure becomes instead a kind of occlusion: revealing subversively becomes reveiling. By the same token, a narrative that seems wholly a collection of exterior manifestations (dates, objects, encounters, events) becomes the most unfathomable process of interiorization, as the project's subject becomes, as it were, secreted, placed outside the speculative invasion of the reader's eye.

Perhaps even this discourse of the seen and the hidden, with its structure of inside and outside, fails to clarify the way *People Who Led to*

My Plays explores a new mode of self-representation by discrediting the available models. Just how tenacious this demystification is can be felt by setting the book's concluding entry against our memory of the prefatorial self-inauguration:

> *Myself:*
>
> We sailed back to New York on the *United States*. I had a completed play in my suitcase. How could I know it would establish me as a playwright and change my life? After years of writing, I had finally written of myself and my family and it would be on a stage and in a book too, and I would be on the pages of *Vogue* and in Leonard Lyons's column.
>
> And in a few months I would climb the steps to the Circle in the Square theater where I would see this play inside my suitcase performed, become a member of the Actors Studio (where Brando had been) and become a part of the Off-Broadway theater movement...a movement that in itself would come to occupy a powerful place in American theater history.
> (*People*, 125)

Is this a satire of the narrative implicit in the opening invitation for self-display, that reifying quest for value in the public exchange of recognizable personalities whose devastating costs of mutilated consciousness are explored so hauntingly in the very triumphant writings being brought "home"? What effect does the echo of the slave narrative's topos of climactic self-realization in the acceptance of representativeness, marked by a merging of personal and public "places" on the historical scaffold, have upon such an evaluation?[7] Or ought we rather ask, might the implicit tension between the definitively subjective entry title, myself, and the diffusion of that potent locus of well-catalogued desires, interests, possessions, wounds, expectations, and so forth, into the narrowed expression of public notice signal an unresolved conflict of self-representational decorum, a conflict that makes of the subject a peculiar rhetorical predicament? Form and consciousness, self and representation, structure and agency can be seen by the end of *People*, not as the unified, consumable entity complacently presumed by the opening query, but as mutually supplemental aspects of a mobile and transformative subject.

Adrienne Kennedy in One Act: The Quest in Excess of Itself

Already, we can say, autobiography is theatricalized, rendered as a play at the borders of revelation and concealment. The pronominal shifts and instability of tense evident in *People's* framing passages alert us to the self's constitutive movement between the other's interrogating gaze, with its demand to render the self as a tellable entity—who influenced you? who are your favorite[s]?—and the ideal of subjectivity seeking an alternative space of enactment and, so, possibly, an alternative (kind of) story. Demanded disclosure threatens the closure of a misrecognition, but it is nonetheless the instigator of the quest for a less visible position of self-enunciation. The autobiographical project is inescapably, if indeterminately, dialogic, its scene a multivoiced nexus of subtle conflicts and purported confluences.

The Preface to the Minnesota edition of Kennedy's one-act plays (intriguingly entitled *Adrienne Kennedy in One Act*, in subtle affinity with the works' emphasis on the self's quest for an almost classically austere and definitive enclosure, a carefully furnished though generally distorted "room of one's own") seems again a response to a query:

> More than anything I remember the days surrounding the writing of each of these plays...the places...Accra Ghana and Rome...the shuttered guest house surrounded by gardens...the sunny roof of the apartment on Via Reno...our wonderful brand new apartment in New York...and the enchanting Primrose Hill in London....Hadn't Sylvia Plath lived across the way in Chalcot Square?...
>
> Without exception the days when I am writing are days of images fiercely pounding in my head and days of walking...in Ghana...in Rome...in London, Primrose Hill (hadn't Karl Marx walked there?)...all of which seem to put me under a spell of sorts....(*Adrienne Kennedy in One Act*, Preface)

In languid, almost hypnotically recursive phrasing, Kennedy suggests how these plays are precipitates of a personal quest for the continuity of self in time. Personality and history reflect one another as persistent, but self-interrupting, discourses (the ellipses are, for the most part, Kennedy's own), a series of phenomena whose center lies in a recurrent questioning of their possible underlying necessity. Structured by a symmetry of personal re-locations and ghostly summons, this Preface seems obsessed by evocations of an Other at once radically distant (as markers of specific, historicized, even monumentalized figures) and potentially self-mirroring (as anterior editions of the author's own perambulations and, covertly, ambitions). The unifying thread of these reflections is the juxtaposition of memory's pleasant resituation of activities *surrounding* writing's effects to what Lacan termed *aphanisis*, or the incipient panic of a fading from presence of those inspiriting authorities that legitimate one's enunciations. By evoking Plath (with her problematic identities as woman, writer, wife, American, modern) and Marx (an exile revolutionary who died at his desk), Kennedy formulates the precariousness of the author's own writing subjectivity, which takes up uneasy (and temporary) residence along several locations of marginality. Seeing herself as if from the other's vantage, or as if recognized as an effect of another's incantation, Kennedy enmeshes the remembered writing subject in an irresolvable drama of identifications and distinctions. Catching glimpses of herself in the fading traces of such richly provocative spirits, she resists any precise self-location (spatial or temporal, psychic or political, formal or thematic), while teasing our own desire to resolve the quest in some specific ideological or biographical predetermination.

The implications of such insouciant exilic self-displacement are further "spelled" out in the Preface's final lines:

> ...I am at the typewriter almost every waking moment and suddenly there is a play. It would be impossible to say I wrote them. Somehow under this spell they become written.

Is the author, then, merely a per-sona, a mask through which language(s) (whose? from where?) speak(s)? And are we to understand such a spoken subject in a Plathian manner, as a willing if troubled participant in a pluri-voiced struggle for expression's grace, or in a Marxist sense, as a pure position within a system of utterances wherein subjectivity is only a phantasm of ideology? Thus fragmented into the writing itself, the quest outlined by the Preface's narrative of writing's genesis is emptied of its presumed intentionality. Or, rather, that intentionality is deconstructed, distantiated as the product of the very discourse it would claim to wield. Kennedy performs for us the structural dependence of the subject on some relation to an other, its constitution as a locus of voices variously competing for presence and self-authorization...even from beyond the grave. Seen in this way, the subject is not an essence reporting on its self-discovery but a process of invention arising as a relation with itself that is mediated by time and circumstance. It is an infinitely open semiosis, a body and a ghost all at once, a maddening interchange of repetition and substitution. And, "naturally," it cannot help but be inadequate and excessive to its own scene or "home."

Deadly Triplets: The Double Scene

This generative motif of narrative staged as endless self-supplementary quest is given sharper imagistic focus in the Preface to Deadly Triplets, a self-consciously disjointed fiction-cum-journal in which theatre, autobiography, meditation, and mystery mix into a generically fragmenting, thematically phantasmagoric enigma. Continuously rehearsing the book's own defining tensions between unity and dispersal, continuity and contingency, the "Real" and the Imaginary, story and detail, this Preface finds compelling focus in moments of recollection, where memory and writing compete for the still-elusive center of the author's attention:

> This book contains two very different, though connected, writings that deal with my experience of London and the theatre. Although a theatre journal

and a theatre mystery may seem an unlikely combination, they are united in the attempt to write about a time and set of experiences that for me continue to be significant. The real mystery is why London has occupied such an important place in my imagination and why it continues to haunt me....Although I thought the sketches [vignettes of theatre personalities, echoing the style and format of *People Who Led to My Plays*, that make up *Deadly Triplet*'s second section] I had written on London were complete, four years later when I reread them I decided the sketches only reminded me of the mystery I still felt existed around London and my three-year stay there in 1966–69....I decided to try a short mystery novel. Perhaps fiction in this form would finally capture the complexity of my feelings toward London. (*Deadly Triplets*, viii; hereafter cited as DT)

The laconic style, which lends each compositional and even "experiential" decision an air of casual improvisation, is belied by the "haunting" sense of writing's endless struggle to contain the excessive imaginative dis-ease that is, ironically, writing's very spur. A pattern of desire and frus-tration inaugurates the book's effort to settle the self's accounts with time and place: desire for containment of experience's "significance" in some formal mode, frustration at the inevitable rupture of narrative by those unnameable clusters of associational feelings whose appearance, in the *fort/da* rhythm of inscription and rereading, in turn produce more narrative. And so the quest for, and of, narrative begins as the staged return to a doubled scene of writing:

> Writing short sketches on people had seemed natural to me so I had been surprised when a friend...asked me why I had written sketches rather than a long continuous piece. I think I had written sketches because the people I met in the theatre seemed to be dream interludes in my life. My real continuous story seemed to be that of my family....The real me went out to Actor's Studio worrying about what to wear, running across the street to the cleaners, waiting for the babysitter, and met Geraldine Page, Rip Torn, Molly Kazan. These wonderful interludes of people excited me. But they were not quite real. Even with the passage of time most often the people I've met in the theatre seemed no more real to me than people I'd seen on stage at the old Palace Theatre in Cleveland when I was a kid. (DT, viii)

The putatively real, anchored by the quotidian and the familial, becomes entangled, even syntactically, with the theatrical; repeated, doubled, the real and the "seeming" mirror one another in an obfuscating, iterative play, and distinctions of locale, time, and their memorializations (whether in dream or in the already quasi-hallucinatory or shadowy impressions of "sketches") begin to be blurred—again (as in the opening to *People Who Led to My Plays*) under the slyly factitious pressure of arresting, if "friendly," inquiry. The theatre, a site of masks and illusions neither true nor false (*"not quite* real"), is itself characterized as an "interlude," an entr'acte interrupting and reflecting a presumably larger encompassing drama, that of the purportedly "real" life story in which the act of doubling dramatic scenes by means of the quasi-performative mode of the "sketch" (the splash of pictorial representation) seems quite "natural." Impelled beyond the apparent security of domestic structure by some unspecified desire, the author experiences the intrusion into that realm's routinized histrionics (marked by the primordial theatrical signifiers of dressing and waiting) of another order of personality and place, so that no absolute present or past is established. Rather, the present is suffused by the otherness of several alternative stages, and the self is, like its story, always incomplete, its "significance" always an effect of narrative's partiality and excess.

Strangely compressed, specific yet eccentric and mesmerizing in its repetitiousness, Kennedy's prose suggests here an almost therapeutic scene at which layers of past experience refuse repression by any systematic ordering of significance or any unbroken temporal schema. The author embarks on a quest for encounters in the giddy world of theatrical "recognition" that would simultaneously derealize and establish her own identity as mother, wife, playwright, public figure.[8] But as the divisions or boundaries between private/public and real/hallucinatory dissolve into a montage of impression and recreation, we find ourselves everywhere in the domain of the Imaginary, where identity is structured as a phantasmatic scene that the subject immediately (though unsuccessfully) disavows. It is no wonder, then, that the Preface in *Deadly Triplets* proceeds to a series of doublings and reflections, replete with imagery of enclosure and alienation, that manage to complicate the very coordinates of identity they would firmly anchor:

> My plays were filled with the intricacies of race in my life. Why had I refused? [I.e., to write of race autobiographically when asked to do so.] Was it because at that moment I had not wanted race to separate me from the Brontës, Wordsworth...Tintern Abbey? (I often felt deep down that I had once lived in Haworth.)...In Accra, Ghana, my husband and I had driven past the enclave of British homes surrounded by walls where British families had lived separate as they colonized the West African. Although in 1961, Nkrumah was Prime Minister, these enclaves still existed, and when we first arrived in Accra we even lived briefly in a section of the city that had once been populated by Europeans, a district of large homes, walled in, gardens tended by Ghanaians. I used this experience as the basis for plays and stories. (DT, viii–ix)

But what, exactly, is "this experience"? On the one hand, it seems reasonably clear that two disparate and antipathetic political and cultural matrices compete for power and centrality in both landscapes. But, as with Kennedy's own efforts to write of memory's continuity in the present's disjunctive moment (recorded in the Preface's opening ruminations on the form and origin of *Deadly Triplets*), we discover a haunting continuity of effect despite apparent revolutionary change. Not only do the architectural configurations of colonial rule remain in place, their arrangements of labor and social hierarchy still effective, but, perhaps even more disconcertingly, the author's own placement within that labyrinthine system of "separations," protections, and containments stands in disturbing relation, first, to a lingering wish to close the distance between herself and an imagined Anglocentric ancestry, and then, to a structural replacement of those European masters among their African servants. "Race," a barrier to the black American woman's "momentarily" idealized self-realization in the English domain, stands in analogical relation to the Ghanaian walled garden, which, paradoxically, enforces the suppression of the African by the European. And this remains so even when the African has, presumably, undertaken a triumphant action of reversal. But the irony of this oppositionality, too, is precisely to the point: whoever stands within the enclave, under whatever empiric sign, the *structure* of differences remains the same.

It is perhaps a strategic necessity that race remain inflected within a structure of difference in such a way that, given a resistance to the logic of reversibility, its value cannot be too easily calculated. Standing somewhere *between* African and European (in racial, historical, and physical terms),[9] the author suggests that the work of self-representation arises along an ever-shifting boundary "separating'" the vague evocations of a literary tradition and the concrete (if still undecidable) data of political event. What gives "unity" to such projections of contrast, repetition, and irony is the structure of doubling itself, the compulsion to continuous transferences and transformations that, though intoxicating in their proliferation, create the illusion of balance, of a wholeness composed of fused oppositions—a wholeness economically labeled "this experience." Once again, we might think of this kind of seductively circumstantial exposition as a *staging* of narrative self-exploration, a simulated inquiry into the definitive coordinates of the self understood as both consciousness and as social construction. Once again, the "self" is above all a dramatic proposition, a derivative of movement between positions, a series of displacements that adhere only if seen simultaneously from differing perspectives of culture, temporality, and place.[10]

It is also in this sense of writing-the-self as the scene of self-writing, as a restorative and effacing movement of an impossible self-scrutiny, that Kennedy's Preface becomes a confrontation with the historicality of self-construction. For race, nationality, gender, and other categories of recognition and mis-construal appear in these pages as alternative modes at once of representing experience and of experiencing the self *as* a representation. "History," like its subjects, becomes then an irresolvable layering, or friction, or accretion among elements that might be at one moment felt as representation, at another termed experience. (It is for this reason that the Preface moves with obsessive nervousness from capturing experience in the discourse of writing—*sketches, rereading, writing* itself—and attempting to locate an exact experiential ground for the present's *activity* of writing.) The personal and the political become inextricably entangled, not because the self is either beyond or utterly produced by ideology and tradition, but indeed because it is the ongoing effort to locate itself between determinations, an effort that writing seeks ever to record and thereby materially enacts.

Thus problematizing the scene of its own enactment, Kennedy's Preface (dis)locates the self as something both within and beyond the discourse of self-representation, just as she was both in and absent to the legacy of Haworth, both within and foreign to the ambiguous walled gardens of postcolonial Ghana. The subject's formation is a conceptual dilemma of specific historical texture, since its failure to achieve satisfying harmony questions the violent closures of both traditional (imperial, romantic) order and its transgression by revolutionary replacement. On the one hand, as Kennedy suggests in the conclusion of the Preface, the old economy of colonial authority remains a fading but still enrapturing phantasm, a memory in dissolution, a literally in-spiriting landscape of the past's ghostly reinscription:

> Now I felt I did not know the English. I remembered all of this. I remembered...[and used as] the setting for my mystery novel:...squares shrouded in mist, fog rising over Primrose Hill, stories of dead writers, dead Kings and Queens, landscapes with names like Gloucester Gate,... murders,...betrayals,...all of it still mesmerized me. (DT, x–xi)

On the other hand, still arrested by the spectacle of tradition's mutilations, secrets, and ravishments, the author suggests that contemporary subversions of this fading dream of feudal narrative figuring an exchange of power cannot yet offer any truly alternative "names" of self-empowerment. Stripped of any aura of natural cultivation either in the security of European lineage or the liberatory assertion of African sovereignty, the self, in its continued search for origination, becomes an unavoidably but undecidably political crux.

In this sense, too, Kennedy's "experience" in Accra is paradigmatic: presenting a poignant juxtaposition of "home" and exile, this anecdotal hinting at a perpetual foreignness is everywhere duplicated in *Deadly Triplets*, especially in the Preface's own doublings in the opening paragraphs to each of the book's two main sections and in the framing epilogical entry. "Part One," the "mystery," is prefaced by the following account of an uncanny repetition, replete with the temporal confusions and spatial dislocations already familiar to us:

> Last night John Lennon was murdered at the Dakota apartment...four blocks from where I am now living. I find it a strange and terrible coincidence that several years ago I started writing a play based on Lennon's nonsense books...in a studio at the top of the Dakota apartments and that the writing of that play led to my being involved in a mysterious and brutal death. A murder most unexpected.
>
> My theatrical producers, who let me use the studio in the Dakota to write, put me in touch with Lennon's English publisher. The publisher liked the pages of the play I had written. This, and some reasons that I myself was not entirely aware of, reasons that dealt with the strange demise of my adopted mother years ago in England, convinced me that London was the place I wanted to go. I brushed aside the unfulfilled longing and curiosity that I had never satisfied about my adopted mother's illness and last days and accepted the more obvious reasons: I was recently divorced, in the throes of a new career...that was bringing me recognition....I was entangled in the deadly ambitions and desires of other people I was yet to meet. (DT, 5–6)

The clichéd outline of a murder mystery's mise-en-scène notwithstanding (and that parody is itself characteristic of the book's constant evocation and displacement from its ostensibly enabling genres and voices), the passage again instances the I's diffusion in a miasma of dislocations, refracted desires, dispersed projects, and incomplete perceptions. Typically, the subject introduced is occluded by the juxtapositions of portentous exposition and petty ambition, of self-assertion and self-deferral. Does the voice, or character, presented here consist merely in a range of impulses and movements, a process under constant erasure? Or is there a motivating center behind the I's furtive gestures preserved apart from the continuing drama of separation and resituation? Though syntactically (even, on the page, visually) central, that I is perhaps superfluous or resistant to the symbolic order it variously invokes (as repository of careers, relationships, protections, judgments, recognitions, etc.), unable or unwilling to take up a determinate position within it.

In the book's next prefatorial entry, the opening of the second section or "Theatre Journal," we see repeated the desire to repeat the self as the story of its telling:

> In 1981 when I was teaching at Berkeley, I decided to write a piece entitled *People I've Met in the Theatre*. One evening [my writers' group] asked me about

winning the Obie....|O|ne of them said what a "glorious past" you've
had....So now sitting...in a lovely room facing a redwood tree and a creek,
I started the first sketches about Off-Broadway, choosing what I felt to be
exciting moments of my life....One of the reasons I chose sketches was a
book I read when I was twenty-one, by Daniel Blum, called *Famous People in
the American Theatre*. How I had loved the short, dense paragraphs about the
actors and actresses accompanied by a black-and-white photo. How I had
longed to be in that book. (DT, 99–100)

The doubling of the prefatorial justification of *People Who Led to My
Plays* is cannily further layered by the expressed desire to discover oneself
in the enclave of another's account of oneself, to reside in the "book"
of fame as character and commodity. In a sense, Kennedy here calls
upon the conventional notion of identity as a reciprocal social construction, though here it is an exchange of representations that produces the
thrill of identity. Or perhaps we should rather speak, with Elin Diamond,
of Kennedy's desire for identification,[11] that mode of identity-as-reading
in which the subject is both present and estranged, its presence an effect
of that very otherness, of its (mis)recognition by the other-as-reader.
Kennedy here further delineates her earlier expressed "entangle|ment|
in the desires of other people" by suggesting how the self and its longings
can reach fulfillment only by knowing itself in another place and by
accepting the conflict between consciousness and its formal embodiment
that lies at the core of mimetic desire. Where else can the author wish
to be but "in" the book? But once in the book, however condensed and
spatialized its form (the proclivity for the sketch and the photo expressing
a resistance to invasion by narrative temporality), how can the authorial
subject hope to escape the contingencies imposed by readers with their
own inevitably transformative and unmastered desires?

Deadly Triplets concludes with a stunning answer to this perplexing
contradiction of scriptive containment and transcendence; not surprising,
it is in several senses a reflection and duplication of the strategies
organizing the book's prior prefatorial performances, not so much an
answer, in fact, as a response:

In one of my stories I gave myself an estranged twin sister, an actress
whom I saw on stage (not realizing she was my sister because of her
elaborate disguise). My children and I were also continual characters in my
stories....On some nights I wrote mystery stories...and made myself and
the children characters. One included a description of our real house.

"Chalcot Crescent was beautiful:...It was furnished and belonged to an
English family that was in Nigeria. The faded parlor faced a wild garden
with a brick wall....The children were thrilled because the television series
'The Avengers' was filmed on the Crescent."

Soon there would be rallies in Trafalgar Square against the war in Vietnam. More than once Vanessa Redgrave led them.

The crazed old woman living in the house on Rothwell Street screamed,...."Go back to India where you belong." Despite the enchantment, there was a subplot to England that I couldn't perceive. And although I could never admit it, the hurt over the breakup of my marriage had never healed. I thought: Perhaps I should go home. And I did. (DT, 121, 123–24)

Like the uncanny mists of the old English landscapes or the enclaves of colonial structure, the major thematic, imagistic, narrative scenarios of Deadly Triplets arise once again, enfolding one another in a dizzying play of the "real" and the represented so that writing becomes, as if for one "last" performance, its own ghost, its own simulacrum, its own empty excess. Race, revolution, history; motherhood, marriage, authorship, career; nature, technology, commodification; discrete encounters, mass actions, uncertain relations—every category of self-constitution, every perceptual and representational strategy, and indeed every specific nexus of cultural and personal experience called upon heretofore to organize the book's rehearsal of a proper subject is once again summoned on stage, "twinned" to a funnyhouse profusion of such evocations and projections. Kennedy stages a metanarrative of multiplied depictions and receptions such that the referent of any given instant in this climactic self-explanation is both an "experience" (meticulously dated and located) and a previous description of such "experience" (available not only in Deadly Triplets itself but in other works bearing Kennedy's signature). Jostling for primacy are the effort to tame alterity's threatening potential by various tactics of containment and the concurrent urge to undo the strictures of such domestication by acknowledging a residue of uncertainty. The book ends in yet another reiteration of its inability to fully begin, for despite the marvelously productive intention to turn all desires and all strangeness into the tractable material of drama and story—to effectively confuse the boundaries of work and world and thereby formalize the characterological quality of any identity—despite this imperialist annexation of experience by fabulation, the countervailing intuition of an otherness that remains unconditioned by the author's powers of appropriation saves the book from any complacent and deadly closure. Put differently, in more ideological terms, the self now emerges from the failure of the procedure of identification that gives rise to the "journal" of personal images, anecdotes, and other reflections, becoming instead a (re)commitment to its absence from any absolutely understood locale or relation. "Home" and the unheimlich become not so much fixed and mutually exclusive places of legible definitions and events as differential elements in a continuing entanglement of conflicting desires, plots, structures, affiliations. "Home" names the site of the next adventurous rearticulation of the subject in question; like "self," it names what is never there but always about to be.

Preface: II

The "mystery" persistently presented in *Deadly Triplets* emerges as the quest for an authentic source of the book's own mimetic intention amidst the swirling welter of social, political, historical, psychic, familial, and cultural markers by which Kennedy seeks to "recognize" herself and gain recognition from others. Each scene of origination conjured as explanation of writing's responses to puzzlements of memory and desire can only repeat the subject's irresolution in a vertiginous play of inscriptions and mirroring revisions. In this sense *Deadly Triplets*, like *People Who Led to My Plays*, is composed of a *series* of mutually qualifying "prefaces," a succession of textual masks confusing the order of "author" and "character," reified book and exorbitant world.

Similarly, Kennedy's prefaces, taken together, repeat the desire for a subject that is somehow both reliably essential (repetition bespeaking the desire for the stability in time conferred by ontological continuity) and unpredictably inventive (the impossibility of fixing the self being the one reliably repeated topos). For her readers, such rigorously and openly contradictory "self"-exploration provides an instructive exemplum (this, too, a paradox, given the spectral quality of her own exemplars). We are enjoined to suffer the inadequacy of any narrative of the works' intentions, while standing warned that only silence, mutilation, or death can substitute for this disruptive process of hermeneutic displacement. More concretely, no discussion of Kennedy's work can fail to address her protagonists' arduous quests for anchoring signatures of time and place (be they sexual, familial, racial, or cultural), and no such discussion can fail to entertain risk of privileging a single order of significance in the desire to redress or cure or avenge those enduringly hopeful, if apparently unrealizable, explanatory journeys. For the quest, the hope, and even perhaps the endurance is ours, as well. And so we, too, begin to preface the subject...again.

Notes

1. Among the more insightful and stimulating thematically oriented studies of Kennedy's work are the following: Paul Carter Harrison's effort to locate an Africanist modality throughout Kennedy's drama, in *The Drama of Nommo* (New York: Grove Press, 1972), 216–20; Robert L. Tener's discussion of various mythic topoi in Kennedy's work, in "Theatre of

Identity: Adrienne Kennedy's Portrait of the Black Woman," *Studies in Black Literature* 6 (1975): 1–5; Geneviève Fabre's examination of racial ambivalence and Kennedy's "hallucinatory" dramatic imagery, in *Drumbeats, Masks, and Metaphor*, trans. Melvin Dixon (Cambridge, Mass.: Harvard University Press, 1983), 119–22; Herbert Blau's reading of Kennedy's "politics of the unconscious," in "The American Dream in American Gothic: The Plays of Sam Shepard and Adrienne Kennedy," *Modern Drama* 27 (1984): 520–39; Timothy Murray's analysis of the mediation of the "historical," in "Screening the Camera's Eye: Black and White Confrontations of Technological Representation," *Modern Drama* 28 (1985): 110–24; Rosemary K. Curb's interpretation of Kennedy's exploration of the temporality of identity, in "Re/cognition, Re/presentation, Re/creation in Woman-Conscious Drama: The Seer, the Seen, the Obscene," *Theatre Journal* 37 (1985): 302–16; Margaret B. Wilkerson's comparison of interiority in Hansberry and Kennedy, in "Diverse Angles of Vision: Two Black Women Playwrights," *Theatre Annual* 40 (1985): 91–114, reprinted as chapter 5 of this volume; Elin Diamond's situation of Kennedy's dramas of identity with respect to a feminist critique of mimesis, in "Mimesis, Mimicry, and the 'True Real,'" *Modern Drama* 32 (1989): 58–72; Jeanie Forte's related study of subversive desire in Kennedy's plays, in "Realism, Narrative, and the Feminine Playwright—A Problem of Reception," *Modern Drama* 32 (1989): 115–27; and Diamond's rereading of Kennedy in terms of "history" and "hysteria," in "Toward a Politics of Identification: Brecht, Freud, and Kennedy" (forthcoming).

2. Adrienne Kennedy, *People Who Led to My Plays* (New York: Knopf, 1987), *Adrienne Kennedy in One Act* (Minneapolis: University of Minnesota Press, 1988), and *Deadly Triplets* (Minneapolis: University of Minnesota Press, 1990).

3. See Kennedy's "A Growth of Images," *Drama Review* 76 (1977): 43–48. Elin Diamond, "An Interview with Adrienne Kennedy," *Studies in American Drama* 4 (1989): 143–57; and scattered remarks on compositional method in *People Who Led to My Plays* and *Deadly Triplets*.

4. See Stephen Greenblatt, *Renaissance Self-Fashioning* (Chicago: University of Chicago Press, 1980), especially chap. 6.

5. Lesley Wheeler, in an unpublished paper, "Autobiography and Adrienne Kennedy's *People Who Led to My Plays*," has, for example, suggested a synecdochic relation between the opening's striking image of a shuffling of Old Maid cards and the autobiography's persistent thematic tension between control and disruption.

6. Cf. Leo Bersani's discussion of realist Ideology of character in his *Baudelaire and Freud* (Berkeley: University of California Press, 1977).

7. The classic theatricalized instance of this topos is to be seen at the conclusion of Frederick Douglass's *Narrative* of 1845, but it is present as well in such narratives as those of Harriet Jacobs, William Wells Brown, and Samuel Ringgold Ward.

8. Here, a confession: the most difficult interpretive dilemma faced in reading both *People Who Led to My Plays* and *Deadly Triplets*, I have found, is evaluation of authorial *tone* in the heroine's gushing recollections of awards garnered, compliments gleaned (no matter how trivial or ambiguous), encounters with renowned figures, and other detritus from the journey through the Anglo-American culture of celebrated achievement. Indeed, penetrating reflections on matters of race and politics are often interrupted, even disrupted, by a return to enumeration of the author's adventures in an almost comically Baudrillardian funnyhouse of fetishized, commodified, self-caricaturing realm of "fame" and "success" (e.g., a discussion of the trial of Michael X is framed by comments on, first, what Bianca Jagger wore to the opening of *Hair* and, next, the domestic charms of the John Arden household |*Deadly Triplets*, 120|). The inference that irony is in the air is an effect entirely of narrative juxtaposition and readerly desire rather than any rhetorical performance—an effect that makes the reader uneasy, perhaps even exposed, in her effort to stabilize the text's ethos through assertion of that inference.

9. Near the end of the preface Kennedy records the following scene (a scene echoed in the book's final paragraph |124|): "During my time |in England| no one except a very old crazy woman in Rothwell Street had spoken to me negatively about race. And she in her half-consciousness had referred to me as Indian. Yet race was present in our consciousness. We talked about...Malcolm X, Martin Luther King,...went to the Ambiance and saw plays by Ed Bullins, discussed Michael X. At the same time I was treated grandly as a Guggenheim Fellow" (DT, x). Here, again, we are in a liminal and contestatory arena where "*half*-consciousness" marks an otherness that invades and even seeks to define one's own "consciousness," where authority remains ambiguously distributed across many voices, and where the author's own "race" is pointedly, if comically, located along a boundary between absolute terms ("Indian" suggesting a figural, if nonlogical, mediation of black and white). The alternation between political concern and personal aggrandizement and comfort (discussed in the previous note) only heightens the rhetorical aura of indeterminacy.

10. The possibilities of feminist appropriation of such displaced self-stagings are provocatively explored by Barbara Freedman in "Frame-Up: Feminism, Psychoanalysis, Theatre," *Theatre Journal* 40 (1988): 375–97.

11. Diamond, "Towards a Politics of Identification." Diamond's argument derives from a subtle effort to expose Brechtian theories of distantiated performance and Freudian notions of self-transformation to the pressure of mutual critique, resulting in the startling formula of a "hystericized/historicized" spectator. In the terms we have been exploiting above, we might say that Diamond posits a disruption of the classic subject-stage opposition that has structured Marxist and psychoanalytic accounts of reception alike, if from diametric perspectives.

10

Mimesis in Syncopated Time
Reading Adrienne Kennedy

Elin Diamond

"As long as I can remember I've wanted to be Bette Davis." [Pause.] "I
still want to be Bette Davis." I am quoting Adrienne Kennedy, at least I
think I am. On the printed page, packed snugly between diacritical marks,
these words are granted an undeserved truth. For in her public interview
at my university—an unusual format that Kennedy prefers to lecturing—
we, neither my colleague who asked questions nor I who sat eavesdrop-
ping in the audience, thought to bring a tape recorder, the machine that
would play back to us, in a reassuring space far from the seductions of
presence, Kennedy's precise words, her true utterance.[1] Then, too, diacritical marks, this written essay, erase a deliberate impersonation: at
the conference for which this paper was written I appropriated Kennedy's
pronominal before an audience of mostly white feminists and theatre
scholars.[2] Hence two performances of a line about Bette Davis, one
authorized by a celebrated black dramatist, the other impersonated by
a white critic, both recollected for a new site, a critical anthology designed
to present critical truths about a significant writer. I mark this process
of representation, this "coming to truth," because reception desire is
precisely what is elided in most scholarly work, and because Kennedy's
theatre texts make such issues necessary and important.

If her exact words during the interview elude me, I remember that
Kennedy's audience laughed at the comparison she seemed playfully to
invite. Impeccably attired in a dark suit and ruffled white blouse, Adrienne
Kennedy called to our collective mind the celluloid image of Bette Davis,

and taught us, in that moment, the racism embedded in mimesis. For not only did the subject of enunciation not resemble her model or object, Bette Davis, but also it was unacceptable in the cultural discourses through which we think, speak, and see that she could represent her. Dressed in black and white, Kennedy performed the Ur-text of her play *A Movie Star Has to Star in Black and White* without the comforting frame of the stage. It is important to note that Kennedy did not say, "I want to be *like* Bette Davis." She vaulted the model-copy structure of mimesis and spoke desire: "I want to *be*...." And here we learned that the language of ontology is no match for the ideology of glamour—"being" with its problematic relation to time provokes only the greatest yawn next to movie-star perfection. The power of glamour is to produce an imaginary being that transcends the real conditions of a spectator's life. This is not mimesis, or same*ness*. This is not being in the world or with others: this is being Bette Davis.

Let me distill two ideas from these observations. The first concerns the mimetic assumptions that often govern critical thinking and writing. What I will call "mimetic criticism"—and its "syncopated" subversion—will constitute the main body of this essay. The second idea, addressed at the end, concerns the potentiality of mass mediations. Kennedy doesn't make common cause with Bette Davis; rather she purloins a cinematic image for her fantasy life as a way of telling us about her life. She both identifies and deploys her identification, producing a space of connection—or ironic disconnection—between herself and others.

Mimetic Criticism

> However unfeasible and inefficient it may sound, I see no way to avoid insisting that there has to be a simultaneous other focus: not merely who am I? but who is the other woman? How am I naming her? How does she name me? Is this part of the problematic I discuss?[3]

As much recent discussion of the topic has elaborated, mimesis is not simply a morphological issue, proposing likenesses between made objects and their real or natural counterparts, between celluloid images and real women. Mimesis is also epistemological, a way of knowing and therefore valuing.[4] Whether we consider such "objective" standards as the inherent perfection of Platonic forms or neo-Platonic discourses on nature, or such subjective standards as the romantic artist's soul, mimesis relies on the idea of universal models, assumed truths, rules of inclusion and exclusion by which a text, be it the text of a play or the text of someone's behavior, is judged. Mimetic criticism not only accepts such rules as unquestionable, it assumes a stable subject position and a reliable linguistic field by which truthful judgments can be made.[5] Perhaps feminism's oldest, and still most valuable, project has been to demystify the male gender bias of that stable subject, to borrow deconstruction's strategic subversion of humanist concepts, such as the masculine cogito that traditionally stands in for God the Father.

But feminism is also, unapologetically, a political practice, and is willingly seduced by the referent. Feminist critics will select desirable models—positive images of women some years back; self-reflexiveness, formal rupture, and split subjectivities more recently—and seek appropriate objects for illustration. But isn't there a narcissistic component to this selection? If poststructuralist psychoanalysis has taught us anything, it's that the critic's imaginary is reading as attentively as her consciousness. What I am suggesting is that if mimetic criticism posits a stable relation of resemblance between object and world, object and model, it also, more insidiously, assumes a mimetic relation between subject and object, between I who write and the object I write on—which turns that object into a projection, the image into one of my imagoes. When I, a white critic, approach the plays of Adrienne Kennedy, a black artist, am I not interpellating her texts with my models, making her and them into something ideologically comfortable to deal with?[6] Am I not instead obligated to ask, as Gayatri Spivak does in the epigraph above: who is the other woman? How am I naming her? How is she naming me?

The title of this essay, "Mimesis in Syncopated Time," comes from Gertrude Stein's lecture "Plays," in which she complains of being made "nervous" at the theatre because "the thing seen and the thing felt about the thing seen [were] not going on at the same tempo."[7] The scene as depicted on the stage "is more often than not one might say it is almost always in syncopated time in relation to the emotion of anybody in the audience."[8] No one and nothing could interpellate Gertrude Stein, hail her into imaginary identifications with characters through whose specular wholeness she could find completion. But syncopation made her nervous. The contracture of fictional time that constitutes the stage event produced a conflict with the temporality of her emotions. Her solution, of course, was to spatialize the temporal, to refuse the aggregation and accumulation by which the subject/spectator makes meanings.

Stein's landscape plays would eliminate, she hoped, the anxiety of syncopation. However, I am not in a hurry to do so. Syncopation comes from the Greek *syncoptain*: to strike, chop off, to shorten, but the musical sense is more to the point: placing of an accent or accents on parts of a bar that are not usually accented. According to my music dictionary, if a syncopated rhythm is continued for more than a bar, it has the effect of a displaced meter superimposed on the basic meter. This is in effect

Stein's problem: the theatre fiction accented certain rhythms in disturbing syncopation to her own. One became superimposed on the other: "the thing seen and the thing felt about the thing seen [were] not going on at the same tempo [and this is] what makes the being at the theatre something that makes anybody nervous."[9]

Mimetic criticism eliminates the syncopation between subject and object, because it needs to appropriate the object for the enterprise of critical truth-telling. In the name of truth the critic mystifies her desire in relation to the texts she studies. If I am a mimetic critic, the objects I recognize and privilege not only illustrate selected models, but fundamentally illustrate me—are continuous with my values and perspectives. Mimesis in syncopated time is therefore an impossibility in feminist practice but a theoretical goal: a means of acknowledging the feminist tendency to think mimetically along with the imperative to acknowledge difference, not just between objects produced, but between subjects producing them. As black feminists have explained to white feminists for at least a decade in the United States, a white critic cannot hope for, nor is it desirable for her to assume, a simple continuity between her analyses and the cultural and political subtleties of texts by black women.[10] Rather than bridge the gap of cultural difference, I might stress the syncopatedness between Kennedy's images and my readings. That is, I might try to represent not Kennedy's truths, or the truths of her text, but the otherness constructed for me by her texts. I might try to hear the syncopatedness and construct a criticism from that pleasurable and unstable rhythm.

The plays of Adrienne Kennedy would seem to be ideal objects of study if I were content simply to thematize the syncopation metaphor. Sarah and Clara, the protagonists of *Funnyhouse of a Negro* (1964) and *The Owl Answers* (1965), are afflicted with Gertrude Stein's nervousness. Out of sync in their temporalities of consciousness, they fail to imitate or validate social and cultural norms. Sarah, "the Negro" of *Funnyhouse of a Negro*, is split into, and inhabits, various cultural icons, what Kennedy calls "selves": the Duchess of Hapsburg, Patrice Lumumba, a hunchbacked Jesus, Queen Victoria—who through monologue and incantatory repetition circulate a traumatic story of rape and miscegenation. Obsessed with her "yellow" skin, with her hair falling out, her history an uncanny return of repressed racial and sexual violations, Sarah claims, "I want not to be," and indeed her "I" occupies no ontologically secure space.[11] Rather her selves disperse her amidst swarming ravens, floating skulls, ebony masks, a statue of Queen Victoria, and white friends whose (Victorian) culture "keep me from reflecting too much on the fact that I am a Negro" (*Funnyhouse*, 6). Ultimately, the repetitions of her selves become superimposed on the rhythms of her monologues. Like so many nervous moderns who want not to be, Sarah commits suicide.

Syncopation is particularly thematized in *The Owl Answers*, in which discrete selves are encased in one entity—for example, "She Who is Clara Passmore who is the Virgin Mary, who is the Owl"—a kind of parody of ontology. This play generates another violently skewed family romance, here with a poor black mother impregnated by the Richest White Man in Town. Gradually a story emerges of a bastard daughter, adopted by the Reverend Passmore and renamed Clara, who carries her black mother's color and a passion for her white father's culture, the England of "dear Chaucer, Dickens and dearest Shakespeare."[12] These white literary fathers merge with those of Christian myth, but on a fantasy trip to England they lock her in the Tower of London: having colonized her desire, they deny her white ancestry. Culture and history are disjunctive, desperately out of sync.

But I will not go on with this exercise in mimetic criticism. My model, syncopation, is producing its own readings, as though the plays and not I were speaking. The white cultural hegemony that produces, I think, the orderly rhythm against which the Sarah/Clara characters register their syncopations is the rhythm I need to hear. No doubt any text by a woman of color would ask me to do this, but Kennedy's most insistently. It is almost too tempting to narrativize these surreal plays, too easy to tell the story of their alienated subjectivities, as I have just done, with the ulterior motive of giving readers a point of reference. But if I choose not to fill in the gaps in Kennedy's subjects, if I can see and hear the play as an address from a multiple and complex "I" whose truth, whose difference I can recognize but not fully know, then I will be able to allow difference (otherness) to inform my criticism.

Mimesis in Syncopated Time

Let me return to *Funnyhouse of a Negro*, a play whose dominant trope is the mirror. Amidst Sarah's "selves," there are two white characters, one a landlady with the resonant name of Mrs. Conrad, and the other Raymond, the Jewish boyfriend, also designated the Funnyhouse Man. How as a spectator and critic do I name the experience of watching this play without acknowledging that as a white Jewish woman I am presented with certain identification problems? For if the vestiges of my psychic history propel me toward Sarah's perverse family romance, her obsession and fascination with a mother's raving, such identifications have to circulate through Raymond, as well. Because Raymond, Sarah tells her audience, is "very interested in Negroes" (*Funnyhouse*, 6). Dressed in

Hamletic black, this Funnyman, not Sarah, is the artist, a trafficker in the mimetic arts. The walls of his room, behind the blinds, are all mirrors, endlessly reflecting and splitting Sarah into distorted fragments, while he, like God the Father, remains coherent and consistent. While Sarah and her "selves" lose their hair, Raymond questions, admonishes, judges, and, at the end, *"observing"* the hanged woman, puts closure to her torment, giving, at least in its position in the play, the final and truthful version of her story: "Her father never hung himself in a Harlem hotel when Patrice Lumumba was murdered. I know the man" (*Funnyhouse*, 23).

Do I know Raymond? Perhaps, syncopatedly. In a play about *his* funnyhouse, he might be the one losing his hair. But in a text that investigates the multiple identities of a young black woman, he is for me an uncomfortable object. I can historicize Raymond, situate him in the context of Jewish liberalism of the 1950s and 1960s, which enlisted early in civil rights struggles, without perhaps fully examining the class inequalities that fostered racial divisions. I can recall that among New York beat poets, musicians, and artists, racial/cultural lines, especially between blacks and Jews, were frequently intertwined. I can enjoy these mimetic comparisons, but Raymond causes me to place myself in syncopation with the protagonist's suffering, causes me to acknowledge early identifications with something called "being a Jew" or "being a Caucasian." When I recognize the pull to identify with Raymond, to enter not his gendered space, but his cultural space, do I find myself implicated in the funnyhouse? Do I partially control the mirrors—the images—by which black women construct themselves in this culture? Am I among the repetitive agonized voices that constrict the fictional Sarah, and by extension, Kennedy? With such questions, my contingency as a critic becomes a datum of critical perception: I must place myself within, not above, the cultural conflux that this play dramatizes, and that, through my reading and teaching of it, it continues to shape.

Which brings me briefly to *The Owl Answers* and the white literary fathers—Chaucer, Dickens, and dear Shakespeare—who have colonized the desire of the schoolteacher Clara. Reading this syncopatedly, aware of the hegemonic superimpositions that Clara suffers, do I name myself a first-world professor in an English department at a major U.S. university with privileged access to any object of study? Or do I name myself, ironically, a feminist teacher who supports a curriculum dominated by Eurocentric models of disciplinary specialization, most notably the English department, consecrated by its very title to perpetuating a cultural identity historically invested in imperialist policies, the effects of which are still being felt in the nonwhite world? If Kennedy's Clara, through private symbols, manages to dismantle the transcendental signified ("I call God and the Owl answers" |Owl, 43|), she is also in the Shylockian position of loving Anglo-Saxon culture when it doesn't love her. Or more accurately she constitutes the otherness whose exclusion helps to define that culture's literature. A syncopated reading of The Owl Answers would, then, focus on the canon and on canonical curricula—in which Kennedy's own oeuvre has, until recently, occupied a peripheral position.[13]

From the canon to mass culture, Kennedy carries over the family romance, but in A Movie Star Has to Star in Black and White (1976), the protagonist's otherness and my own are worked through a theatricalizing of the cinematic image. If the other texts, in their longing for a social and subjective coherence, invited a mimetic criticism, a filling in of narrative gaps or an illustrative discussion of modernist fragmentation, Movie Star and Kennedy's canny autobiography People Who Led to My Plays (1987) divert mimetic criticism into postmodern cul-de-sacs. These texts are no longer fragmented but decentered. In the autobiography the black woman's "I" is displaced onto a disparate array of personal and cultural simulacra including language, drawing, and photographs of movie stars and family members. Clark Gable, My Mother, Jesus, Lena Horne, Hitler, My Father, Old Maid Playing Cards, and scores of other signifiers precede a colon mark, generally followed by brief lines of impressionistic description. No distinction is made between things or people, or between races—all are objects "mingling in my life, my thoughts, my imagination."[14] Interestingly, in an entry on the film version of Williams's Streetcar Named Desire, the autobiography's narrator recalls that Marlon Brando "was the first movie star (in the dorm) that both my white and my Negro friends had loved equally, at a time when we seemed to have little in common except our passion for 'engagements' and engagement rings" (People, 78). The way in which mass culture idols have shaped the imaginary of consumers across boundaries of race and class has often been broached.[15] Here Kennedy proposes that Marlon Brando provides an unexpected link between black and white students in the generally racist environment of a midwestern dormitory in the 1950s. But in the aleatory mode of the autobiography, the passage on Brando is less a positive image than a moment of syncopated memory—one rhythm among many.

In the remarkable play A Movie Star Has to Star in Black and White, Kennedy both thematizes and mobilizes syncopation. The title refers both to the technology of filmmaking in the great period of Hollywood narrative cinema and to the racial semiotics Kennedy constructs for the play's white spectator-readers. Kennedy seems at once to demonstrate the power of mass culture narratives not simply to reflect but to produce our lives ("|Clara's| movie stars speak for her").[16] Yet she co-opts the spectacular surface of the cinematic image: the white movie stars, retaining the appearance, rhythms, and gestures of their roles in three major Hollywood films (*Now, Voyager, Viva Zapata! A Place in the Sun*), speak not their movie script lines but rather tell the stories of black Clara's life. As Anna Deveare Smith has written, signification in this play arises at the level of rhythm, not voice.[17] Or, in the terms of this essay, in the contested rhythms of syncopation.

Moreover, Kennedy defies the phonocentrism of realist cinema as well as the titillating alienation we experience during theatrical cross-dressing. "Character" in A *Movie Star* is based not on gender and race, but on Hollywood's glamorized version of gender and race—the text directs that "*'Leading Roles' are played by actors who look exactly like: Bette Davis, Paul Henreid, Jean Peters, Marlon Brando, Montgomery Clift, Shelley Winters.*" Exploiting the ontological present of the stage, Kennedy makes it possible for Clara to be subsumed by Bette Davis and to remain herself. (Clara is *"totally preoccupied,"* the stage directions tell us, writing in her notebook. Evidence of her production—citations from previous Kennedy plays—occur in her "own" lines, while the movie stars are consigned to relating family history.) Colonized by these glamorous images, Kennedy in turn remakes and re-presents them in a contingent context that bears the materiality of her consciousness (her language), if not her color. Clara's movie stars are proximate and continuous with her, but in a mimetic relation that creates, rather than elides, difference.

And what is the otherness inscribed for the white feminist spectator in this text? I might expect the iconic disjunction between movie image and theatrical performance, but the whiteness of the performers also becomes a datum, perhaps *the* datum, of critical perception. It never occurs to a white spectator when she sees Bette Davis in *Now, Voyager*, Jean Peters in *Viva Zapata!*, or Shelley Winters in A *Place in the Sun* that these actresses are white. Only when they speak the history of the visible black woman is that fact foregrounded. Moreover, to identify with whiteness in this play is to identify with an image, to see whiteness as an image and not an origin, and that is a vital alienation. At the same time Kennedy has retrieved a spectator position that feminist film theory had written off years ago. Two of the female roles—Bette Davis in *Now, Voyager* and Jean Peters in *Viva Zapata!*—are classic invitations to masculine visual pleasure and fetishization. Bette Davis's Charlotte leans over the ship railing with Paul Henreid's character after being transformed by a male doctor, the signs of her sexual repression—dowdy dress, thick eyebrows—transformed into a glamorous Hollywood face. The Jean Peters character, sexually glamorized on her wedding night, teaches Zapata to read. Purloined from their contexts—and from the contexts in which I viewed them—speaking the life of an ordinary woman, these "characters" are returned to me as social, not cinematic, constructs. Moreover, building on these hybrid images, I learn that the pregnant Clara projects her ambivalence about pregnancy by drawing on movie scenes in which female sexuality is marred by repression (Bette Davis's shipboard confession in Now, Voyager); displaced onto reading (Jean Peters teaching Marlon Brando's Zapata in Viva Zapata!); or repellently and pathetically represented (by the pregnant Shelley Winters in A Place in the Sun).[18]

Are these readings the result of a naive mimetic criticism? Yes and no. The hermeneutic pleasure of renting videos of old films and reading them into the text hardly requires theoretical sophistication. Yet the syncopatedness of black and white is the impetus for these descriptions, or, to put it another way, the archival work that this play demands brings me face to face with the racist erasure of difference perpetuated by a powerful culture industry: the Hollywood narrative film. Yet Kennedy's text invites another question: does the cinematic image of Bette Davis, which Kennedy invoked in her interview (above), serve as a kind of fulcrum, a point of connection between black writer and white reader? Cultural consumers both, are we not linked by our desire to be Bette Davis? Hers is, after all, an image in black and white—although, of course white is the "color" we see.

Better, I think to look at Kennedy's Bette Davis, not Hollywood's. Here is an image in black and white but a radically unstable one: I have no means of consuming it, fetishizing it, or reproducing it. I cannot identify with it. But I can produce a discourse alongside of it, in syncopation with it. A discourse not in black and white, but in black…white.

Notes

1. The event took place on April 19, 1989 at Rutgers University, where Adrienne Kennedy was Visiting Professor in the English Department. Also featured were readings from Kennedy's plays and from her People Who Led to My Plays by members of the Crossroads Theater Company of New Brunswick, N.J.

This description of Kennedy's interview and its aftermath, as well as parts of the following analyses of Funnyhouse of a Negro, The Owl Answers, and A Movie Star Has to Star in Black and White have been drawn from a longer paper, "Rethinking Identification: Brecht, Freud, Kennedy," which focuses not on mimetic criticism but on the related issue of identification in reception.

2. The Association for Theater in Higher Education (ATHE), August 1989, New York City.

3. Gayatri Chakravorty Spivak, In Other Worlds (New York: Methuen, 1987), 150.

4. In "The Mimetic Bias in Modern Anglo-American Criticism," Herbert Lindenberger is less concerned with different manifestations of Western mimetic theory than with its persuasive function. Citing critics like Eliot, Leavis, Milton, and Lewis, he notes that appeals to "nature," "life," and "human" serve as indisputable honorifics (in Mimesis in Contemporary Theory, ed. Mihai Spariosu [Philadelphia: John Benjamins, 1984], 1–26).

5. See Homi K. Bhabha, "Sign Taken for Wonders: Questions of Ambivalence and Authority under a Tree outside Delhi, May 1817," *Critical Inquiry* 12, no. 1 (Autumn 1985): 144–65.

6. Louis Althusser's term for the process by which ideology constitutes individuals as social subjects: "Ideology hails or interpellates concrete individuals as concrete subjects" (see "Ideology and Ideological State Apparatuses," in Althusser, *Lenin and Philosophy and Other Essays* |London: New Left Books, 1971|, 162ff.

7. *Gertrude Stein: Writings and Lectures, 1909-1945*, ed. Patricia Meyerowitz (Baltimore, Md.: Penguin, 1967), 60.

8. Ibid., 59.

9. Ibid., 60.

10. See, for example, Barbara Smith's early essay, "Toward a Black Feminist Criticism," in *All the Women Are White, All the Men Are Black, but Some of Us Are Brave*, ed. Gloria T. Hull, Patricia Bell Scott, and Barbara Smith (New York: Feminist Press, 1982), 157–75: "When white women look at Black women's works they are, of course, ill-equipped to deal with the subtleties of racial politics" (159). See also Audre Lorde, "The Master's Tools Will Never Dismantle the Master's House," in *This Bridge Called My Back: Writings by Radical Women of Color*, ed. Cherríe Moraga and Gloria Anzaldúa (Watertown, Mass.: Persephone Press, 1981), 98–101; and bell hooks's more recent reminder: "Black women with no institutional 'other' that we may discriminate against...often have a lived experience that...may shape our consciousness in such a way that our world view differs from those who have a degree of privilege (however relative within the existing system)" (*From Margin to Center* |Boston: South End Press, 1984|, 15). Finally, see the testimony of Ellen Pence, a white feminist and activist: "As white women, we continually expect women of color to bring us to an understanding of our racism" (*Some of Us Are Brave*, 46).

11. *Funnyhouse of a Negro*, in *Adrienne Kennedy in One Act* (Minneapolis: University of Minnesota Press, 1988), 5. All further references are to this edition and are cited in the text.

12. *The Owl Answers*, in *Adrienne Kennedy in One Act*, 31. All further references are to this edition and are cited in the text.

13. *The Norton Anthology of American Literature* (1989) now includes Adrienne Kennedy's *A Movie Star Has to Star in Black and White*.

14. Kennedy, *People Who Led to My Plays* (New York: Knopf, 1987), 110. All further references are to this edition.

15. See Joan Rockwell, *Fact From Fiction* (London: Routledge and Kegan Paul, 1974); and (for related morsels) Richard Dyer, *Stars* (London: British Film Institute, 1982). See also the interview with Raymond Williams by Stephen Heath and Gillian Skirrow in *Studies in Entertainment*, ed. Tania Modleski (Bloomington: Indiana University Press, 1986), 3–17, especially Heath's comment: "In one sense what you're saying is that we should resist mass culture, all along the line: the assumptions built into it, the terms of its production... though recognizing that mass culture now carries elements of a popular culture, *that it also produces representations that do make connections, that can be read in other ways*" (my italics, 14).

16. Kennedy, *A Movie Star Has to Star in Black and White*, in *Adrienne Kennedy in One Act*, 87. All further references are to this edition.

17. Anna Deveare Smith, "Towards a More Expressive Actor" (paper delivered at the ATHE in San Diego, California, 1988).

18. Kennedy's modifications are revealing. The Jean Peters character is never bloodied in *Viva Zapata!*, nor do she and Marlon Brando change black (blood-encrusted?) sheets. Rather the bleeding (which is Clara's) comments on the problematic female agency within patriarchal constructions of the maternal. The cultural agency achieved by Zapata's bride

in the "teach-me-to-read" is later erased in the film's diegesis by her subsequent sterility—bleeding, not reading, is what she ought to be good at, especially on her wedding night. The drowning of Shelley Winters in A *Place in the Sun* signals the full immersion of the young male protagonist George in a regressive fantasy of plenitude; this is of course the moment when Clara's family learns that Wally will be paralyzed, when as it were the family closes in on Clara, forcing her movie stars out of the frame.

11

(Hetero)Sexual Terrors in Adrienne Kennedy's Early Plays

Rosemary Curb

Adrienne Kennedy creates decentered subjects who are never fully present at any moment as individuals. Rather her characters exist as conscious
sites of invasion and colonization, battlegrounds for wars of race, class,
and gender in contemporary U.S. culture. In her early plays, which focus
on fragmented female characters, Kennedy deconstructs ordinary narrative process. The lack of linear narrative and of integrated characters
disrupts the spectator's scopophilic expectations and denies the spectator's entry into the text.

In the disturbing no-exit-but-death-or-madness narratives of four
1960s plays (*Funnyhouse of a Negro, The Owl Answers, A Rat's Mass*, and *A
Lesson in Dead Language*), Kennedy's female characters fear physical invasion by (hetero)sexual intercourse. I embed the prefix *hetero* within the
word *sexual* as signifier of the mainstream conflation of sexuality into
heterosexuality. Through heterosexual activity Kennedy's characters make
family and cultural connections with past and future generations. Initiation into heterosexuality not only signifies an individual physical and
social rite of passage but also an entry into history. Kennedy's characters
are forced to enter what is presented as real history but what is ultimately
illusory and disempowering. This is so because North American Eurocentric racist heteropatriarchy attempts to deny, distort, and thwart the
struggles of African-American women to understand and celebrate their
own history. If they connected with their heritage, they would be affirmed
as part of a people. In order to maintain the status quo, the dominant

system of power denies their moral agency.

In order to illuminate Kennedy's characters' paralysis or lack of moral agency, I am also employing Sarah Hoagland's concept, *heterosexualism*: "a way of living...that normalizes the dominance of one person in a relationship and the subordination of another" and that thereby undermines female agency.[1] Hoagland further demonstrates how the system of heterosexualism makes colonization seem natural and normal. Colonizers dominate supposedly defenseless peoples in the guise of protection. In fact, adapting the ideas of Walter Rodney, Hoagland argues that colonizers are "de-skilling" native peoples by imposing the civilization of the colonizer in much the same way that men force "protection" on women and then maintain their dominant position through violence.[2] Through the device of metonymy, the bodies of black women in Kennedy's plays become sites for the reenactment of the European imperialist colonization of Africa. Hoagland's theory explains the common metonymy in Eurocentric art and literature whereby virgin or "undeveloped" land is represented symbolically as a female body.

My essay analyzes three interrelated consequences of (hetero)sexual terrors: (1) obsessive fear of rape, (2) guilt stemming from culturally learned dualisms, and (3) loss of history, ancestry, identity. Kennedy's foregrounding of women's terrors disrupts dominant ideologies of gender, race, and class rooted in heterosexualism.

Fear of Rape

Although present-day psychologists may label obsessive fear of rape pathological, black women in the United States have the dubious heritage and collective memory of institutionalized rape by white masters during slavery. As bell hooks asserts:

> Racist exploitation of black women as workers either in the fields or domestic household was not as de-humanizing or demoralizing as the sexual exploitation....The female slave lived in constant awareness of her sexual vulnerability and in perpetual fear that any male, white or black, might single her out to assault and victimize.[3]

Rape of black women did not stop with slavery. Paula Giddings notes that during the whole suffragist movement, African-American women primarily sought the vote as a means of ending their sexual exploitation.[4] Jacquelyn Dowd Hall asks whether attention given to lynching of black men during Reconstruction may have obscured the sufferings of black women during the same period:

> Lynching served primarily to dramatize hierarchies among men. In contrast, the violence directed at black women illustrates the double jeopardy of

race and sex. The records of the Freedmen's Bureau and the oral histories collected by the Federal Writers' Project testify to the sexual atrocities endured by black women as whites sought to reassert their command over the newly freed slaves. Black women were sometimes executed by lynch mobs, but more routinely they served as targets of sexual assault.[5]

Susan Brownmiller describes rape, especially during war or between different races, as a crime of one man against another, using the bodies of the women raped as battleground and proof of the conquered men's impotence to defend their women.[6]

One of Kennedy's recurring motifs is fear of rape leading to death or a state worse than death, such as bestial metamorphosis. Both Sarah the Negro and She who is Clara Passmore who is the Virgin Mary who is the Bastard who is the Owl were conceived by rape and, as a consequence, hold themselves to blame for their mothers' suffering.

According to repeated narrations, the rape drove Sarah's mother mad, and she was sent to an asylum. In the opening mise-en-scène the Mother appears as archetypal madwoman in a white nightgown mumbling to herself and, as a grotesque suggestion of dismembered and decaying bodies, "carrying before her a bald head."[7] Kennedy's suggestion of necrophilia here not only conjures up images of gothic horror but is also reminiscent of Georges Bataille's theory of death as erotic union.[8] "A violent death disrupts the creature's discontinuity," says Bataille.[9] Through death one can satisfy the yearning to escape from the discontinuity of individuality into the continuity of life unindividuated and lost by coming into consciousness as a separate being.[10]

In a later appearance Sarah's mother speaks her only line, an ironic and internalized racist echo of the "Black sheep, black sheep" English nursery rhyme: "Black man, black man, I never should have let a black man put his hands on me. The wild black beast raped me and now my skull is shining" (Funnyhouse, 4). Note the cultural overdeterminism and redundancy of the term "black beast" in this context, where to be black carries the cultural weight of bestiality.

In her second monologue Sarah the Negro supplies the additional information that in Africa her father "started to drink and came home drunk one night and raped my mother. The child from the union is me" (Funnyhouse, 14). She narrates her childhood fear that the father would rape her as he did her mother because he sometimes came home "struggling to embrace me. But I fled and hid under my mother's bed while she screamed of remorse" (Funnyhouse, 15). Creating the darker father as rapist of the lighter-skinned mother and potential rapist of the daughter disturbs spectators by embedding a social reality within a racist cultural myth. Men do rape women, including their wives and daughters. However, it is a distortion fabricated by phobic white racists to imagine that the darker the man the more likely he is to rape and the lighter the woman the more likely she is to be the victim.

Both during and after slavery, "the rapist became not just a black man but a ravenous brute."[11] Whipping white racist terrors into a frenzy likely to provoke random violence against black men, the president of the University of North Carolina preached in 1901, "The black brute is lurking in the dark, a monstrous beast, crazed with lust. His ferocity is almost demonical."[12] Kennedy parodies this obsession that led to the lynching craze in the South by having the "the wild black beast" from the jungle threaten to invade the enclave of Victorian sexual prudery and phobia. As Michel Foucault demonstrates, sexual repression is hardly a modern invention but rather the fundamental link involved in controlling people's power and knowledge since the Western classical age.[13] The Duchess of Hapsburg throws up her hands in mock horror to Queen Victoria: "How dare he enter the castle, he who is the darkest of them all, the darkest one?" (Funnyhouse, 3). Note the racist and perhaps Dantean metaphor that equates dark with bestial. Sarah's other selves echo the rape fear by embodying in Sarah's father the white southern racist myth of the bestial black rapist lusting after white women. In fact, most rapes in the United States are intraracial. During slavery interracial rape was far more likely to be white against black.

The Bastard's Black Mother fanatically tries to keep her daughter virginal. "I cry when I see Marys, cry for their deaths," she tells her daughter over and over. The corrupted state of owldom associated with black female carnality leads inevitably to death. The description by She of sexual initiation recalls Leda's rape by Zeus in the form of a swan: "He came to me in the outhouse, he came to me under the porch, in the garden, in the fig tree. He told me you are an owl, ow, oww, I am your beginning, ow" (Owl, 35). She cannot escape capture and violation. Her rape, suggestively forced and painful ("Ow, oww"), initiates her into the dark, carnal, nonhuman world of owldom.

The more realistic sequence of the Negro Man's attempted rape in the final scene may seem less horrifying to spectators than the narrative of archetypal remembered rape because the subway scene seems almost salvific in its naturalism. At first, the Negro Man tries to seduce She who is Clara Passmore on the New York subway, but finally he forces her down in a Harlem hotel room on a bed that becomes the high altar of St. Paul's Chapel and her funeral pyre. Bataille compares the orgiastic ecstasy of animal sacrifice in religious ritual with rape:

> The act of violence which deprives the creature of its limited particularity and bestows on it the limitless, infinite nature of sacred things is with its

profound logic an intentional one. It is intentional like the act of the man who lays bare, desires and wants to penetrate his victim. The lover strips the beloved of her identity no less than the blood-stained priest his human or animal victim. The woman in the hands of her assailant is despoiled of her being.[14]

Although the language of the translation ("lover" and "beloved") denies the reality of the force and violation, Bataille describes precisely the final mise-en-scène of *The Owl Answers* in which She becomes an owl.

In both *The Rat's Mass* and *A Lesson in Dead Language* the large menacing figures are female. The Medusa-like Italian girl Rosemary with worms in her hair seduces Blake, Brother Rat, to act out her will that he rape his sister Kay, Sister Rat, on the playground slide. Atop the slide Rosemary occupies the masculine and even pornographic position of ownership of the gaze and the act. E. Ann Kaplan perceives the one initiating the scopophilic desire to be always in the masculine position.[15] Even though Rosemary is female, she acts out the dominant or colonizing side of Hoagland's system of heterosexualism.

Speaking to his absent sister (in a hospital having their baby or in an asylum for the insane), Blake confesses, "After you lay down on the slide so innocently Rosemary said if I loved her I would do what she said" (*Rat's Mass*, 59). Narrating the incident later in the play after Kay has returned from the hospital, he tries to shift the guilt: "I told myself afterward it was one of the boys playing horseshoes who had done those horrible things on the slide with my sister" (*Rat's Mass*, 63). As a result of her rape, Kay has a mental breakdown and has to be taken to a hospital in an ambulance. Nevertheless, she blames neither her brother nor Rosemary, but as discussed below, incorporates the guilt into her body. "Every sister bleeds and every brother has made her bleed" (*Rat's Mass*, 58), she says, as if rape were a natural female rite of passage.

In *A Lesson in Dead Language*, the menacing figure of the larger-than-life White Dog threatens the pupils with punishment. Their bright red blood-soaked white dresses may suggest sexual violation but more likely the onset of first menses. Nevertheless, the appearance of blood in the play signifies guilt associated with violence.

Dualism and Guilt

Under the system of heterosexualism, Kennedy's characters exhibit guilt for manifesting a down side of dualisms. Racist sexist culture always privileges white over black, male over female, European over African, human over animal. Black and white women have also become culturally and symbolically separated, thanks to the classist "cult of true womanhood."[16] According to Paula Giddings, white women were thus reduced to "an image of frailty and mindless femininity."[17] Barbara Omolade notes that "the white man's division based on race meant that he alone could claim to be sexually free...[and] the goodness, purity, innocence, and frailty" of white women was contrasted with "the sinful, evil strength, and carnal knowledge" of black women.[18] According to bell hooks, black women thus became the repository of the gynophobia of Western culture:

> As white colonizers adopted a self-righteous sexual morality for themselves, they even more eagerly labeled black people sexual heathens. Since woman was designated the originator of sexual sin, black women were naturally seen as the embodiment of female evil and sexual lust. They were labeled jezebels and sexual temptresses and accused of leading white men away from purity into sin.[19]

This male projection of guilt not only blames the victim for her own violation but positions her as an original-sinning Eve.

Hortense Spillers perceives the dualistic split going beyond male/female, white/black, good/evil, spirit/flesh, to human/nonhuman:

> Slavery did not transform the black female into an embodiment of carnality at all, as the myth of the black woman would tend to convince us, nor, alone, the primary receptacle of a highly-rewarding generative act. She became instead the principal point of passage between the human and the non-human world. Her issue became the focus of a cunning difference—visually, psychologically, ontologically—as the route by which the dominant male decided the distinction between humanity and "other." At this level of radical discontinuity in the great chain of being, black is vestibular to culture. In other words, the black person mirrored for the society around her and him what a human being was *not*.[20]

Thus racism urged black women to forgive the white men who sexually exploited them and to internalize dominant gynophobic values. Darlene Hine and Kate Wittenstein demonstrate that "the white master's consciously constructed view of black female sexuality...was designed...to justify his own sexual passion toward her [and to blame her] for the sexual exploitation which she experienced."[21] Condemned by the hypocrisy of this double dualism, black women are invited to internalize the white European and Victorian value system that projects carnality on them.

Kennedy's characters escape either into a nonhuman world or into nonbeing itself. Sarah, for example, incorporates opposing dyads in her own psyche and condemns herself to death. She blames herself not only for her father's rape of her mother and her mother's madness, but also for her rejection of her father and his consequent death either directly at her hands by bludgeoning him to death with his own ebony mask (a wish-fulfilling fantasy of vengeance for her mother's sufferings by having his own blackness kill him) or indirectly by prompting him to hang himself. At her first entrance she appears with a hangman's rope around her neck, the image of the lynch victim condemned for being black. Throughout the play Sarah repudiates her blackness as the evil inherited from her father. In the end her blackness and whiteness destroy each other.

Sarah takes on guilt for both sides of the duality. As her father's daughter, her very existence proves her collaboration in her mother's contamination. In her first monologue as the Negro and again as her Lumumba self, she expresses hatred of her blackness: "I am the black shadow that haunted my mother's conception" (*Funnyhouse*, 12). Disguising her blackness under the theatricalized fake mask of white makeup in order to pass for the white Duchess, she makes herself a fetish by striking a seductive pose for the benefit of Sarah's boyfriend Raymond, also known as the Funnyhouse Man, who says, "I always knew your father was African" (*Funnyhouse*, 9). The Duchess joins Raymond in laughing at her father (denying her African heritage) for "devoting his foolish life to the erection of a Christian mission in the middle of the jungle" (*Funnyhouse*, 9), emphasizing in the phallic metaphor the sexual violation of Africa by European religion. In an earlier article I state that Sarah's selves "are not the historical persons whose names they carry and whose costumes they wear, but fragments of Sarah's mind so real as to seem separate persons."[22]

Sarah's father, who never actually appears in the play, blames himself for betraying his mother, for sending his wife to an asylum, and for making his only daughter despise him. His guilt leads him to hang himself, to be the subject and object of his own lynching. By hanging herself, Sarah incorporates her father's guilt. Sarah accuses the father not only of sullying European whiteness with African blackness (raping his almost white wife and siring a mulatto daughter) but of failing to save Africa from colonialism (rape by Europe). Sarah's repeated narratives portray the father as obsessed with guilt over his failure to "be Christ," as his mother had desired. Sarah narrates her father's recurring phobia of soldiers coming to find him and nailing him to a cross. Sarah's Jesus self states, "I am going to Africa to kill this black man named Patrice Lumumba" (*Funnyhouse*, 19). In her two male selves, Sarah replays her father's white racist (Jesus) Christian destruction of his pagan African (Lumumba) nationalism.

She who is Clara Passmore also feels guilty from birth. "Bastard," coldly shout Shakespeare, Chaucer, and William the Conqueror, as they surround and imprison her in the Tower of London of her imagination. Does she pass for white more in England than at home? What English "legitimacy" does Clara seek? In Clara's matrilineage are women up-rooted from African culture and in her patrilineage are rapists white men? Her violent patrilineage challenges and condemns her victimized matrilineage.

She displaces her guilt for being the timid Savannah schoolteacher, Clara Passmore, her mother's Bastard, and the sullied Virgin Mary, on to her Owl self—that is, her black, African, Negro side and her evil, sensual, bestial female side. Clara Passmore, riding the New York subway at night to pick up Negro men to take to a Harlem hotel room, is an unusual Kennedy creation: a potentially desiring agent. For this she condemns herself. According to Marina Valverde, in the popular "domino theory" of the passions, the merest sensual thought can lead the innocent down the slippery slope to perdition.[23] She has slid down into sensuality because she has lost her connection with the good, white, European, and male-approved side of her dualistic nature. She says, "I call God and the Owl answers" (Owl, 43). When the Owl personality assumes dominance, her metamorphosis is complete.

In A Rat's Mass, Brother and Sister Rat have part human, part rat bodies. Blake, costumed with rat head and tail, thinks and acts like a rat. Kay, on the other hand, becomes the passive receptacle of ratness with her impregnated rat belly. Representing the dualistic halves of incomplete genders, thinking and acting masculinity meets feeling and receptive femininity. Driven by guilt, Brother and Sister Rat cry, "We want to hang ourselves" (Rat's Mass, 57). Blake's incest with his sister sharply divides the life of the rat children into the innocent prelapsarian golden age before their fall into the original sin of knowing themselves in the mirror of the other. In their unredeemable sinful present state they are pursued to the death by avenging gray cats, who are also Nazis. Sister Rat recalls their past bliss: "Remember...we lived in a Holy Chapel with parents and Jesus, Joseph, Mary, our Wise Men and our Shepherd. People said we were the holiest children" (Rat's Mass, 56–57). Together they recall, "When we were children we lived in our house, our mother blessed us greatly and God blessed us" (Rat's Mass, 58). But all the bliss has vanished since their fall from grace. "Now they listen from the rat beams" (Rat's Mass, 58).

As in the Adam and Eve story, willing sinful knowledge accomplishes a spiritual and psychic metamorphosis. Sin opens their eyes to their true bestial state. It opens their ears as well, since they listen to gnawing above their heads and say, "It is our mother." Before carnal knowledge they had not recognized that they and their parents were rats. Afterward they know ancestral guilt and horror. "Our father gives out the Communion wine and it turns to blood, a red aisle of blood" (Rat's Mass, 58). In my article "Lesson I Bleed" I analyze various associations of Kennedy's blood imagery: slippery playground slide, red church carpet, communion wine.[24] The grotesque metamorphosis or transubstantiation makes rat blood an emblem of guilt. Brother Rat says, "Everywhere I go I step in your blood" (Rat's Mass, 64).

Since Rosemary has been the instigator of their fall, Blake begs her in garbled Christian catechism jargon: "Atone us. Deliver us unto your descendants....If you do not atone us Kay and I will die" (Rat's Mass, 60). Consistently cruel and sadistic, she taunts him in terms of his own religious fears: "Perhaps you can put a bullet in your head with your father's shotgun, then your holy battle will be done" (Rat's Mass, 61). Not only does Rosemary abandon them after she has had her way, but the Christian statues withdraw grace and protection: "Goodbye Kay and Blake. We are leaving you" (61). When the statues return at the end of the play, they have been nightmarishly transformed into the Nazis that gun down the Rat children. The final obscene spectacle suggests the Devil card of the Tarot, with Rosemary as presiding devil/celebrant. The Rat children are condemned to exhibition in their bondedness to each other and in their bondage to the flesh.

Blood also signifies guilt for the pupils in A Lesson in Dead Language. Circles of blood on the white communion dresses widen as the ritualized Latin class progresses, increasing evidence of guilt. Theatrical emphasis on the white of the dresses foregrounds the racist notion of goodness and innocence being equated with whiteness. The lesson for the day seems to be an unusual chain of causality leading to the pupils' collective guilt as conspirators plotting the overthrow of white European ancestral authority. "Lesson I bleed," announces the White Dog as teacher.

Bleeding exposes the pupils to ridicule and censure as women, collectively blamed for the murder of the White Dog, an emblem of authority. Killing the White Dog is equated with assassinating Julius Caesar and destroying whatever Roman civilization signifies, including its descendant ideology, Christianity. The pupils' lesson recalls that Caesar's wife Calpurnia had a precognitive dream of a pinnacle tumbling down but did not use her knowledge to prevent Caesar's murder. Calpurnia bleeds like all women, including the pupils. By association, they share her responsibility and guilt. Blood on the dresses indicates disloyalty to civilization, to borrow Adrienne Rich's phrase, especially white Western civilization, represented by the phallic pinnacle capable of being toppled. Since no pupil will step forth to confess her individual crime or take on the role of scapegoat, the White Dog announces that all will share punishment:

"We will all bleed, since we do not know the one, we will all be punished" (*Lesson*, 49). The pupils, however, like the Rat children, trapped in history, mourn prelapsarian bliss: "I am a pinnacle tumbled down" (*Lesson*, 52). As in the other plays discussed, the final spectacle exposes the guilt of the pupils, sisters of the original sinning Eve.

Loss of History, Ancestry, Identity

Heterosexualist terror finally leads Kennedy's characters to loss of history, ancestry, identity. They live perpetually on the edge of death and metamorphosis, rape and original sin. Following Bataille's notion of death as escape from the discontinuity of individuality into the continuity of life lost by coming into consciousness as a separate being,[25] Kennedy's characters flee the discontinuous body prison through death or metamorphosis. However, as they may shed culturally ingrained internalized guilt, violence ultimately leads to separation from self and history. Kimberly Benston notes:

> For the Afro-American, then, self-creation and reformation of a fragmented familial past are endlessly interwoven: naming is inevitably genealogical revisionism. All of Afro-American literature may be seen as one vast genealogical poem that attempts to restore continuity to the ruptures or discontinuities imposed by the history of black presence in America. [In] the slave narrative,...we find most explicitly the need to resituate or displace the literal master/father by a literal act of unnaming.[26]

Both because of and as a result of guilt and terror, Kennedy's characters cannot mend their genealogical discontinuities.

The character of Sarah the Negro is a consciousness set on three continents at war among themselves. As both rapist and raped, Sarah's body recapitulates the rape of Africa by white Europeans. In relation to her parents, Sarah is both betrayer and betrayed. Kennedy mocks the hypocrisy of her four historic selves in the penultimate jungle scene by having them appear with nimbuses as "saviors" of Africa, still obsessively narrating the story of the father's rape of the mother.

The mundane descriptions of Sarah the Negro's life as an English major, as a mechanistic poet in imitation of Edith Sitwell, and as an anglophile who fawns on white friends create a mask of the soulless pallid Negro projected by mass media. This is as much a theatrical construction as the more flamboyant historic selves. The metaphor of flying objects in the opening scene and especially in the jungle scene presents the Negro self exploding outward from an empty center. Deliberately resisting self-consciousness, the Negro states, "I find it necessary to maintain a stark fortress against recognition of myself" (*Funnyhouse*,

6). Simply to call herself "the Negro" assumes a mask of anonymity. Eschewing moral agency, she states, "I want to possess no moral value, particularly value as to my being. I want not to be" (*Funnyhouse*, 5). As noted above, the denial of moral agency in Kennedy's characters through the erasure of their history also denies the spectators' entry into the narrative.

She who is called the Bastard and Owl Mary Passmore incarnates a slightly different collection of warring dualities in her search for ancestry. Her (un)names suggest paganism and animalism rising to resist pallid Christianity, the passivity and hetero(non)sexual receptivity of the virgin mother, and the white dominance of effete English aestheticism strangling African identity. Clara Passmore's ambiguous parentage generates not only her confusing sense of self, but also her guilt for simply being. The three guards whom she imagines as representatives of the "lovely English" accuse her of being an imposter because of her race. They reverse the historicity of genealogy: "If you are his ancestor why are you a Negro?" (*Owl*, 28).

She searches for but never locates the desired mother. As product of her white father's rape of her mother who worked as his cook, She is bastard. Whereas from slavery to the present black women who must work in white kitchens in order to survive are prey to the predatory lust of white men, they and others blame them for the assaults they suffered.[27] The character called Bastard's Black Mother obsessively mourns her own and her daughter's loss of virginity: "I cry when I see Marys, cry for their deaths" (*Owl*, 30). As the Reverend's Wife, she carries a vial of what she calls "owl blood," or "the fruits of my maidenhead" (*Owl*, 30). In all three personalities as the Bastard's Black Mother who is the Reverend's Wife who is Anne Boleyn she eludes the search of She for an approving helping mother by continually changing personality.

Benston ruminates that this complex intertextual mirroring typical of Kennedy's characterization is common in African-American literature:

This primary speculation of an alternative configuration of the self comprises several scenarios: the shock of one's reflection in the father's or the mother's face, the glance of self-discovery or dissociation in the mirror, the confrontation with the face of mastery, the encounter with some emblem of communal visage. Such scenes present a simultaneous enactment and theorization of consciousness taking place at key textual moments. Here African-American identity looks on an image of being at once external and internal to itself, an echo or reflection that it must revise in order better to see itself. The specular event captures a pivotal instant in which the black self may experience an epiphany about its relation to the starkly coded black-and-white world of received figures, a vision that, whether substantive or heuristic, can result in a formative narrative or ideology.[28]

Through her fragmented selves Kennedy dramatizes all of the scenarios Benston describes. With her funnyhouse reflections she explodes the expected codes of narrative and ideology.

In Clara's search for identity, Kennedy also parodies patriarchally "sacred" themes of male-identified Eurocentric literature celebrating heterosexual genealogy such as the search for the father (*Oedipus Rex*), son avenging his father's death (the *Oresteia* and *Hamlet*), need for recognition of ancestry (Shakespeare's history plays). Clara's fiancé, Professor Johnson, and relatives in Jacksonville, Georgia, ridicule her search for a white father: "London, who in the hell ever heard of anybody going to London?" (*Owl*, 38). As a rude contrast to her genteel fantasy of "wandering about the gardens" with her father in London, she recalls, "I met my father once when my mother took me to visit him and we had to go in the back door of his house" (*Owl*, 36).

Both mother and daughter find release from their irreconcilable warring selves through death. "I know the way to St. Paul's Chapel," the Mother repeats before stabbing herself with a butcher knife, a kitchen variant of Juliet's dagger. The daughter escapes rape in the manner of many of Ovid's canny maidens in *The Metamorphoses*: she changes into a nonhuman. Note Hortense Spillers's analysis of dualism under slavery quoted above. Owls, however, have more significance than simply as stock gothic haunters of the night. They carry divine mythic associations. According to Barbara G. Walker, owls retain a remnant of women's ancient psychic oracular power to draw out secrets and signify the untamed powers of the banished Lilith who refused to submit to patriarchal authority.[29]

Brother and Sister Rat yearn to return to a lost paradise before their incest, when they had parents, home, and religion to console them. However, loss of innocence turns Christian icons into a firing squad sent by their beloved betrayer Rosemary. Like She who succumbs to the seductive suggestion that she belongs to the owls, Brother and Sister Rat discover their inheritance as animal cannon fodder.

The pupils in *A Lesson in Dead Language* have no individual identities nor any apparent race or ethnicity in their identical white organdy communion dresses as school uniforms. As pupils they inherit Roman history and Latin language along with collective guilt for the murder of Caesar and Christ. They address the grotesque White Dog as Teacher and Mother, suggesting that the dog costume may be the medieval nun's habit in Catholic schools, not an unlikely site for Latin recitations and moralistic accusations of collective guilt.

Conclusion

Kennedy's plays dramatize heterosexualism and its consequent terrors: fear of rape, guilt arising from dualisms based on dominance and submission (white over black, male over female, colonizer over colonized, European over African), and loss of history, ancestry, and identity.

Beyond the overt pessimism of Kennedy's defeated characters and her endlessly deferred narratives, the feminist reader remains fascinated with the political accuracy of Kennedy's art. No doubt her plays fail the liberal feminist's search for role models of women winning. In commenting on black female characters in current novels by black women, Sondra O'Neale deplores the train of self-destructive maniacs, pitiful victims, whores, and tragic mulattoes that present a false picture of isolation, loneliness, and marginality of "black women who have never been wrapped in the heart of black communal love."[30] In fact, Kennedy's exaggerated spectacle of women destroyed by self-hatred and paralyzed by fears of heterosexual abuse foregrounds a core historic oppression of women. Denial of moral agency leads to loss of self and history. Just as African-American women in North American heterosexist society are denied moral agency to be real African-American women, spectators of Kennedy's drama are denied access to a linear narrative with the consoling closure of catharsis.

The plays foreground not only gender but the inextricable matrix that it forms with race and class. Kennedy's plays leap beyond Elizabeth V. Spelman's caution to avoid what she calls "the ampersand problem" or the "additive analyses of identity and of oppression"[31] by always dramatizing the multidimensional matrices of African-American women's oppression. Furthermore, Kennedy fulfills Jill Dolan's goals for materialist feminist theatre: "to disrupt the narrative of gender ideology, to denaturalize gender as representation, and to demystify the workings of the genderized representational apparatus itself."[32] Kennedy's layering of theatrical devices (changing costumes, repeated narratives) deconstructs the false simplicities. The theatricality of grotesquely fake makeup, masks, and costumes exaggerates whiteness, femininity, and royalty in the identical costumes of Queen Victoria and Duchess of Hapsburg. Having a single actor shift back and forth along a spectrum of class and color within a gender, as does the Bastard's Black Mother who is the Reverend's Wife who is Anne Boleyn in *The Owl Answers*, disrupts gender ideology in the context of race and class and demystifies gender representations. Characters such as the absent dead but returning rapist black father and the evasive dead but reviving wealthy white father offer comic commentary on symbolic patriarchal potency. Perhaps the performance text might be more "readable" than the written one because meaning depends as much on mise-en-scène as it does on the verbal text.[33] However, the written text alone conveys Kennedy's matrix of oppressions.

Personal, political, and intellectual vicissitudes alter the ways spectators read a character such as Sarah the Negro. Enthusiasts of the 1960s black revolution could hardly be expected to applaud a suicidal schizophrenic "tragic mulatto" torn between her African roots and European intellectualism. Do spectators of a later generation have more aesthetic distance? Successive waves of liberation movements have splintered into factions and formed coalitions. Kennedy's drama continues to disturb, if not terrify, spectators into a heightened consciousness of the complex weave of American history and culture and the legacy of injustice that every American carries.

Notes

I wish to thank Diedre Crumbley for suggesting additional readings by Africana women, Twila Papay for encouraging my writing and for organizing faculty writing support groups at Rollins College, and Bette S. Tallen for her suggestions of resources and insightful feminist analysis. Writing this essay has been challenging for me as a white woman. I am trying to resist "the habit of false universalism" and "whitewashing" my critical interpretations to fit my white experience (cf. Marilyn Frye, "On Being White: Thinking toward a Feminist Understanding of Race and Race Supremacy," in Frye, *The Politics of Reality: Essays in Feminist Theory* [Trumansburg, N.Y.: Crossing Press, 1983], 117). Although I would not do it today, sixteen years ago I wrote a doctoral thesis on African-American drama in an all-white English department where no courses in African-American literature were taught. Coming out as a lesbian while writing the thesis expanded my "outsider" perceptions. Not that I equate racism and heterosexism, but, as a lesbian, I shared the rage and frustration I read in 1960s black revolutionary writers at the arrogance and ignorance of the dominant white male heterosexist system. Studying African-American literature has expanded my consciousness of systems of oppression and helped me confront my racism.

1. Sarah Hoagland, *Lesbian Ethics: Toward New Values* (Palo Alto, Calif.: Institute of Lesbian Studies, 1988), 29.

2. Ibid., 32–34.

3. bell hooks, *Ain't I a Woman: Black Women and Feminism* (Boston: South End Press, 1981), 24.

4. Paula Giddings, *When and Where I Enter: The Impact of Black Women on Race and Sex in America* (New York: Bantam, 1984), 121.

5. Jacquelyn Dowd Hall, "'The Mind That Burns in Each Body': Women, Rape, and Racial Violence," in *Powers of Desire: Politics of Sexuality*, ed. Ann Snitow, Christine Stansell, and Sharon Thompson (New York: Monthly Review Press, 1983), 332.

6. Susan Brownmiller, *Against Our Will: Men, Women and Rape* (New York; Bantam, 1975), 31.

7. *Funnyhouse of a Negro*, in *Adrienne Kennedy in One Act* (Minneapolis: University of Minnesota Press, 1988), 2. All further references to Kennedy's plays are from this edition and are cited in the text.

8. Georges Bataille, *Erotism: Death and Sensuality*, trans. Mary Dalwood (San Francisco: City Lights, 1986), 24.

9. Ibid., 22.

10. Ibid., 14.

11. Hall, "'The Mind That Burns,'" 335.

12. Ibid., 347.

13. Michel Foucault, *The History of Sexuality*, vol. 1, *An Introduction*, trans. Robert Hurley (New York: Random House, 1978), 5.

14. Bataille, *Erotism*, 90.

15. E. Ann Kaplan, *Women and Film: Both Sides of the Camera* (New York: Methuen, 1983), 29–30.

16. Barbara Welter, "The Cult of True Womanhood: 1820–1860," *American Quarterly* 18, no. 2 (1966): 151–74.

17. Giddings, *Where I Enter*, 54.

18. Barbara Omolade, "Hearts of Darkness," in *Powers of Desire*, ed. Snitow, Stansell, and Thompson, 352.

19. hooks, *Ain't I a Woman*, 33.

20. Hortense Spillers, "Interstices: A Small Drama of Words," in *Pleasure and Danger: Exploring Female Sexuality*, ed. Carol Vance (Boston: Routledge and Kegan Paul, 1984), 76.

21. Darlene Hine and Kate Wittenstein, "Female Slave Resistance: The Economics of Sex," in *The Black Woman Cross-Culturally*, ed. Filomena Chioma Stead (Rochester, Vt.: Schenkman Books, 1981), 290.

22. Rosemary Curb, "Fragmented Selves in Adrienne Kennedy's *Funnyhouse of a Negro* and *The Owl Answers*," *Theatre Journal* 32, no. 2 (1980): 182.

23. Mariana Valverde, *Sex, Power and Pleasure* (Toronto: Women's Press, 1985), 150–55.

24. Rosemary Curb, "Lesson I Bleed," in *Women in American Theatre*, ed. Helen Chinoy and Linda Jenkins (New York: Crown, 1981), 53.

25. Bataille, *Erotism*, 14–15.

26. Kimberly Benston, "I Yam What I Yam: The Topos of Un(naming) in Afro-American Literature," in *Black Literature and Literary Theory*, ed. Henry Louis Gates, Jr. (New York: Methuen, 1984), 152.

27. Hooks, *Ain't I a Woman*, 34.

28. Benston, "I Yam," 99–100.

29. Barbara Walker, *The Woman's Encyclopedia of Myths and Secrets* (San Francisco: Harper and Row, 1983), 754–55.

30. Sondra O'Neale, "Inhibiting Midwives, Usurping Creators: The Struggling Emergence of Black Women in American Fiction," in *Feminist Studies/Critical Studies*, ed. Teresa de Lauretis (Bloomington: Indiana University Press, 1986), 141–42.

31. Elizabeth Spelman, *Inessential Woman: Problems of Exclusion in Feminist Thought* (Boston: Beacon Press, 1988), 115.

32. Jill Dolan, *The Feminist Spectator as Critic* (Ann Arbor, Mich.: UMI Research Press, 1988), 101.

33. Jeanie Forte, "Realism, Narrative, and the Feminist Playwright—A Problem of Reception," *Modern Drama* 32, no. 1 (1989): 125.

12

Kennedy's Body Politic: The Mulatta, Menses, and the Medusa

Jeanie Forte

Rather than viewing Kennedy's protagonists as tragic, lost figures who cannot overcome the condition of their color, I am interested in how these figures demonstrate points of resistance against racist assimilation, how they operate both to frame and deconstruct history and perceptions of race. In this effort, which is more attempt than execution, the hope is to initiate an undoing of racist and/or limited interpretations of Kennedy's work.

In a recent essay, Sondra O'Neale charges that most fiction by black American women has presented a very narrow and mostly negative portrait of black women, showing their readers primarily alienated, warped, or maladjusted creatures who frequently cannot relate to their own black community. As O'Neale points out, such images serve to support racism, affirming that it must indeed be impossible to be black in white culture, being forever misfit, permanently handicapped. Also, she notes how conveniently the dominant culture valorizes these texts, whose images thus maintain a stasis of power structures. O'Neale challenges black American fiction—"Where are the Angela Davises, the Ida B. Wellses, and Daisy Bateses of black feminist literature? Where are the portraits of those women who fostered their own actions to liberate themselves, other black women, and black men, as well?"[1] O'Neale accurately delineates the black woman as she has been portrayed in American fiction by white and black men, most notably as the emasculating mammy, the revered grandmother/matriarch, or the "tragic mulatto." But what she

157

finds even more surprising and discouraging is that in current black women's fiction, most black female characters are presented as

1) suffering rejection from black males who are smothered by the male's longing for idealized white beauty, and thus force the women themselves into a hopeless longing to be white; 2) maladjusted tragic mulattoes, who cannot find identity or acceptance in either the black or the white worlds; or 3) "normal"-looking black women, who are triumphant heroines because they have found avenues of escape from their supposed lack of desirability, and consequently from society's rejection.[2]

Making a bold statement about the inauthenticity of these characters, O'Neale says that "black women do not go around all the time thinking about white women, wanting to be like them, or look like them or think like them. Black women just want the freedom, and the economic where-withal, to be themselves."[3]

On the surface, Kennedy's plays seem to be guilty of every charge in O'Neale's essay, unable to provide anything other than tragic or unten-able images for black women, focusing as they often do on women who seem to want nothing more than to erase their blackness, to somehow become white, claim a white heritage, run from raping or impotent black men and suicidal black mothers. Far from meeting O'Neale's challenge, Kennedy's heroines seem hopelessly impaired, regressive in their desire to be legitimized in the white world, and in fact, would, at face value, appear to reinforce white culture's negative images of blacks and black women. That is, each fulfills the dominant image of a marginalized, incomplete, compromised personality, one who suffers utterly from vic-timization and low self-esteem, totally incapacitated by her blackness. Yet, Kennedy's plays are too disturbing, too passionately stubborn in their refusal to submit to any single analysis, too contradictory and puzzling for this to be the whole story, the last word.

What is it that redeems Kennedy's plays from these charges? Most immediately, her "heroines" (and I use this term quite loosely, for want of a better shorthand when speaking of the extremely complex and irreducible figures that move across Kennedy's stage) are not merely tragic characters; rather, they frame/demarcate the problematics of a specific historical juncture, operating as tropes of resistance within that historical context. In addition, Kennedy's textual strategies serve to name structures of oppression not only in terms of dominant over subjugated but also within the subjugated community itself, and the problems pre-sented specifically for the black woman's struggle for identity.

These heroines do not lend themselves to conventional analysis, such as "character analysis." The surreal quality of the plays invites a formalist approach, but this also proves impossible; traces of common themes and coherent meanings run through the plays like Hansel's bread crumbs—you can follow them only so far, then they disappear, or transmute, and suddenly the ground has shifted. In a postmodern age, Kennedy's texts seem quintessential: fragmented, decentered, nonlinear, marked by marginality and alterity, begging for comprehension and simultaneously defying it, haunting a search for meaning and identity in a world where all such categories have been rendered mobile, elusive. Rather than providing a realistic scenario, the work moves via images and associations, registering as an experience of consciousness effected by representations in literature, pop culture and film, as well as by the movement of history.

Projecting O'Neale's observations onto Kennedy's heroines would not be not totally inaccurate, but would not provide the perspective for the whole picture. Negro-Sarah of *Funnyhouse*, She Who Is in *The Owl Answers*, Clara in *A Movie Star*, and to some extent, the brother and sister protagonists of *A Rat's Mass* invite the reader to "subject" them—that is, to attempt to construct and read their subjectivity, only to prove, ultimately, that it is an unfinishable task. Indeed, this appears to be their function. As an example, She who is Clara Passmore who is the Virgin Mary who is the Bastard who is the Owl encompasses and suggests multiple personae within a single figure, defying the construction of a "personality" that might be read psychoanalytically. Their indecipherability as whole characters, combined with their "content" (again, an inadequate term) as figures, moves the reader/viewer to a consideration of historical parameters, in a fashion as unlike Brecht as it is unlike realism.

A major trope in this operation pivots around body imagery, particularly in terms of skin color. The "pallid" color of Kennedy's undeniably mulatta heroines, sometimes called "yellow" or "high yellow" or "yellowish alabaster," specifies the ambivalent history of the neither/nor. During the days of slavery, the mulatto (male) was often considered desirable chattel because of his supposed combination of strength and intelligence, the infusion of white "blood" supposedly serving to create a superior laborer. The derivation of the term, most likely from the Spanish for mule,[4] even designates a creature bred for one purpose, to do hard work, and also implies sterility. This parameter of the term, although patently false when applied to humans, required active maintenance in both attitude and law; any transgression meant harsh penalty, usually death. In stunning contrast, the mulatta (female) was frequently praised for her beauty (by white standards), but also embodied the wild, exotic sexuality attributed to African women, posing a threat to white home life by her mere presence.[5] To further clarify the basis for this contrast, note that, insofar as gender-making proceeds from modes of dominance, gender can be observed "as a special feature of a racialistic ideology."[6] In a culture dependent upon slavery and its attendant racism, women are cast(e) into a "drama of exchange value," based on their particular usefulness to the dominant male: to illustrate, Hortense Spillers quotes one of Faulkner's characters, who itemizes the "three dimensions of female being—'the virgins whom gentlemen someday married, the courtesans to whom they went while on sabbaticals to the cities, the slave girls and women upon whom the first caste rested and to whom in certain cases it doubtless owed the very fact of its virginity.'"[7] In racist ideology, only the first group is granted the role of mothering, designated for continuing the patrilineal line, but is paradoxically robbed of its sexual pleasure, in service of "a transcendent and opaque Womanhood." The third caste, assigned the plenitude of female sexuality, is equally robbed of any expression of its own pleasure, in unremitting, always accessible service to the dominant male. As Spillers notes, however, "the ways and means of domination are not adopted with culture/historical subjects-become-objects in mind, nor is 'gender' here any more than, or other than, an apt articulation of a divided male heteroticism."[8] The mulatta occupies some uncharted middle ground in this division, "allowing the male to have his cake and eat it too," joining the "woman" with the "female", the vaginal/uterine and the prohibitive pleasure.[9] The mulatta thus registers as the visible evidence of the privilege of the phallus, "[demarcating] those notions of femaleness that would re-enforce the latter as an object of gazing."[10] But she is only of value in a sexual economy that simultaneously pursues her and renders her invisible, nameless. She must be available as the site of sexual plenitude for the dominant male, but must disappear as the evidence of his transgression. She is there to confirm his virility and to support racist classism against the subjugated community (see below), but does not exist within the whole of culture, which indeed would deny her existence. As Spillers notes, the mulatta "has no personhood, but locates in the flesh a site of cultural and political maneuver."[11] Her body becomes the precise site of unassimilable difference; it has no resting place, no definition other than as neither/nor.

It is this condition of "mixed blood" that cannot be resolved which frustrates Kennedy's heroines in their desire for a place, or perhaps a "race," of their own. As Negro-Sarah says, "I long to become even a more pallid Negro than I am now."[12] Negro-Sarah also accurately describes her particular condition of "homelessness": "I know no places. That is, I cannot believe in places. To believe in places is to know hope and to know the emotion of hope is to know beauty. It links us across a horizon and connects us to the world'' (*Funnyhouse*, 7). The mulatta's search for origins and insistence on claiming her white heritage destabilizes the terms of the sexual economy that birthed her, inducing white anxiety for threatened structures of family (tied indubitably to capitalistic enterprise) and patrilineal dominance. It is key that "blood," in racist geneology, follows the *maternal* condition, a fact that is not lost on Kennedy's heroines. They persist in challenging this genealogy by searching for fathers, fathers who would presumably grant them a different heritage, although this, too, proves futile.

The "tragic mulatta" claimed a central place in American fiction prior to 1950, even in black women's writings; the writers themselves were often mulattas, and they wrote of heroines who experienced social difficulties primarily with the white community and their white or black lovers.[13] These works did little to erode a racist standard of acceptable beauty and behavior. As Barbara Christian notes, "Most novels published before the 1950s embodied the tension between the writers' apparent acceptance of an ideal of woman derived from white upper-class society and the reality with which their protagonists had to contend."[14] Both Christian and O'Neale cite Gwendolyn Brooks's novel *Maud Martha* as the only glaring exception to this trend, wherein an "ordinary" black woman struggles against the limits set on her by "her family, her husband, her race, her class, whites, [and] American society."[15] She is not triumphant, nor is she destroyed; but her persistent struggle and refusal to be tragic does set a new standard for the discussion of black women's lives. (Interestingly, *Maud Martha* is the only novel by a black woman cited by Kennedy in her book, *People Who Led to My Plays*.)[16]

While clearly having absorbed "the emphasis on community and culture...as a prerequisite for self-understanding"[17] that is evident in *Maud Martha*, Kennedy's work yet reflects an assimilation of the tragic mulatta tradition and a struggle with its unexamined implications. Her mulatta heroines still desire further assimilation within white culture, but their visibly "tainted blood" makes that impossible. At one point in *The Owl Answers*, She Who Is reveals a blacker body in contrast with her pallid face (42). While this might be a reference to the earlier practice among some black women of tinting their facial skin "to make themselves more acceptably white for black men,"[18] it also makes visible (literally) the impossible lie of "passing"—that no matter how pale the face, the body (the entire figure) must read black in a racist culture. Blackness, as constructed by the dominant group, is literally determined, one might say "figured," in the blood. Claiming whiteness is impossible with even one "drop" of black blood. Yet the *maternal* heritage, referring back to blackness and African origins, is bankrupt in these plays. Not peopled by strong, self-sacrificing matriarchs, freedom fighters, or escapees from slavery, this "black" heritage is no more accommodating than the white one is remote. Africa itself sometimes emerges in the plays as a romanticized land of both dreams and strength, a beautiful land both desired and feared;[19] but the various mothers of Kennedy's plays are weak, passive figures, unable to escape either white or black abuse, unable to give positive guidance to their offspring, usually recommending suicide (as with the mother of *The Owl Answers*, who kills herself, saying it is the "way out of Owldom," the way "to St. Paul's Chapel" [43-44].) Africa, in *Funnyhouse*, is "where my mother fell out of love with my father" (14), where the mother's hair begins falling out—the dream of saving the race dies hard in this Africa, and spells the end of the parents' marriage (15-18). Kennedy here resists the early rhetoric of the 1960s black community, in its passionate return to African roots, through the vivid portrayal of the mulatta's neither/nor status—outsider to both the black and white communities, as well as the emblem of the black community's tendency to be "colorstruck."[20] In this, she prefigures the black women's novels of the early 1970s, such as Morrison's *The Bluest Eye* and Walker's *Grange Copeland*, in which the black community itself comes under critique for its own racism and sexism.[21]

Spillers points out that the intrusion of a middle term, or middle ground, figuratively, between subjugated and dominant interests, proves advantageous for the class in power, allowing for the "[orchestration of] otherness through degrees of difference."[22] By creating and valorizing "literal shades of human value," the subjugated community, "potentially insurgent," is thus turned furiously back on itself, colluding unsuspectingly with its own oppression. Kennedy gives us a blatant example of this in *A Movie Star Has to Star in Black and White*, when Clara's Mother and Father argue over the dissolution of their marriage:

> MOTHER: I have never wanted to go back to the south to live. I hate it. I suffered nothing but humiliation and why should I have gone back there?
>
> FATHER: You ought to have gone back with me. It's what I wanted to do.
>
> MOTHER: I never wanted to go back.
>
> FATHER: You yellow bastard. You're a yellow bastard. That's why you didn't want to go back.
>
> MOTHER: You black nigger. (*Movie Star*, 96)

In another passage, from *Funnyhouse*, Negro-Sarah says that every time her mother talked to her, "she saw I was a black man's child and she preferred speaking to owls" (15)—this from a mother with long straight hair.

In the forties and fifties, the mulatta might experience difficulties, either passing for white or reconciling herself to her ambivalent status, but was still usually held up as a standard of beauty, an object of pursuit and envy within the black community itself. In the sixties, Kennedy's violent depiction of the mulatta's unresolvable dilemma, challenging the black community, might have seemed regressive to a movement then focused on "black is beautiful."[23] (It might seem regressive even now, but for the contrary evidence in, for example, the films of Spike Lee, or popular television sitcoms that perpetuate racist standards of acceptable black beauty; all of which reveal the extent to which the black community is still "colorstruck.") Sarah/Clara's search for definition, for a heritage free from racism (characterized as "anonymity" by Sarah), becomes a poignant cry of resistance, a refusal to name themselves wholly African-American or to ignore their white heritage; a refusal to "settle" for a definition of self forced upon them by a racist interpretation of blood. In this, Kennedy's heroines continue to defy, regressively or otherwise, the prevailing sentiment of her black and female literary colleagues since the mid-1970s. As Barbara Christian notes, in most novels since that time, the female protagonist chooses to rebel in some way against the identity provided her by her community, but

> it is |still| important that...these women claim their heritage. |They| are who they are because of their *maternal* ancestry and their knowledge of that ancestry; and it is from their mothers that they acquire their language.... |A|lthough these characters are critical of their own communities, they come back to them and work out their resistance in that territory.[24]

In marked contrast, claiming this heritage is not possible or desirable for Negro-Sarah or She who is Clara Passmore who is the Virgin Mary who is the Bastard who is the Owl; even their names reflect the racist underpinnings of such claims and the inescapable body politics for the mulatta.

The mulatta body politics of Kennedy's plays also includes sexual politics. These figures are objects of desire for both black and white men, not by virtue of some individual attraction, but because of the sexuality imputed to their skin color. In *The Owl Answers*, She Who Is is pursued nearly to the point of rape by a nameless Negro Man for whom she too is apparently nameless, since they seem to meet anonymously on the subway (26). In *Funnyhouse*, Negro-Sarah lives with Raymond, a white Jewish man who "is very interested in Negroes" and who accuses her of cruelty when she refuses to accept her black heritage. ("Hide me from the jungle" |*Funnyhouse*, 10|.) They variously appeal to their fathers for a rape-free heritage, which, again black or white, is depicted as an impossibility. Rather than celebrating their own sensuality, a commonality in contemporary black women's writing noted by Susan Willis,[25] these figures are almost adamantly unsensual and asexual, caught up in the commodification of their desire in the context of male privilege. Sex outside of marriage is depicted as rape; sex within marriage, as in A *Movie Star*, is unsatisfactory and leads to ambivalent childbearing. In this latter instance, Kennedy does seem to touch on a theme consonant with the black women novelists of the seventies and eighties, hinting at "the contradictions that heterosexuality and childrearing bestow on women."[26] Kennedy's heroines, share with later heroines, such as Sula, Nel, or Meridian, a recognition of "the imprisonment that adult female heterosexuality means for women in this society, and for black women in particular."[27] This ambivalence, it should be noted, is also evident in other plays by black women, as in *For Colored Girls* by Ntozake Shange and *Unfinished Women Cry in No Man's Land While a Bird Dies in a Gilded Cage* by Aishah Rahman.

It must be emphasized that this essay does not intend to produce an exhaustive or totalizing study of "body imagery" in Kennedy's plays. Such an endeavor, even if it were possible, would run counter to the fragmentary and surrealistic nature of the work. Rather, it is more like sifting the aforementioned breadcrumbs, finding some that stick together, some that don't; and each sifting is likely to produce new combinations. However, what I find most compelling at this stage of my encounter with these plays is that these texts and the figures within—multiple selves, fantastic creatures, monstrous and mundane—always send me, *not* into dreams or musings on the improbable, but into history, into the critical examination of historical parameters of specific cultural conditions. In this way Kennedy's work vividly illustrates Adrienne Rich's "politics of location," the necessity for naming one's position in history, which she says must start, for women, with the politics of the body.[28] What is the "location" of Kennedy's central figures, or from Rich's perspective, in what way is Sarah/Clara's body a political identity? To the expected parameters of race and gender we must add geography—the pursuit of a Eurocentric heritage reveals both the twin continents of the body's origins and its impossible condition, invoking the regressive term *mulatta*. In this context Clara and her counterparts become more clearly historicized—not just "victims" of white oppressive culture (the "tragic mulatta"), but literal embodiments of resistance as well: their search for identity cannot possibly end up in another black/white opposition, but must create new ground, even new terms of the debate. This, it seems to me, is more than the postmodern split self, more than fragmentation; it is tantamount to dropping a nuclear bomb into culturally held concepts of race, gender, and identity, and then making everyone else deal with the fallout (e.g., hair falling out). This "bomb" also gets everyone quite bloody.

If "history is what hurts,"[29] Kennedy's figures are the walking wounded—these bodies bleed so freely, so often, that one must suspect irony; like slasher films, the gore can become routine. But unlike Sweeney Todd or Freddy's nightmares, there is no reference in these texts to a "real" person/character (bleeder or bleeding) for whom we are to feel shock or sorrow. Instead, the reference is to history—that which hurts— and our shock and horror are reserved for hard looks at the violence underpinning a culture dependent upon racial domination, hard looks at one's own position within that culture. In the case of the mulatta, the mensurable properties of "blood" (as in the blood that "taints," Faulk- ner's "outcast blood," the "mixed blood," the demarcation of one-half, one-fourth "black blood," etc.) are literally laid waste by the visible leakage of red, that is, "human," blood from black bodies.[30] The racist preoccupation with blood, the mystification of its properties, foregrounds the ideological construction of "community," here determined (as al- ways?) by the manipulation of "knowledge" by the dominant group.[31] In A *Movie Star*, the ambivalence and pain of childbearing for black women, noted earlier, is made literal through Jean Peters's repeated bleeding through her skirts and the changing of bloodied sheets related to dialogue about Clara's miscarriage and failed marriage (87-91). Perhaps one of the most compelling stagings of blood occurs as the focusing image of A *Lesson in Dead Language*, when all the female pupils stand to reveal bloodied skirts. An obvious reference to menstruation and its fearful properties for young girls, the larger context is historical—Caesar, Pompeii, Christianity—grounding their experience of their bleeding in Western culture (which, it should be noted, appears as a "dead language") and rooted in the ideological state apparatus of education: the girls are literally taught to menstruate ("Lesson I bleed"), learning the requisite social stigma/stigmata of being female (47-53). Once again, Kennedy makes gender visible as a process of culture in relation to the female body; like the mulatta's skin color, the evidence of menstruation, over which they have no control, entraps females in a particular cultural condition, situates them in history.[32]

Closely related to the bloodiness is the seeming obsession with hair— the figures of *Funnyhouse* have "wild, kinky hair," massive manes that then proceed to fall out in giant handfuls, or hair matted with blood; in this and other plays, there is described the rapacious black man, a "black beast with shining skull," and then there is Rosemary, a little white Catholic girl with worms in her hair. Historically, hair frequently connotes power or the lack of it, as with Sampson, or the convention of shaved pubic hair for female nudes in art. In *Funnyhouse* and *The Owl Answers*, hair is a signifier for mulattaness, for the inescapable black "blood," the visible marker of race, hence locator within a specific network of relationships with black and white communities. That it falls out in dreams, or is matted with blood, or refuses to straighten pertains to the figures' "ill health," or one might say their lack of power. In the case of Rosemary, her wormy hair conjures images of a modern Medusa, signifying disease in a horrifying vision, a killer with a look (racism being predicated on the specular, the visibility of skin color). She seems to exercise hypnotic power over her subjects, inciting them to evil and fatal acts; to see her— to believe her—is to court a certain kind of death. She is a scourge, diseased, a plague, but she is a plague in power—and herein hangs another "tail."

The play A *Rat's Mass* offers another stunning and perplexing study of bodies "located" in history. Rather than seeing Brother and Sister Rat purely as victims of their oppressors, the discussion of A *Rat's Mass* must shift, I think, to Kennedy's interrelational positioning of historical entities/ events (religious figures, Nazis, etc.)—a kind of "layering of oppressions" whose intersection provides new perspectives for viewing the structures of oppression and the apparatuses that supply reinforcement. Brother and Sister Rat are afloat in a sea of oppressors; groundless, "location-less," without "place," like Negro-Sarah. Yet they are ensnared within culture—they are "rats" like rats caught in a trap; like rats, the scavengers of cities (homeless); like rats, animals in a lab experiment (Rosemary's experiment, analogous to cruel slavers, colonizers, missionaries, carrying out their agenda at the expense of the objectified "thing," object of their experiment);[33] like rats, lowly, "dirty," despised, feared—the carriers of "dis-ease" in a "pure" society. Nazis (and by inference, fascism in any guise), keepers of racial purity, must eliminate the rat peril, the "breeders" of disease. That the Nazis are represented by central figures of Christianity glaringly highlights the intersection of state apparatuses—here the military and religious institutions—in supporting the dominant ideology. Kennedy reveals the fascism of a socioeconomic structure founded on colonialism, racism, and slavery, and names the oppressors in all their guises.

However, the Rat siblings also demonstrate the complex phenomenon of apparent collusion with their oppression, in their repeated protestations of love for Rosemary, their desire for her white, Eurocentric heritage and her mysterious religious rituals, in a sense sealing their own deaths.[34] In this, Kennedy's perceptions would seem to parallel those of Foucault, who speaks of power, not as a force possessed by one group and wielded over another, but as a relational network of institutions, groupings, technologies, and practices.[35] Foucault notes that:

> power comes from below; that is, there is no binary and all-encompassing opposition between rulers and ruled at the root of power relations, and serving as a general matrix....One must suppose rather that the manifold relationships of force that take shape and come into play in the machinery of production, in families, limited groups, and institutions, are the basis for wide-ranging effects of cleavage that run through the social body as a whole....Major dominations are the hegemonic effects that are sustained by all these confrontations.[36]

This understanding of power relations contextualizes Brother and Sister's persistent belief in Rosemary and their poignant confusion over what has happened. Brother Rat says:

> God, I think of Rosemary all the time. I love her. I told myself afterward it was one of the boys playing horseshoes who had done those horrible things on the slide with my sister. Yet I told Kay I am her keeper yet I told Rosemary I love her. It is the secret of my battlefield. (*Rat's Mass*, 63)

Brother's battlefield is marked by "all these confrontations," by the relational nature of power; Brother and Sister's love for Rosemary makes them submit to her demands, after which they are bewildered and ashamed, yet they continue to believe in her, and beg Jesus et al. not to leave them. As with the mulatta's ambivalent position within the black community, Kennedy again imparts a sense of power relations that is localized and complexly interwoven through the fabric of identity, demarcating sources of oppression within the community itself. In this context, the act of incest, instigated by Rosemary and performed by Brother and Sister, becomes a perfect physical trope for the mechanisms of power and oppression within the culture of a nondominant group.

The persistent body violence of Kennedy's plays—exploding bodies, decapitations, executions, suicides, rapes, excessive bleeding, and the like—emerges as a textual strategy of resistance. For these figurative bodies, war is waged on the intensely personal site of the physical, as evidence of the intersecting and conflicting strategies of power and resistance. Ideology reaches fulfillment in bodily practice, in the neither/nor status of the mulatta, or the gendered framing of menstrual blood, and it is only through graphic violence at the specific site of these practices that resistance finds visibility.

Kennedy's plays thus offer no comfort for those who would consign her heroines to "tragedy" or who would condemn her work for its "negative" imagery. The violence of this textual body defies such a reduction, proffering its bleeding wounds as evidence of conflict and contradiction, as emblem of complex power relations across racial lines. As a strategy of resistance, Kennedy's "body politic" bleeds, but is not broken.

Notes

1. Sondra O'Neale, "Inhibiting Midwives, Usurping Creators: The Struggling Emergence of Black Women in American Fiction," in *Feminist Studies/Critical Studies*, ed. Teresa de Lauretis (Bloomington: Indiana University Press, 1986), 139.

2. O'Neale, "Inhibiting Midwives," 144.

3. Ibid., 149.

4. See "mulatto," *Webster's Ninth New Collegiate Dictionary* (Springfield, Mass.: Merriam-Webster, 1983).

5. Katherine Fishburn, *Women in Popular Culture: A Reference Guide* (Westport, Conn.: Greenwood Press, 1982), 10-11.

6. Hortense Spillers, "Notes on an Alternative Model—Neither/Nor," in *The Difference Within: Feminism and Critical Theory*, ed. Elizabeth Meese and Alice Parker (Philadelphia: Benjamins, 1989), 170.

7. Spillers, "Notes" 171, quoting from Faulkner's *Absalom, Absalom*.

8. Ibid.

9. Ibid.

10. Ibid., 173.

11. Ibid.

12. *Funnyhouse of a Negro*, in *Adrienne Kennedy in One Act* (Minneapolis: University of Minnesota Press, 1988), 6. All subsequent references to the plays are to this edition and will be cited in the text.

13. See O'Neale, "Inhibiting Midwives," 152: "From [Iola] Harper's novel up to and including the Harlem Renaissance, the black woman writer tended to come from a very small sector of the upper-middle-class elite, who were usually mulattoes themselves. Thus, the black woman reader could seldom approach a text that presented her as a desirable heroine unless she was depicted as having light hues and long hair."

14. Barbara Christian, "Trajectories of Self-Definition: Placing Contemporary Afro-American Women's Fiction," in *Conjuring: Black Women, Fiction and Literary Tradition*, ed. Marjorie Pryse and Hortense J. Spillers (Bloomington: Indiana University Press, 1985), 237.

15. Christian, "Trajectories," 238.

16. Adrienne Kennedy, *People Who Led to My Plays* (New York: Knopf, 1987), 99.

17. Christian, "Trajectories," 240.

18. O'Neale, "Inhibiting Midwives," 148.

19. *Funnyhouse*, 14: Africa is a land of revelation, "golden savannas, nim and white frankopenny trees, white stallions roaming under a blue sky." There lies the search for Genesis, that is, origins, Eden.

20. I am indebted to Paul K. Bryant-Jackson for pointing out Zora Neale Hurston's devising of the term *colorstruck* to describe the issue and conflict of complexion within the African-American community.

21. Granted that there are obvious differences between plays and novels and that any analysis should not loosely equate the two, nevertheless such differences are somewhat elided in this essay for the sake of concision as well as for embracing the now-recognizable tradition of black women's writing in the United States, of which Kennedy is undeniably a part.

22. Spillers, "Notes," 178.

23. I say "might" because I have no specific evidence to support this supposition. I observe, however, the frequent omission of Kennedy's work from the small number of published anthologies of black American plays and the lack of critical discussion and recognition heretofore. As an example, I cite the otherwise excellent critical anthology, *The Theatre of Black Americans*, ed. Errol Hill (New York: Applause Theatre, 1987); in the entire book, there is only one single-line reference to Kennedy, and in the chronological list of "Important Events," Kennedy's Obie award for *Funnyhouse* in 1964 is curiously absent.

24. Christian, "Trajectories," 241–42.

25. Susan Willis, "Black Women Writers: Taking a Critical Perspective," *Making a Difference: Feminist Literary Criticism*, ed. Gayle Greene and Coppelia Kahn (New York: Methuen, 1985), 211–37.

26. Ibid., 232.

27. Ibid., 233.

28. Adrienne Rich, "Notes Toward a Politics of Location," in *Women, Feminist Identity and Society in the 1980's*, ed. Myriam Diaz-Diocaretz and Iris Zavala (Amsterdam, Philadelphia: Benjamins, 1985), 7–22.

29. See Spillers, "Notes," 173; and Frederic Jameson, *Political Unconscious: Narrative As a Socially Symbolic Act* (Ithaca, N.Y.: Cornell University Press, 1981), 102.

30. For example, the bloodied hanging scar around Negro-Sarah's neck in *Funnyhouse*, or the vaginal bleeding in *Lesson in Dead Language* and *A Movie Star Has to Star in Black and White*.

31. See Spillers, "Notes," 182–83, for an extended discussion.

32. See Susan Bordo, "The Body and the Reproduction of Feminity: A Feminist Appropriation of Foucault," in *Gender, Body, Knowledge*, ed. Alison M. Jaggar and Susan R. Bordo (New Brunswick, N.J.: Rutgers University Press, 1989), 13–33, for a discussion of anorexia, bulimia, hysteria, and other particularly "female" disorders as pathological attempts to reclaim control over a gendered body.

33. See Michelle Cliff, "'I found God in myself and I loved her / I loved her fiercely': More Thoughts on the Work of Black Women Artists," in *Women, Feminist Identity and Society*, ed. Diaz-Diocaretz and Zavala, 101–26, for an excellent discussion of the profound effect colonialism and slavery and the subsequent "rewriting" of history have had and continue to have with regard to African art and song and that of its African-American descendants.

See also Spillers, "Notes," for her discussion of Todorov's model of alterity and the construction of blacks as "things," chattel—the process of dehumanism endemic to slavery.

34. It is important to note that, while Kennedy's heroines may intensely desire a white heritage, or more white skin, actually obtaining that heritage would not be sufficient redemption, either: for example, Negro-Sarah's fictive white friends will be "shrewd, intellectual and anxious for death," self-despising and morally bankrupt, "out of life and death essential" (*Funnyhouse*, 6).

35. Michel Foucault, *The History of Sexuality* (New York: Random House, 1978), 93–94.

36. Ibid., 94.

13

"A Spectator Watching My Life": Adrienne Kennedy's A Movie Star Has to Star in Black and White

Deborah R. Geis

> ...Hollywood
> laughs at me,
> black—
> so I laugh
> back.
> —Langston Hughes, "Movies"

> ...She was never able...to look at a face and not assign it some
> category in the scale of absolute beauty, and the scale was one she
> absorbed in full from the silver screen....There the black-and-white
> images came together, making a magnificent whole.
> —Toni Morrison, The Bluest Eye

Adrienne Kennedy's 1976 play A Movie Star Has to Star in Black and White is located at a complicated point between the sardonic detachment of the Hughes poem and Morrison's cautionary description of Pauline Breedlove's immersion in Hollywood ideology. The "Leading Roles" of Kennedy's drama are played by actors "who look exactly like" Bette Davis, Paul Heinreid, Jean Peters, Marlon Brando, Montgomery Clift, and Shelley Winters, while the "real" characters (designated as the "Supporting Roles") are the mother, father, and husband of Clara, a thirty-three-year-old black woman.[1] Clara herself, the ostensible heroine, only plays "a bit role," as the narrating Columbia Pictures Lady tells us (Movie Star, 81). The play's narrative itself consists of the words of Clara and her family (mostly as "excerpted" from what appears to be Clara's journal), but the movie stars "play out" these dramas from Clara's life for her and occasionally for her family members. That is, Jean Peters, Bette Davis, and the others appear in their movie-star roles, but they speak Clara's

Robbie McCauley and C. S. Hayward in the New York Shakespeare Festival production of *A Movie Star Has to Star in Black and White*, November 1976, Joseph Chaikin, director; Joseph Papp, producer. Photo by George E. Joseph.

words in her place. The result is not intended to be a camped-up spoof of Hollywood imagery; Kennedy indicates in her opening stage directions that "[t]hese movie stars are romantic and moving, never camp or farcical, and the attitudes of the supporting players to the movie stars is deadly serious" (*Movie Star*, 80). Yet even these last two words hint at the ominous side of this movie-star world: the seriousness with which the black "supporting players" regard those who play the leading roles may indeed be "deadly." This essay argues that the tension between immersion in and angry confrontation of the Hollywood world experienced by Clara in this play embodies the ambivalent spectatorial status of the African-American woman whose subjectivity risks being undermined by her identification with an exclusionary cultural apparatus. The clear disjunction between the "romantic" demeanor of the movie-star figures, who "play" scenes from *Now, Voyager*, *A Place in the Sun*, and *Viva Zapata!*, and the events of Clara's narrative (her father's suicide attempt, her hemorrhaging during pregnancy, her brother's coma) suggests that however compelling the movie-star fantasies may appear to be, their attractiveness originates from a Hollywood world sustained by a mythology that is ultimately oppressive in its unassailability.

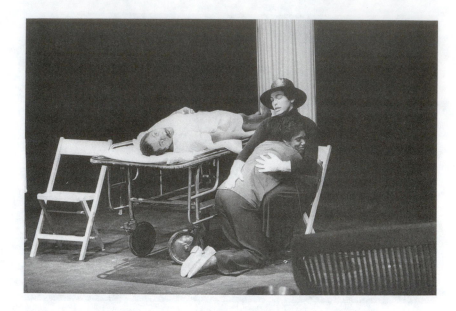

Robbie McCauley, Gloria Foster, and Frank Adu in the New York Shakespeare Festival production of *A Movie Star Has to Star in Black and White*, November 1976, Joseph Chaikin, director; Joseph Papp, producer. Photo by George E. Joseph.

For Kennedy and for her alter ego Clara, the Hollywood films of the 1940s contain the promises of fulfillment and female power (as embodied in, for example, the persona of Bette Davis) that permit the potential artist and dreamer/moviegoer to be a sort of visionary. Kennedy's own verbal scrapbook, *People Who Led to My Plays*, attests repeatedly to the powerful fascination that Hollywood held for her ever since her early childhood. Of Bette Davis in *Now, Voyager*, she writes:

> In this avid dream of transformation I still also daydreamed of myself as this character. She was plain. She was troubled. She was controlled by her mother and then one day she took a trip on an ocean liner and total fulfillment came to her because of this trip on the ocean. She became beautiful and loved. One day I'm going to take a trip on an ocean liner, I thought, and all of my dark thoughts and feelings, all my feelings that I don't belong anywhere, will go away.[2]

Kennedy's memoir is sprinkled with reflections of this sort, beginning with her comment that her mother told her as a child that she had even been named for a movie actress, Adrienne Ames. The imagery of the passage I have just cited reveals, I think, a subconscious division between the Bette Davis identity and Kennedy's African-American identity in her desire to banish the "dark" thoughts and feelings, that is, those which on some level she associates with her blackness. In almost an "enactment" of Lacan's mirror stage, Kennedy/Clara turns to the symbolic realm of the movies to find a mirror, and instead sees the reminder of her Otherness; she writes, "My father often called me good-looking when in the mirror I saw a strange-looking face" (*People*, 41), and—interestingly—includes at an earlier point in the book a picture from the Disney *Snow White* cartoon showing the evil stepmother confronting the mirror in which she is being told that she is no longer "the fairest of them all" in comparison to Snow White. This image of the mirror turns up repeatedly in Kennedy's plays, most powerfully in *Funnyhouse of a Negro*, where the divided "selves" of "Sarah the Negro" (who, Kennedy has said, is an earlier version of Clara), the Duchess, the Queen, Jesus, and Patrice Lumumba examine their faces repeatedly in the mirror. In this case, the "funnyhouse" suggests the ability of the funhouse mirror to distort, to reshape, and (as Herbert Blau points out) to entrap within an infinite series of replications.[3] Laura Mulvey's pivotal essay, "Visual Pleasure and Narrative Cinema," argues that the form of pleasure-in-looking that Freud calls "scopophilia" is predicated on the eroticism of subsuming ego identification into the spectatorial mode of objectification. Narrative cinema, suggests Mulvey, has thus manipulated our sense of visual pleasure through the coercive act of "cod[ing] the erotic into the language of the dominant patriarchal structure."[4] My point in evoking Mulvey's article here is to suggest that her sense of the simultaneous ego loss/ ego reinforcement that occurs when one observes the "mirror" of the cinema screen has powerful implications not just for female spectatorship (which is, of course, also applicable to Kennedy's play), but for the spectatorial situation of the black filmgoer searching for an "ego ideal" in the cinema, as well. One can see Kennedy's/Clara's position, or for that matter Pauline Breedlove's, in Mulvey's description of the mirror stage's onset:

> The mirror phase occurs at a time when the child's physical ambitions outstrip his motor capacity, with the result that his recognition of himself is joyous in that he imagines his mirror image to be more complete, more perfect than he experiences his own body. Recognition is thus overlaid with mis-recognition: the image recognized is conceived as the reflected body of the self, but its misrecognition as superior projects this body outside itself as an ideal ego, the alienated subject, which, re-introjected as an ego ideal, gives rise to the future generation of identification with others.[5]

Thus, when Clara says at the beginning of *A Movie Star*, "Each day I wonder with what or with whom can I co-exist in a true union?" (*Movie Star*, 82), her words represent the position of the "alienated subject," which seeks to re-inscribe itself as the ego ideal, but which can only do so at the imperfect level of identification with an object. Clara's longing is marked with an intrinsic awareness that the "true union" she desires is as unlikely as the possibility that she could "become" her Bette Davis/ Jean Peters persona.

Clara's status as alienated subject can now be contextualized in Althusserian terms, wherein subjectivity is itself a "socializing function" set into motion by the dominant means of production. As Bill Nichols puts it:

> The imaginary does not…pass away after the mirror-phase and the emergence of the symbolic realm; it continues to reappear in new guises, often infiltrating the symbolic to reduce it to the imaginary, most notably through the workings of ideology.[6]

Kennedy's play repeatedly invokes the effect of this ideological "infiltration" of the symbolic, particularly through images of the power of the camera itself. Speaking through the Columbia Pictures Lady, Clara compares the photograph of her producer in *Vogue* to the way she has actually seen him: "In the photograph Joel's hair looked dark and his skin smooth. In real life his skin is blotched. Everyone says he drinks a lot" (*Movie Star*, 81). Similarly, she adds, "My father once said his life has been nothing but a life of hypocrisy and that's why his photograph smiled" (*Movie Star*, 81). The ironic resonance of these two passages, of course, is that to whatever extent Clara harbors an awareness of the camera's "lying eye," her movie-star fantasies reveal the extent to which her own system of representation depends upon it. The camera "eye," as Jean-Louis Baudry has demonstrated, perpetuates its own authoritative status by manufacturing the belief that its monocular perspective, as a replication of the human eye, allows us to define that which can be seen as central to human agency.[7] This belief, which Timothy Murray calls "visibility as ideology,"[8] causes us to have inestimable faith in the "truth-value" of the camera. Clara's eagerness to depend on the camera's monocularity, then, is predicated on her desire to control an uncontrollable world by circumscribing her vision. At the same time, to do so is to place herself outside of history, a history partially revealed nevertheless through moments of her narrative, as when Clara's mother describes the segregation in her Georgia town:

> When a Negro bought something in a store he couldn't try it on. A Negro couldn't sit down at the soda fountain in the drug store but had to take his drink out. In the movies at Montefore you had to go in the side and up the stairs and sit in the last four rows.
>   When you arrived on the train from Cincinnati the first thing you saw was the WHITE AND COLORED signs at the depot. White people had one

waiting room and we Negroes had another. We sat in only two cars and white people had the rest of the train. (*Movie Star*, 84)

We are beginning to see the ways that Clara's desire to insert herself and her family into the context of the Hollywood narratives is a longing for the seamlessness and coherence promised by the machinations of the visible, the eye/I of the camera. To inhabit the world of cinematic representation is to seek the pleasure of "translating" one's experience into the experience of the idealized Subject. As Nichols puts it, "The pleasurable reflux of self-recognition helps guarantee the obviousness of ideology, its disappearance behind the inevitable, for who in the midst of pleasure would seek to disrupt it by analyzing its source or consequences?"[9] But Clara's attempts at immersion in this pleasure are consistently undermined by the inability of her *histoire* to fit her *discours*,[10] by the extreme differences that characterize her "black" narrative (her depression, her bleeding, her brother's car accident) and her "white" (Hollywood) one. By the end of the play, it is as if even the Hollywood fantasies themselves cannot satisfy the needs that Clara calls upon them to fulfill; as the play closes, Montgomery Clift stares impassively at the drowning Shelley Winters, who cannot cry aloud for help.

Is the sense of the finale, then, that Clara will only avoid a similar "drowning" if she is able to swim away from the "dark boat...done with lights and silhouettes" (*Movie Star*, 80) of the Hollywood cinema? If this is the case, then Kennedy's title quickly becomes an imperative, a reminder that Clara's attempt to make her movie stars "star in black" (by using their on-screen characters to act out the scenarios of her life) only underscores the disparity between those scenarios and the actual "white" ones of the films themselves. More important, the play's narrative structure and Clara's status as playwright provide indications that Kennedy does indeed participate in undermining these ideological structures "from within."

First, the narrative structure of A *Movie Star*, like that of *Funnyhouse of a Negro*, *The Owl Answers*, and most of Kennedy's other plays, resists the temporal linearity of the classic realist narrative; rather than proceeding from point A to point B in the process that Teresa de Lauretis has described as the Oedipal "discovery" narrative,[11] Kennedy's play is anachronistic, collagelike, and filled with lacunae or ellipses. Jeanie Forte's description of this structure in *The Owl Answers* is also applicable to A *Movie Star*:

> In Clara's case, the Oedipal narrative is absolutely oppressive, in that she is locked outside of it and within it, by virtue of her race/gender doublebind. The play's ambiguity and near-incomprehensibility articulate the

impossibility of identification with a narrative position, least of all one which might provide closure, or the fiction of a coherent self. Clara... instead traverses narrative, zig-zagging across various systems of signification, seeking herself in the gaps, the spaces of unnarrated silence wherein her persistently elusive subjectivity might be found.[12]

However, Forte goes on to argue that because of the ultimate "unreadability" of The Owl Answers, the play may depend upon the performance situation to guarantee a certain degree of comprehensibility, which in turn may undo the politically subversive aspect of its refusal of realism.[13] Here, I believe, is where A Movie Star has a rather different effect. Because the movie stars and the settings from Now, Voyager and other films preexist for the audience as reassuringly "familiar" components of Hollywood narrative, the subversiveness of Kennedy's narrative strategy lies in the refusal of these temptingly familiar, even dazzling, images to cohere into a "satisfactorily" romantic or straightforward narrative "whole." Furthermore, we mustn't forget that what we are seeing in A Movie Star are not filmic images, but staged ones. As Blau, Murray, and others have pointed out, live performance foregrounds the corporeality of the actors in ways that cinematic performance cannot.[14] One might argue, then, that Kennedy's "translation" of the dreamlike Hollywood fantasy images into live, staged ones has another potentially disruptive effect, preventing the spectators from entering into the same specular relationships as they would with characters visible on a screen. A further reflection of Kennedy's "diffused" narrative might be that the staged image resists, to some extent, the "monocular" view of the camera that I have already mentioned.

Finally, it is striking that within A Movie Star, emerging out of the fantasies of transformation on board the craft of Now, Voyager, we find Clara struggling to define her own "craft": that of the playwright. The suggestion is that Clara, as Kennedy's surrogate, embodies the African-American artist who faces the challenge of "writing her way out of" Hollywood's insidiously appealing dream factory. At the beginning of the play, we see Clara in a maternity dress, and she says, "I'm terribly tired, trying to do a page a day, yet my play is coming together" (Movie Star, 82). Thereafter, in most of the sequences where Clara speaks for herself instead of having her movie stars speak "for" her, we hear her reading passages from her play, which turns out to be Kennedy's actual play The Owl Answers. It becomes clear, especially in a sequence where Jean Peters (as one of Clara's movie-star personae) recites from The Owl Answers following an argument between Clara's mother and father, that Clara uses an allegorized form of her family life to create her play, just as Kennedy uses both this poetic allegory and, of course, the duplicate allegory of A Movie Star to articulate her own dramatic voice. However, the traditional association of writing and pregnancy or reproduction, introduced through the passage I have mentioned showing Clara in a maternity dress, develops into a disturbing set of images. Just as Clara has explained that she must stay in bed because she is hemorrhaging and has already had one miscarriage before, the Marlon Brando and Jean Peters "wedding night" scene from *Viva Zapata!* emerges late in the play as a cyclical sequence in which the Jean Peters character continually bleeds black blood onto the sheets, while Marlon Brando pulls them out from under her and throws them on the floor, over and over again, as the play progresses. It is at this point that Jean Peters mentions another play that she (or, in fact, Kennedy) is writing: "It's going to be called a Lesson In Dead Language. The main image is a girl in a white organdy dress covered with menstrual blood" (*Movie Star*, 94). This conflation of menstruation, deflowering (the "wedding night"), and pregnancy as expressed through blood imagery pervades Kennedy's plays, as Rosemary Curb has discussed.[15] Curb, however, does not point to the powerful association Kennedy establishes between bleeding and artistic creation, especially in A *Movie Star*: the sheets strewn on the floor around the bed are covered with black blood and link imagistically to the sheets of writing paper that Clara/Kennedy attempts to fill as she writes her play. The ink, like the blood, is black—a source of pain in the sense that Clara/Kennedy is "writing her wounds," but a source of power in the sense that she is creating, in black, something that comes from inside of her.

To return to my opening citations, then, I would not want to say that Clara has succeeded utterly in finding a way to "laugh back" at Hollywood the way that Hughes claims to do in "Movies." Rather, she—and, by extension, Kennedy—has accepted the immense difficulty of this challenge in a culture that, in adopting Hollywood cinema as its source for standards of "beauty" and "romance," has embraced what Morrison reminds us are "probably the most destructive ideas in the history of human thought."[16]

Notes

1. A *Movie Star Has to Star in Black and White*, in *Adrienne Kennedy in One Act* (Minneapolis: University of Minnesota Press, 1988), 80. All subsequent references are to this edition and will be indicated in the text.

2. Adrienne Kennedy, *People Who Led to My Plays* (New York: Theatre Communications Group, 1987), 91. All subsequent references are to this edition and will be indicated in the text of the essay.

3. Herbert Blau, "The American Dream in American Gothic: The Plays of Sam Shepard and Adrienne Kennedy," *Modern Drama* 27 (Dec. 1984): 532; reprinted in Blau, *Blooded Thought: Occasions of Theatre* (New York: Performing Arts Journal Publications, 1982).

4. Laura Mulvey, "Visual Pleasure and Narrative Cinema," *Screen* 16 (Autumn 1975), 8.

5. Ibid., 9–10.

6. Bill Nichols, *Ideology and the Image* (Bloomington: Indiana University Press, 1981), 35.

7. See Timothy Murray, "Screening the Camera's Eye: Black and White Confrontations of Technological Representation," *Modern Drama* 28 (March 1985), 113–14.

8. Ibid., 119.

9. Nichols, *Ideology and the Image*, 41.

10. For a discussion of the difference between *histoire* and *discours*, see Annette Kuhn, *Women's Pictures: Feminism and Cinema* (London: Routledge and Kegan Paul, 1982), 49–52.

11. Cf. "Desire in Narrative," Chap. 2 in Teresa de Lauretis, *Alice Doesn't: Feminism, Semiotics, Cinema* (Bloomington: Indiana University Press, 1982), 103–57.

12. Jeanie Forte, "Realism, Narrative, and the Feminist Playwright—A Problem of Reception," *Modern Drama* 32 (March 1989): 121.

13. Ibid., 124–25.

14. See Murray, "Screening the Camera's Eye," 116; see also Blau, *Blooded Thought*, cited in Murray.

15. Rosemary K. Curb, "Lesson I Bleed: Adrienne Kennedy's Blood Rites," in *Women in American Theatre*, ed. Helen Krich Chinoy and Linda Walsh Jenkins (New York: Theatre Communications Group, 1981; reprint, 1987), 50–56.

16. Toni Morrison, *The Bluest Eye* (New York: Washington Square Press, 1970), 97.

14

Critical Reflections: Adrienne Kennedy, the Writer, the Work

bell hooks

GLORIA WATKINS: Speak about the appeal of Adrienne Kennedy, her plays.
BELL HOOKS:[1] Kennedy's work seduces readers by its appeal to the enigmatic. She shrouds the work in mystery. And yet, since much of it is autobiographically based, the reader senses that something is revealed and not revealed at the same time. It is this characteristic that gives the work its strange yet familiar appeal. There is always something in it that you recognize, and something that catches you unaware. Kennedy's work problematizes the question of identity, black subjectivity, in ways that do not allow for a simplistic understanding of "blackness," of race, of what it means to be a black woman in the United States and abroad.
G. W.: How did you come to Kennedy's work?
HOOKS: Since childhood (like Kennedy) I have had this obsession with drama. Acting in plays from grade school and all through high school, I knew early that I wanted to be an actress. And since I attended segregated schools, there was no sense in my mind that race was going to inhibit that. It was desegregation, going to the predominately white schools that brought home that a black woman actress always existed on the margins of white people's plays. I could be in *Member of the Wedding* because there was this ever-faithful black mammy-like character. As a black woman actress I was always on the outside of exciting plays. How I longed to be at the center of Lillian Hellman's *The Little Foxes* but—no. These places were reserved for white girls. I went to college to study drama, to act. And though I worked with a group for a while that was following Jerry

179

Grotowski's method of guerrilla theatre, I was always appalled by the racism—by the difficulty of making a place in that theatre system. Ultimately, I gave up on acting and decided to be a playwright.

That's where the search for black women writers who had charted the journey began. And of course I found Lorraine Hansberry before discovering Kennedy's work. There is that lovely tribute Kennedy gives her in *People Who Led to My Plays* when she says, "I had abandoned playwriting by the time Lorraine Hansberry made her sensational entrance into the Broadway theatre with the classic A *Raisin in the Sun*, because I thought there was no hope; but with Lorraine Hansberry's success, I felt reawakened. I read every word about her triumph and took heart."[2] This quote moves me because it captures what I felt when I came to Kennedy's work. Because I was more familiar with the linear narratives Hansberry worked with, more familiar with the form and content, but Kennedy was different; she was all over the place. And I was moved by her work to reconsider my narrow senses of drama. She was on the edge, out there, daring to be avant-garde and that was thrilling.

G. W.: What was the first Kennedy play you read?

HOOKS: Oh, *Funnyhouse of a Negro* and it really disturbed me in the way Kennedy's plays do. This passage stayed with me:

> It is my dream to live in rooms with European antiques and my Queen Victoria, photographs of Roman ruins, walls of books, a piano, oriental carpets and to eat my meals on a white glass table. I will visit my friends' apartments which will contain books, photographs of Roman ruins, pianos and oriental carpets. My friends will be white.
>
> I need them as an embankment to keep me from reflecting too much upon the fact that I am a Negro. For, like all educated Negroes—out of life and death essential—I find it necessary to maintain a stark fortress against recognition of myself.[3]

G. W.: Why did this passage strike you?

HOOKS: Kennedy grapples in this play with the issue of black intellectuality. Few writers have focused, as she has, on the place of black thinkers in a white world, in an educational system that is always looking to Europe for directions and definition. *Funnyhouse of a Negro* is, in that way, a great companion piece for Baraka's *Dutchman*. When I first read *Funnyhouse of a Negro*, I was mesmerized. First by the sheer sense of daring—of fun and play. Kennedy's plays always have that ritualized "play." Let's face it! Few recognized African-American dramas have so relentlessly refused the linear narrative that makes everything clear and explicit. Most African-American drama remains a drama of the story, it's naturalistic, it's realistic. But Kennedy's plays call us to celebrate her creative daring, her willingness to take artistic risks, to do on paper what the surrealist painters did in their work. Her plays remind me of Salvador Dali's painting. And when I went to the Dali museum in Spain, it could easily have been a set for an Adrienne Kennedy play.

G. W.: Say more! What do you mean "creative daring"?

HOOKS: It's about the wonderful movement away from simple realism in her plays, that willingness to play with form and content, like in *The Owl Answers*, and even in the way she revisions those Greek tragedies. Kennedy's use of autobiography definitely makes her work unique—less so now than when she first began (by that I mean more contemporary African-American playwrights make use of their own life stories). She was breaking new ground in the beginning, though. Kennedy's work is so important to the development of contemporary American drama because of her willingness to be experimental, and she most definitely charts new journeys for aspiring black women playwrights. Though I dream of writing plays that are experimental, avant-garde in a contemporary sense, so far the plays I have written have linear narratives. Kennedy's work has always urged playwrights to move in new directions—to move beyond even where she started out.

G. W.: As a feminist critic, a feminist theorist, how would you locate Kennedy's work?

HOOKS: Immediately what comes to mind is the critical focus on confessional writing by women—on autobiography. Many of the critics writing on women's autobiography are white women (with exceptions), and few of them who are doing such work on women of color call attention to Kennedy. Any feminist discussion of female subjectivity (and particularly black female subjectivity) would be enhanced by a discussion of Kennedy's work.

G. W.: Which works in particular?

HOOKS: *People Who Led to My Plays* and "Theatre Journal" at the end of *Deadly Triplets* and all the plays. Feminist critics could really use these works to discuss the development of the woman artist in the way that we have traditionally, in academic circles, talked about Virginia Woolf's *A Room Of One's Own*. Kennedy's work is as much about the development of a woman playwright as it is about a vast array of other concerns. That's what makes the work so fascinating—it is multi layered. But always there is that autobiographical subtext.

G. W.: Are you saying that her work is explicitly "feminist"?

HOOKS: If we think of the feminist movement as I defined it in *Feminist Theory: From Margin to Center*, as a movement to resist sexism and sexist oppression, we could surely do a critical analysis of Kennedy's work that would show how her focus on the construction of "femininity" subverts traditional paradigms. But the point I want to make is not to focus on the work as overtly feminist, it is to suggest that there is an emergent perspective on woman's identity—on her quest to create literature in this work—that can be read as linked to a growing political concern in the fifties and sixties with female identity—with women's efforts to come to voice—to establish a writer's identity, and this concern is there in Kennedy's work. And she is different from, say a Hansberry, growing up on the South Side of Chicago. Even though she was in Cleveland, there is a southern influence that shapes her perceptions of reality, her aesthetic vision. Kennedy is a product of the great migration of blacks from the South, but there is a lot of southern sensitivity in her plays.

G. W.: What distinguishes Kennedy's construction of femaleness from say that of a Lillian Hellman in *Pentimento*?

HOOKS: Obviously, Kennedy was able to write about the way race informs the construction of a female's identity in a way that few women writers have. Since so many white women want to deny that race shapes how they see themselves, there is an honesty, a stripping bare in the white and black female dramators in Kennedy's work. Whereas many black women feel estranged from cultural representators of white femaleness, Kennedy lets readers know that at an early age certain notions of beauty and desirability emerge from white culture—and white womanhood—in a way that few black women writers have, past or present. An interesting dimension of her/the work (which seems utterly *alien* to me) is the fascination and to some extent the love of white culture that she expresses in her work, her almost reverent worship of England. Unabashedly, she admits to being obsessively curious about "these people who had conquered the world." There is this powerful nostalgic remembering of England in the "Theatre Journal," poignantly expressed in a passage where she writes of London:

> The city in February, the early darkness, walks in the rain excited me. It made me feel that just beyond that darkness was a completed person, a completed life. I felt the city held a key to my psyche. And apart from literature and my constant interest in British writers I felt too these were the people who had colonized my West African ancestors. What were these people like?[4]

G. W.: Are you suggesting that Kennedy is interested solely in the construction of blackness in relation to whiteness?

HOOKS: No, not at all. What makes her treatment of these issues complex is that she acknowledges this obsessive fascination with Europe, with white people on the one hand, but on the other, she is politically aware, conscious of the importance of antiracist struggle, of black tradition. In this way she reminds me of black intellectuals, like Du Bois, and even

Martin Luther King, who though passionately devoted to the civil rights struggle were truly enamored of white culture. King never writes about his fascination with black music, but he does write about opera. Kennedy always juxtaposes this obsessive interest in white culture with her keen awareness of imperialisms of racism. Her brief accounts of her college experience at Ohio State clearly show that she was deeply affected by white racism, that it assaulted her psyche.

> My dorm mates at Ohio State, often from southern Ohio towns, they were determined to subjugate the Negro girls. They were determined to make you feel that it was a great inequality that they had to live in the same dorm with you...an injustice. This dark reality was later to give impetus and energy to my dreams. (*People*, 69)

When I first read these autobiographical sketches I rushed to phone my play daughter who is in her twenties with whom I have talked at length about white female aggression against black women—particularly at predominately white institutions. I wanted her to read Kennedy, to know that this black woman was naming that reality. For black women have not documented enough the harsh nuances and textures that characterize our relationships to many white women. Black people have not written enough autobiographical works that name the "traumas" that many of us undergo in predominately white settings.

G. W.: Do you see the effect of these settings in Kennedy's work?

HOOKS: Clearly, throughout. In that ambivalent love/hate relationship that is always going on between blacks and white folks in the plays. Of course there are tensions that Kennedy does not resolve or reconcile. Indeed, the work itself suggests these tensions may be irreconcilable.

G. W.: Can we return to the question of feminism?

HOOKS: Sure. What is so important in terms of Kennedy's work, that is the dimension of her work that focuses on the construction of her identity as a "writer." She explicitly names gender issues when she talks about how difficult it was as a married woman with husband and children to establish a writer's identity that people around her acknowledge. In *People Who Led to My Plays*, she lets the reader know that it was difficult to claim that writer's identity, that she had to fight to gain recognition of her work—its value. And it must have been all the more difficult as a black woman who wanted to do something different in the world of theatre. It's interesting that she mentions the white woman poet Sylvia Plath (another writer whose work fascinates me) at the end of *Deadly Triplets*, for Plath's struggle to come to terms with marriage and motherhood was similar to Kennedy's—that need to project the writer's identity but still fulfill many traditional sex role demands. Significantly, Kennedy, unlike

Plath, finds a way to unproblematically ascend her identity as a writer and clearly lets readers/audiences know that creating plays is life sustaining for her. Much of Kennedy's work highlights the struggle of females, often daughters, to be fully self-actualized.

G. W.: Let's return to the question of Kennedy's fascination with white culture. Do you find it problematic?

HOOKS: This obsession/fascination is constructed as problematic in the work. Certainly it should be discussed, interrogated even. When I read Kennedy, I ponder how she could have such keen awareness of the politics of race and gender, globally and in the United States, yet sustain that fascination with all those artifacts of white cultural imperialism. Significantly, in terms of her development as a playwright, it is not the artistic experience of culture that deeply transformed her sense of drama; it was reading Lorca. She says, "His dark complex vision was thrilling and comforting to me" (*People*, 72). Reading Lorca's plays ruptures her conventional way of thinking about drama, enables her to break with certain traditions.

G. W.: Do you have favorite Kennedy works that speak to you more than others?

HOOKS: For me, it is Kennedy's confessional writing that fascinates. There could never be enough autobiographical writing by black women; we have so much to tell the world about our experience, about how we see the world. Few black women would boast as Kennedy can and does that "autobiographical work is the only thing that interests me, apparently because that is what I do best."[5]

I am completely enamored of *People Who Led to My Plays*. Like her drama, this work is experimental, combining visual images with short narratives and fragments. But like scraps pieced into a crazy quilt, these fragments come together and provide an artistic portrait of Kennedy. To read the fragments—to look at the pictures—there is something very infinite about this work. When Kennedy describes her mother and then you see the picture, you can *read* this image in your way, comparing your response to Kennedy's. It's a very powerful representation of her reality.

G. W.: Would you say Kennedy is one of the writers who influenced you?

HOOKS: Yes! Oh yes! Like Kennedy, I am fascinated by the autobiographical, by the urge to both reveal and yet withhold. She does both in her work—always keeping the sense of mystery and magic. And I want to be more experimental—to take risks. It's because her work stimulates my creativity that I want to engage it critically, to learn from it and her. Kennedy has this eclectic approach that aesthetically has not always ensured success; that's another reason to respect her "creative daring." Though I fully appreciate the work of a celebrated playwright like August

Wilson, his work does not break new ground—with thematic consider-
ations being the possible exception. Kennedy is continually playing with
us—making a play within a play—challenging the audience to expand
its vision of what is dramatically possible.

Notes

1. bell hooks is the pen name of Gloria Watkins—Eds.

2. Adrienne Kennedy, *People Who Led to My Plays* (New York: Knopf, 1987), 109: hereafter
cited in the text.

3. *Adrienne Kennedy in One Act* (Minneapolis: University of Minnesota Press, 1988), 6.

4. Adrienne Kennedy, *Deadly Triplets* (Minneapolis: University of Minnesota Press, 1990),
105.

5. Adrienne Kennedy, "Growth of Images," *Drama Review* 21 (Dec. 1977): 41.

PART IV

Performance as a Collaborative Art

15

An Interview with Michael Kahn

Howard Stein

Howard Stein interviewed Michael Kahn on October 9, 1990. Michael Kahn is artistic director of the Shakespeare Theatre at the Folger Library in Washington, D.C., and chairman of the Acting Department of the Juilliard Theatre Center, and serves on the faculty of New York University's Graduate School of the Arts. He directed Adrienne Kennedy's Obie-winning *Funnyhouse of a Negro* (1964) produced by Edward Albee, and directed Kennedy's *Electra* and *Orestes* at Juilliard in November 1980 and again in April 1981. Kahn served as artistic director of the Acting Company (1978–90) and is now a member of its board of trustees; he has been artistic director of the American Shakespeare Theatre in Stratford, Connecticut, and producing director of the McCarter Theatre in Princeton, New Jersey. On Broadway, Kahn directed *Showboat* with Donald O'Connor (for which he received a Tony Award nomination), *Whodunnit*, *The Death of Bessie Smith*, and the musical version of *East of Eden*.

HOWARD STEIN: In 1964, before anybody was doing fragmentation and all that (regardless of how the public talked about fragmentation in Piran-dello), you got a play which is wild as can be: *Funnyhouse of a Negro*, and you go boldly ahead and do it. Then you do *The Owl Answers* as if it was just normal stuff.

MICHAEL KAHN: I just thought it was really interesting. I wasn't sure what it was. I was actually asked to recommend a director for it, and I decided I'd like to do it myself in this playwriting workshop of Edward Albee's of

189

the Circle in the Square where I was teaching at the time. And then I talked to Adrienne, and it just seemed to me—I just understood. I had been really interested in early Cocteau movies and things like that, and there was something about this play that reminded me of that.

H. S.: What most interested you about the script?

KAHN: The imagery, the symbolism. The symbolism of the hair and the writing and the compression of the dialogue. I was also working at that time at La Mama. Adrienne was more poetic than those writers at La Mama; it was such a big time of experimentation that it seemed really— something you do.

H. S.: But when you work with actors—you have to deal with actors who already had fifteen or twenty years of Actor's Studio in America, by the time you come along; naturally they're going to ask you questions about that material [Funnyhouse], and I don't see how the material can answer them.

KAHN: I don't remember it being such a fierce issue at the time. Diana Sands, who was unable ultimately to portray Sarah in the Off-Broadway production due to a commitment to perform in a Baldwin piece but who created the role in the workshop, was...such an imaginative person and understood the emotion of Sarah. The play was quite clear in terms of how it was manipulating the symbols. And I also seemed to have understood all the movie references and everything. I too knew who the Duchess of Hapsburg was; I knew about Carlotta and Maximilian from the film *Juarez* and how white Bette Davis's costumes were. So I was able to communicate that to the actors. It was also a time when people were starting to think about nonrepresentational theatre.

H. S.: It was in the early 1960s, not in the middle 1960s (La Mama only begins around 1960 and Cafe Cino soon after), and it seems to me you were there quite early...before Lanford Wilson or Sam Shepard.

KAHN: We took the workshop production to the playwright section of the Actor's Studio, and they asked questions about moment-to-moment acting. So we showed how we did play situations: we played two people who were fighting or two people who were gossiping or somebody was trying to commit suicide and the landlady was like the animated dummy in a funhouse fortune-telling booth and [in reference to other theatre games:] "as if." We just used a lot of "as if's." That shut them up at the Studio. But I think we all entered into Adrienne's spirit. I think the actors had some difficulty because sometimes it didn't give them an emotional payoff.

H. S.: Did they have the sense of pain that Sarah lives?

KAHN: Diana [Sands] did and later Billie [Allen] did....When we did it Off-Broadway, Billie Allen insisted upon going out after the show—getting all dressed up in a red dress or something like that and leaving the theatre because of what she'd been through. She wanted to reinforce her positive image about herself when she left.

H. S.: It's always seemed to me that the play was a dramatization of a shattered head.

KAHN: Well, there is a shattered head in it, of course. The shattered head of the father which is the African mask which is also the father. It was a very personal and poetic version of a real phenomenon.

H. S.: Would actors ask you what the "funnyhouse" means?

KAHN: I think it was clear that the image of the play was that it was taking place in a kind of Coney Island Chamber of Horrors and the Funnyhouse Man (which André Gregory did in the workshop) or the Funnyhouse Woman were really her landlady and her boyfriend, and were really played like those figures that laugh in booths. So the cast and the production staff knew from the very beginning that the metaphor for the play was a Coney Island Funnyhouse....

When I first met Adrienne, instead of explaining the play to me, she brought me loads and loads of photographs and reproductions of paintings. From that I really understood what the power of the images were for her. And for some reason, even though I was a white boy from Brooklyn, I shared a lot of those understandings of the same images. But that was how she explained the play, and we never really did discuss much of the psychology.

H. S.: And you didn't feel the need for it?

KAHN: No. It seemed clear to me that everybody was an extension of herself and also a projection of her father. And the projection of her father also included the major heroes from civilization that were martyred, Lumumba and Christ. The mother projection was great heroines, romantic heroines. But they were also *all* her. And in order to kill herself, she had to kill them...or they acted upon her. So it was really an interior monologue. It seemed very Jungian to me.

H. S.: And you found a very similar thing in *The Owl Answers*?

KAHN: Yeah. I knew something from Adrienne that Clara was based on her Southern aunt. I felt that Sarah was Adrienne and I knew that Clara was her aunt. But again Adrienne's Anglophilia came through always with grace.

H. S.: She's got it. It's shocking, startling if you really—

KAHN: I thought it was very honest to present that, England being such a colonial power. It was a very honest response to power and glamour and whiteness. It was very honest about all those things which made her get undiscovered in the seventies.

H. S.: You think so?

KAHN: I went to the revival of *The Owl Answers* that Joe Papp put on, not directed by myself, and talked to a lot of the actors who were very angry about being in the play because they felt it was not presenting a positive image of blackness. I think Adrienne was severely ostracized. Her plays were considered neurotic and...not supportive of the black movement.

H. S.: Well, I teach the plays now. Most of the students are dumbfounded by *The Owl Answers* and *Funnyhouse of a Negro*. Some will suddenly, without explaining, just indicate to me that they've been thrilled. But most of the students who are much more pedestrian and prosaic do not have that response, and it's more than twenty-five years later.

KAHN: The plays are symbolic, and the working out is a clash of symbols, and there is a strong emotional connection. There is a real story in those plays that actually can be talked about—a woman who lives in a walk-up flat with a white Jewish boyfriend kills herself—that's the story. Then it's all transformed like a dream into this other story. And I always had both stories working.

H. S.: Well, there are some images and some physicality in *The Owl Answers* that I find just stunning. I don't know how you handled them.

KAHN: I had all the characters made up so that when they turned around one side of their face was black, one side of their face was white, and I think the father was something else.

H. S.: Let me just read to you:

> (The WHITE BIRD flies back into the cage, REVEREND reads smiling, the DEAD FATHER lies on cell floor. The MOTHER, now part the black mother and part the REVEREND'S WIFE in a white dress, wild kinky hair, part feathered, comes closer to CLARA.) (*Owl*, 43)[1]

Now that's very straightforward. But then there are things with respect to the chapel and with respect to physical—

KAHN: I probably didn't do those.

H. S.: Well, she falls down at the side of a burning bed.

> (...The NEGRO MAN backs further up toward the gate. SHE, fallen at the side of the Altar burning, her head bowed, both hands conceal her face, feathers fly, green lights are strong, Altar burning, WHITE BIRD laughs from the Dome. SHE WHO IS Clara who is the Bastard Who is the Virgin Mary suddenly looks like an owl and lifts her bowed head, stares into space and speaks:) Ow...oww. (FATHER rises and slowly blows out candles on bed.) (*Owl*, 45)

All that physical stuff—

KAHN: I did all that stuff, but I didn't have the dome and the chapel. We just had the bed, probably on a white floor. But we had red lights for the burning, and we had a lot of feathers which I remember I stole from

Jean Vigo's film, *Zero de Conduite*. As a matter of fact, I not only stole the feathers from *Zero de Conduite*, but I stole the Bach-Vivaldi music from the film *Les Enfants Terribles*. We had a lot of feathers in the air and then Ellen Holly was covered with feathers at the end. But I reduced a lot of Adrienne's "movie" stage directions because they were simply not possible to do on the stage and found a kind of symbolic version of them. She was writing a movie in a way.

H. S.: She has written a movie script of *Funnyhouse of a Negro*.

KAHN: But I mean, that's a movie already. I think it should have been made into a dance piece. I tried to talk John Butler into doing it once.

H. S.: That's why I also wondered about its appropriateness for the stage; it seemed to me that it goes so far off the stage in its directions. More cinematic than stageable.

KAHN: We did the dome by something representing the church. I think maybe there was a cross. But I wasn't literal.

H. S.: And you were able to satisfy her despite the fact that you weren't doing exactly as the script had stated.

KAHN: I never did the jungle scene in *Funnyhouse of a Negro*, in either of the two productions. I kept saying, "Sorry Adrienne, it just doesn't fit. It takes place in her room, and I don't know how she gets to the jungle." I was sort of literal in that way in those days. So I never did the jungle scene. I never did the Jesus search. Actually, I saw a production of it at Juilliard just a couple years ago in which there were just three or four actors; they did the jungle scene, and it was very effective. They had Sarah playing all the women except for one, and one man playing all the men. It was quite good. I kept telling Adrienne to cut the jungle scene, and she kept publishing the play with it in, and I kept not doing the jungle scene. Because I didn't see how that could be done physically; now I completely would have understood. I thought it moved away from the central metaphor which was that everything took place in Sarah's room around Sarah's bed and the Duchess of Hapsburg and the others were at Sarah's dressing table. We did white face and Bill Ritman's whole set was white, and we had all these white costumes by Willa Kim.

H. S.: In *The Owl Answers* you had to simply go both white and black.

KAHN: *The Owl Answers*—we did costumes—southern costumes.

H. S.: There's a play that you might know about Goya [*The Sleep of Reason*, by Antonio Buero Valliejo, trans. Marion Peter Holt] which takes place in Goya's head when he's about seventy-four and Goya is deaf. In the play, when the characters on the stage speak, when Goya's not there one can hear them, but when Goya is on the stage, you can't hear them because the characters are in Goya's head, but the images on the stage are done on a "cyc." Swoboda was the first to design it. With this material you have a similar kind of condition because it really is *the mind* in both cases. The images and the complexity of them and the abundance of them.

KAHN: I didn't use them all. I had to be selective. I didn't try to deliver on the stage every image that she had.

H. S.: And the play came through anyway?

KAHN: Very strongly.

I think Adrienne is a direct descendent of Lorca....Adrienne is a poet and an imagist, and I understood that. I said, "Gosh, you're a lot like Lorca and a little like Tennessee," and she said, "Those are my idols."

H. S.: In the *Orestes* and the *Electra*, of course, she's much more given to the word.

KAHN: It's very interesting. I asked her to adapt them. Then she worked. It was a very interesting job. She really cut it all the way down. A lot of actual modern Greek in it. It was quite wonderful what she did with it. She took an existing translation, and she really stripped it totally bare in her own particular way. So it read like a Kennedy play. Little sentences, repetitions. And, in a way, I did it as a very primitive play, actually, starting out. Martha Clark and I directed it. [Due to personal reasons] Martha bowed out, and another choreographer, Randolyn Zinn, came in. I explained to them, I said, everything Adrienne writes is compressed.

H. S.: And did she choose which of the *Electras* to do?

KAHN: I asked her to do the Euripides. And I wanted to put *Electra* and *Orestes* together. I wanted to put the two plays together, so it needed to be adapted. I thought what a good idea to ask Adrienne. It was a really interesting experience.

...There was quite a lot in the production at Juilliard. The first part ended with Electra [Linda Koslowski] nursing Orestes [Val Kilmen], suckling her breast, and I made Orestes the god who came at the end of the second play. Orestes appeared as Apollo but was himself in a schizophrenic state, and everybody had paint on their face, and there were very strange dances. We did a lot of rehearsal in the dark about dreams. It was quite an experience. We invented a whole new way of speaking.

H. S.: Well, it just strikes me that the stories are quite real and substantial.

KAHN: I put it in a very primitive period, and I said I wanted to do sort of prepsychological—. We had very interesting rehearsals. I mean we would rehearse rituals, dreams, in the dark. We tried to get in a different mode of thinking....It was to get away from realism and to get to what I thought were these...myths, primal myths...to get to some sort of primal response.

H. S.: Well, it's interesting you see, the Sophocles *Electra* appears to be primarily more of a mythological/sociological study whereas this [Euripides| is much more psychological. She's married, she's going to have a baby...all these realistic conditions that take place in her—

KAHN: But I also think that Euripides is much closer to original myths. The kind of raw power of Euripides is much closer to both the original myths and modern theatre. Sophocles seems to me to be more civilized, less violent. Euripides to me is much more jagged on the edge. Adrienne always understood that. I always thought the power of Adrienne's plays was the underlying myth that she tapped into—I mean, the father figure being like God and the destruction of the father or patricide...I don't think Sarah really kills her father, but in the play, she does, in a sense, kill her father, and it turns out that he's just a black man who knocks at the door. But |Adrienne| gets to the most central theme of killing the father who she makes into God |and into Patrice Lumumba|, and that's getting into some primitive myth. I've always thought that was the power of Adrienne's plays....

H. S.: Shakespeare, she talks so much about Shakespeare.

KAHN: That's why I thought the Greeks were perfect for her.

H. S.: I thought that was much to your credit.

KAHN: What I thought was infinitely stranger was that Adrienne Kennedy should work with John Lennon. I might not have made that leap. Then Adrienne and I were supposed to work on her Charlie Chaplin piece at Albany, but I went to Albany and wasn't terribly happy with the situation at Albany so I declined.

H. S.: So she is a writer to whom you not only have a connection as a director with a writer or as a sensitive human being with another sensitive human being, but you also see her as a writer whose works you take pleasure in directing.

KAHN: Oh, absolutely. I mean that one of the favorite experiences of my life is *Funnyhouse*. And that the beginning of my career was really based on those two things: *Funnyhouse* and *The Owl Answers*. Edward Albee saw *Funnyhouse* and hired me, and Joe Papp saw *The Owl Answers* and hired me, so I owe Adrienne a great deal in that sense.

H. S.: But what you just described to me was the beginning of a long, brilliant, distinguished career. You've been at Juilliard now for twenty years, which is quite a long time, and yet, you tell me that these events in the 1960s were the high points—

KAHN: But I love directing Adrienne's plays because they bring out a particular part of my imagination that I enjoy using and which is very central to me. I have had lots of high points since, fortunately—mostly with Shakespeare and Williams.

H. S.: But I teach writers, Michael, my life is devoted to teaching writers. And the most painful thing of all is to find the writers who have no director. No director discovers them. They don't discover a director, and it goes on and on and on. Once in a very great while that happens;... what happened at Yale...is that a writer did discover a director, and that really was an epiphany. It's one of the most wonderful things in the world to happen in the theatre.

KAHN: But yet when Joe [Papp] started producing Adrienne, Gerry Freedman was his director, and so he gave Adrienne's plays to Gerry. So I didn't work with Adrienne's plays for a long time, not because of anything, but because her producers had other directors to work with.

H. S.: That happened in *Dead Essex* in 1976.

KAHN: And I don't think she was as well served by more realistic directors than me.

H. S.: I don't know if she's ever been served as well.

KAHN: As the case would have it in later years, obligations and conflicting schedules would preclude me from directing her. Otherwise I'd see no reason why Adrienne and I couldn't have done all her plays, to tell you the truth...I was going to do A *Rat's Mass* in Europe for La Mama, but Ellen Stewart was unable to raise the money....

H. S.: I do think that there is something in that leap that you made with *Orestes* that I would love to see nurtured. To take a writer of that consequence and assign to that writer someone else's work, and from someone else's work to design a play, which is a wonderful project. Although there are precedents in America, most notably with O'Neill's *Mourning Becomes Electra*, there's something about the writers in America—they're very reluctant to take anybody else's material. We don't have any history here in America of taking the classics and redoing them. In France they all do that; all the writers do that. It doesn't matter who—the Orestes story was done by Sartre and that's the first thing you would do—there's no question. But in America, you know that *West Side Story* comes out of *Romeo and Juliet*, and *Mourning Becomes Electra* comes out of the Greeks, yet you have a hard time finding the other things because our writers don't cotton very well to that. And the fact that Kennedy was such a strange kind of playwright, [not necessarily mainstream] and *would* "cotton" to it—that very fact engaged me and startled me. And, of course, to come out as beautiful as it did. It's a wonderful piece of work.

KAHN: You know that when you work on a play of Adrienne's you don't rewrite. By the time the play is done by Adrienne, the play is done.

H. S.: She's a poet. That's exactly right.

KAHN: So all I did was edit sometimes, but basically the play is finished when you get it.

H. S.: You know that when O'Neill was doing *Iceman Cometh*, he was in the auditorium one day. He was pacing, and he finally shouted on the stage to Eddie Dowling, "Mr. Dowling, there's a comma in the sentence!" Of course, that's a poet's response to hear that. Most of our writers for the theatre are not like that.

KAHN: Every word for Adrienne counts. But when people ask me to describe her, I always think of a poet, with roots in our own unconscious— it's somehow her unconscious and everyone's. I think that's the power of these plays.

H. S.: But as a poet, she chooses to write in a dramatic form. She can't deal with small talk. She has a difficult time speaking on any level, but whatever she says is considered, and it is said with extreme economy. And that such a person would be writing for actors and for the theatre— that's kind of a contradiction.

KAHN: Yes. I'm glad that people recognize that. I was on a panel recently in Minneapolis, Minnesota, about women and racism....I was pretty pleased to see that this panel was based around a production of *Funnyhouse* at a feminist theatre, At the Foot of the Mountain. I was really pleased to see that people were seeing the play as politically viable and accepting it, because it was politics and commercial liability that got in the way of the real recognition of Adrienne earlier. But I think it was interesting that there was so much appreciation of Adrienne by the sort of white intellectual establishment when she first came out. And I think it was not just because she was a black writer that everyone could accept, but I think that these basic stories struck a chord in everyone even though they could not have been written by a white writer in any circumstance because the experience of the plays is about blackness.

H. S.: In a way, *Dutchman* is not as successful. *Dutchman* is really a black and white story, as primitive as it is, and the work of a poet: I mean look at the title...don't we have a poet? He's deeply involved in symbols and indirect statement as we are with anything that Adrienne Kennedy does.

Her subway is quite different from the subway of *Dutchman*.

KAHN: Yes. But it's interesting these plays were not done so far apart— *Dutchman* and *Funnyhouse of a Negro*.

H. S.: Absolutely. *Dutchman* was the next year.

KAHN: Both in Albee workshops...so I think there was a period when this kind of nonrealism was possible to do....

H. S.: Well, I'll tell you privately that in 1965 Donald Bryant organized an event in Iowa. I was there as his teacher, and he said to me he would like me to participate. I said to him, "you have to understand something, the poet is coming back into the theatre," and he laughed and laughed and laughed at me. I felt as if I was out in left field. I said, "I'm telling you things are happening in the city now, the poet is coming back into the theatre. The William Inges and those prosaic sensibilities of other writers are...not there! The poet is coming back." I was thinking, of course, of Rosalyn Drexler and Jean Claude and Sam Shepard and Rochelle Owens and Adrienne Kennedy—all those people. And they came in a surge—like a huge wave they came over us. It seems to me a source of power for whatever theatre we've had in the 1970s and 1980s.

Note

1. *The Owl Answers*, in *Adrienne Kennedy in One Act* (Minneapolis: University of Minnesota Press, 1988).

16

An Interview with Gaby Rodgers

Howard Stein

Gaby Rodgers started her acting career in the early days of television. One of her first roles was the lead on "Philco Playhouse," opposite Sydney Blament. In her fifteen years in television, she had a chance to work with some of the best directors and writers. On Broadway, she appeared in *Mr. Johnson*, *Heavenly Twins*, and *Hidden River*. She won the Theatre World Award for *Mr. Johnson*. Also, Shirley Booth gave her the Barter Theatre Award. Rodgers's directing started at the American Place Theatre, with Bruce J. Friedman's first play, *Twenty-Seven Pat O'Brien Movies*. She directed Adrienne Kennedy's *An Evening with Dead Essex* at the American Place Theatre, and *A Lesson in Dead Language* for Theatre Genesis at St. Mark's Church in the Bowery. At the Brooklyn Academy of Music, she starred in an original production of Robert Wilson's play *Golden Windows*. Recently, she directed a reading of Harry Kondoleon's play, *The Little Book of Professor Enigma*, and a play by E. L. Doctorow. Howard Stein interviewed Gaby Rodgers on October 2, 1990.

Howard Stein: How do you direct Adrienne Kennedy?
Gaby Rodgers: You let the text direct you. Kennedy's text is very dense, it's poetry. You need to give a theatre audience visual aids to help them understand. In *A Lesson in Dead Language*, the young girls wear white dresses that have red blood stains on the back. The director needs to make this symbol clear, with every possible means: actors, lights, sounds, music. Without interpretation, her plays are not quite accessible to an

audience. But Kennedy allows for interpretation. With us, she seemed to welcome it.

H. S.: It happened with your production?

RODGERS: It was a good collaboration. When we added, visually, the Stations of the Cross to *Lesson in Dead Language*, Kennedy liked the idea. When she spoke to me about the play, she stressed her religious up-bringing. She loved the ceremonies of the church. There was also fear. I can understand the ambivalence. The Bible is full of horror stories. Imagine, a father slaying his son for God. A sensitive girl like Adrienne must have experienced a lot of pain. Not only the pain that comes through religion, but the one that comes from being an outsider. How to fit in when you're made to feel that you're different from others. In an act of despair, the girl in *Funnyhouse* pulls out her kinky black hair.

H. S.: In *Funnyhouse of a Negro*, a young black head is shattered in a black and white society.

RODGERS: She places these traumas in a surreal setting. The emotion lies underneath the images. It's there, the feelings, and strongly so. The director must convey these feelings with everything she's got, all the tools.

H. S.: It seemed to me that there were special visual effects that you tried to capture in your production of *Lesson*.

RODGERS: Absolutely, close to film. The piece was designed frame by frame. Like a story board. Just working with the actors won't get you there.

H. S.: The plays that you directed were A *Lesson in Dead Language* and An *Evening with Dead Essex*. In *Lesson*, was there an effect which you were seeking with the last moment of the play which involves the pupil and the white dog? I am interested in knowing what final effect you want to achieve with your audience. When you are directing a piece like *Essex*, which is not a conventional play at all—

RODGERS: You drive towards the final image of the play, the epiphany. *Lesson* was the terror of a black girl, in a white world. The nun, the teacher of the children, was portrayed as a big, white dog. To show the children's terror of this big white dog/nun, it spoke through an amplification system, and was larger than life, towering over these little girls in their white dresses, drilling them in catechism. It was an intimidation that I found easy to understand. A lot of our early education is a terror trip. The little girls spoke in unison like a corps de ballet, or chorus. Their individuality was practically obliterated.

H. S.: Well then let me ask you, when you were casting a play such as that, what did you look for?

RODGERS: Those were the days of ensemble work—the Open Theater, Grotowsky. We did exercises in preparation for Adrienne's text such as sound and movement exercises. We looked for actors experienced in ensemble work. You always need good actors, of course. We found actors who could do choral reading and singing and chanting. My collaborator was Lamar Alford, a gospel musician.

H. S.: Kennedy's plays have a haunted quality. How does the haunted person externalize the quality of being haunted? How is it in her plays?

RODGERS: The language is often repetitive and circular. This repetition gives the text a traumatized and haunted air.

H. S.: That's a principle in her writing. But that's also a poetic principle as well as a musical one; you have variations on a theme....

RODGERS: Yes, her work lacks relief. Her plays are always short. She must feel instinctively that this density can't be endured for hours.

H. S.: Terrified of oblivion.

RODGERS: A terrified frame of mind. The plays have no linear plot. The terrorizing of the children is shown when the Big White Dog slams a ruler to punctuate the lessons. In our production, we amplified that sound as well.

H. S.: I never have associated Catholicism with Adrienne Kennedy.

RODGERS: There are several religious symbols in her plays. In *Lesson*, there are the statues of the saints. We had living statues. We set them in the Stations of the Cross. Kennedy asked that I go and look at one of her favorite churches on upper Broadway. Church gave her solace as a child and stirred her imagination. Also the black/white conflict entered her religious experience. Growing up as a black woman in a white, male-powered society. In our production, the Big White Dog had a male voice.

H. S.: I did want to get on to *An Evening with Dead Essex* because what interests me is that *Essex* is a piece of work which is quite different from other work Kennedy has done.

RODGERS: Yes, it's in a pseudo-documentary style—with newspaper clippings, stills, and film. We did this play in the basement of the American Place Theatre, at the height of black pride and awareness. It is her first play based on a news incident, the shooting of a black man on the roof of a Howard Johnson motel. She imagines what this man's frame of mind must have been like. It is a violent black experience as seen through the eyes of a black woman poet.

H. S.: But it's based upon a real condition and obviously her feelings about his murder were quite different from the feelings in A *Rat's Mass* or in *Funnyhouse of a Negro* or A *Lesson in Dead Language*. Therefore, let me ask you yet one more thing. There you are a white woman, dealing with the stories of a black man, in addition to everything else.

RODGERS: We were seven black men, one black woman, and me. The story is about a black man. We talked about a white director, me, doing a black theatre piece. We talked about it through opening night. The cast would say, "What do you know about our experience?" I would say, "Teach me what I don't know." Their anger upset me, but we were able to work it all out. I'm proud of that. It was a successful experience in theatre and living in this world together. Everyone brought their own experience to this play, and that's what Kennedy had in mind, anyway. She's a poet who writes about her inner experience. She's not a propagandist.

H. S.: What do you think the actors wanted to teach me, as an audience member?

RODGERS: About their monumental rage and pride. No laughter, no relief. Absolutely no relief. Dense like poetry.

H. S.: The accounting of the forces that help define and determine this young man. Those forces are one of Adrienne's subjects? How people got that way?

RODGERS: Yes, a real experience portrayed by a surrealist.

H. S.: That's the question. I don't know what kind of logic.

RODGERS: It is the logic of dreams, I understand that logic.

H. S.: Instinctively?

RODGERS: I can feel her work. It's in symbols and associations.

H. S.: Peter Brook said the purpose of art is to make the invisible visible. And she's trying to do that very thing....

RODGERS: Yes, she also shows that fine line between sanity and insanity. That moment when someone goes over the rim.

H. S.: Do you think that there was an explanation for Essex in the play?

RODGERS: No. What we went on were the feelings. The images. The accumulation of images. We aimed for a total experience, not a treatise.

H. S.: That's very contemporary.

RODGERS: Kennedy as a writer was way ahead; the work is not long. That's why it is difficult to produce commercially. *Lesson* ran a half hour, that's all. Yet it was a full and memorable experience. You can have that in a half hour, and be bored in a three hour show, we all know that.

H. S.: You can go to fifteen minutes of Beckett, like *Rockaby*, and you have the whole evening.

RODGERS: The Kennedy images stay in your mind. People remember those little girls in their bloodstained dresses. It's haunting.

H. S.: Haunting is not the same as remembering. There are only some people who are haunted. There's a book called *The Haunted Heroes of Eugene*

O'Neill. And the third play in the Mourning Becomes Electra is called The Haunted. Being haunted is a special quality. It's powerful. It doesn't fade into a memory. It's pure…there's a purity to it.

RODGERS: And we were able to do that with her work. You can't do that with a commercial show for Broadway.

H. S.: You come from a very visual background, a very artistic background; you've been raised on paintings, all sorts of visual objects, whereas the people in your cast were interested in the statement, more than the image.

RODGERS: I have a visual background. The African-American experience often is with rhythm and music. We used it all.

H. S.: You expect the audience to accumulate moments rather than go through an experience.

RODGERS: You need to understand that about her work. It takes teamwork and collaboration.

H. S.: That's exploration, and the whole idea of accumulation. In Strindberg's A Dream Play (1888), Indra's daughter says to her father (she, who is outside the human world and living in a transcendental sphere), "Why do human beings complain so much?" Her father says, "Why don't you go down and find out?" So she goes down to earth and after a significant scene that she observes, she says, "Man is to be pitied." Then she sees another scene and another scene; after each scene she says, "Man is to be pitied." When she finally says "Man is to be pitied" at the end of the play, all those "pities" have accumulated! The same words, exactly the same words are said each time, but the accumulation hits the audience in such a fashion that one leaves the theatre not knowing how one will ever recover from the amount of pity that human beings deserve in the nature of existence. That goes back. It's a hundred years now, and we're just beginning to get it.

RODGERS: I've always been attracted to that kind of theatre. Not everything on the surface. It's certainly not a sitcom.

H. S.: Because you're very moved by that kind of experience, the image experience and the accumulation of those stimuli which is not necessarily literal. There is something about the literal stimuli which can be dealt with in a different fashion, which can be dismissed somehow.

RODGERS: Her symbols are complex; sight and sound help to make them clearer to the audience.

H. S.: But of course, poetry is all verbal images. The purpose of words is to create a picture and music—for example, that group of poems of Joyce called "Chamber Music." Strindberg wrote poems and chamber plays. I mean, you are either moving in the music or you're moving in the painting, but there's no other way we're going to feel what is pure than through that of language or words. One of the things that you try to do with words is to make them as absolutely precise as possible.... Conversely you get into silence, which is exactly what Beckett did. We discovered that the pause in Beckett is so thunderous that you'll hear it greater than you would hear any other sound. It's terrifically paradoxical, very ironic.

RODGERS: Chamber music is a fine concept. Her words are also very precise. Everything in her work must be precise. A little like Robert Wilson's work. She's also a woman with a great imagination.

H. S.: *Essex* is down-to-earth.

RODGERS: Is it?

H. S.: What was the reaction to *Essex*?

RODGERS: We got a good review from Michael Smith at the *Village Voice* and the late Harold Clurman said it was the best thing he had ever seen at American Place Theatre. And why did they put us in the basement and not on the main stage? The basement caused a lot of flack from the cast. I myself rather liked it. It was suited to the problem of the play. Outcasts. And we had the freedom to do as we pleased. It helped to make it a strong piece. We did it on a shoestring and all by ourselves.

H. S.: Do you think that Adrienne is interested in a person being an outsider and, as you said, that delicate line between sanity and insanity?

RODGERS: I do. In *Funnyhouse of a Negro*, Sarah, in utter despair, pulls out her hair, like someone possessed. Adrienne shows you how she got that way.

H. S.: Do you think that she does that in *Essex*? Did you have the material to work with in *Essex*?

RODGERS: The structure of the work is very sparse. It requires an intuitive approach. You can't mount this text in a literal way. It won't get you there.

H. S.: Pictures? What else?

RODGERS: Everything you've got. Mary Alice, a very fine actress, now on Broadway, sang a song. She played Essex's mother. Her singing told the whole story. I miss that period in the theatre when we could work together and build a piece in this way. It wasn't all money and business.

H. S.: La Mama wasn't all money and business; Ellen Stewart went past the limitations, and she never denied being a black woman.

RODGERS: Yes, people like them are able to reach out to all people— Ellen and Adrienne. As a black or white person, you can be moved by the work.

H. S.: In *Funnyhouse of a Negro*, Sarah is going through a horror when she tells those long stories. Those are packed with feelings that she has of rage, misery, betrayal, anger, resentment, terror...deception in a world around her that threatens her. She's caught in a madhouse. But the world is not as crazy as [Sarah] is. Now maybe the world is the crazy place and she's sane.

RODGERS: I'll tell you...with this dense text of hers, what comes across is what it feels like to be a black woman in white America.

H. S.: You said that at the end of your production of *Essex* the audience was mesmerized. What caused it to be spellbinding? Was Essex seen as a victim?

RODGERS: And outsider. And Essex is also special.

H. S.: In that he did something that someone else didn't do?

RODGERS: He's special in that he had to make a statement.

H. S.: Do you think there is an explanation for Essex in the play?

RODGERS: She leaves it for you to decide. She doesn't moralize.

H. S.: Yes, you fill in the spaces yourself.

RODGERS: She's created her own kind of theatre. Like Strindberg did. And Artaud.

H. S.: You can't find a model for her.

17

An Interview with Gerald Freedman

Paul K. Bryant-Jackson

Gerald Freedman is regarded nationally for productions of classic drama, musicals, operas, new plays, and television specials. As a leading director of Joseph Papp's New York Shakespeare Festival from 1960 to 1971 (the last four years as artistic director), he directed Adrienne Kennedy's *Cities in Bezique (Two Journeys of the Mind in the Form of Theatre Pieces): The Owl Answers* and A *Beast's Story* (1964), coartistic Director of John Houseman's The Acting Company (1974–77), and artistic director of the American Shake- speare Theatre. An Obie Award winner, Freedman made theatre history with his premiere of the landmark rock musical, *Hair*, which opened Papp's Public Theater in 1967. Freedman made his San Francisco Opera debut staging the world premiere of *Angel of Repose* by Andrew Imbrie. In San Francisco, he also collaborated on several operas with the Cleveland Orchestra's music director, Christoph von Dohnayi, and his wife, soprano Anja Silja. Freedman serves as artistic director of the Great Lakes Theatre Festival, Cleveland, Ohio. He has taught at the Yale School of Drama and the Juilliard School.[1]

(The following is from the director's notebook for *The Ohio State Murders*, Great Lakes Theatre Festival, June 16–17, 1990.)

I have directed and produced two of Adrienne Kennedy's plays and seen or read most of her other plays. She seems to be a poet who writes in play form. Her works are very concentrated and condensed to an essence. She deals in symbols and imagery and rhythm as a writer of poems does, except that she uses and suggests the use of visual elements and sound, in addition to words and verbal images.

This creates a richly layered and textured effect in the theatre. I liken it to collage in visual art: an assemblage of fragments in a fresh or unexpected juxtaposition that creates a new object, perceived and experienced on its own, and yet made up of associative elements that have inherent emotive values from their prior context.

So how do you go about producing and directing an Adrienne Kennedy play? You throw out the rules and "listen" to the text with "all" your senses. You let it work on your unconscious and learn to trust an imaginative level beyond the logical and rational. The theatre experience becomes more than the sum of its parts, not necessarily a linear progression.

I choose the parts from clues in Adrienne's text. The scene changes often. Do you bring scenery on? Do you use literal pictures of buildings and locations? On the other hand, the text talks about the importance of symbols. How do you make an audience aware of their meanings? The "play" [The Ohio State Murders] exists in the present and past. Do you suggest this with body language? Color? And there are many, many more choices on every page.

I assemble the parts. I intuitively put them together guided by Adrienne's script. I try not to be judgmental in any way. I do not change a word of the text or rearrange its order. This means that until all the parts of the "collage" come together, I have no idea what the whole will look like or reveal. As I am writing these notes, I do not have the answers. Only the vision.

I will know more when we put all the parts together with an audience.

On June 16, 1990, I interviewed Gerald Freedman prior to the opening of the workshop production of *The Ohio State Murders* at the Great Lakes Theater Festival.

PAUL JACKSON: You seem to have an affinity with Kennedy. You directed *Cities in Bezique*—

GERALD FREEDMAN: Which was really two of her earlier plays. [*Cities in Bezique*] was the title to the third play.

P. J.: What draws you to her work?

FREEDMAN: Mystery, imagery, flights of imagination, lack of cliché and structure, the unexpected, and the surprise of it. Kennedy makes me work harder, think harder, and go into another part of myself, and I enjoy that. I use less, I think, of my intellect, in some way, and more of my instinct.

P. J.: Let me show you something which will probably bring back lots of memories. It's a program from the original *Cities in Bezique*. You have here at the end of the program this wonderful director's note.[2] Do you remember all of that?

FREEDMAN: No, but I'm still saying that about Kennedy. I wrote the director's note [for *Murders*] and yet, it is not quite so different.

P. J.: You say that Adrienne Kennedy does not create theatre. What is it, then, that Adrienne has created?

FREEDMAN: I say, some people question whether it is theatre, but, in the sense that we were just talking about it, for example, it doesn't have obvious action; characters don't interact in a linear way; it seems to be fragmented: bits and pieces of scenes that suggest relationships. So, it certainly is theatre; we've done it numerous times; the audiences come. So, I meant it in a kind of rhetorical way. The comment has to be examined because really it says, "What is theatre?" Not, are Adrienne's plays theatre, but really, what is theatre? We would say the same thing about Robert Wilson, "Is it theatre?"

P. J.: Exactly. That's where I wanted to go. These program notes were written in 1968—

FREEDMAN: I will stand by those remarks. I would still say the same thing.

P. J.: What was it [theatre] in 1968, before performance art?

FREEDMAN: Thank you, I am glad you remember that....

P. J.: Before all of those things, it seems to me. In retrospect, what we have here with Adrienne is somebody that is really working in a performance genre long before it becomes—

FREEDMAN: Yeah, before the critics gave it a name, a jargon. And that is what I thought was totally original.

P. J.: And you, being on a top of it, said that Adrienne's plays "require new technology, new answers." When you say that, if you were to go back—I am not sure as to when computerized lightboards and all these wonderful kinds of things came into the theatre—would you have staged [*The Owl Answers* and *A Beast's Story*] any differently than originally?

FREEDMAN: No, it's not a thought I have because I don't even remember what I did. Maybe I would do something different now if I was presented with this same script. And as for the new technologies, thank you very much. [Laughter.] Today [in reference to a rehearsal of *The Ohio State Murders*] we are using visuals, and the technology didn't work, and the electronic board kept coming up with signals that we couldn't figure out. So, we threw out [the new technology] and we did it lit with just work lights, and it still worked. [The new technology] enhances it and would help it, but I would use whatever is at my fingertips. I mean, Adrienne's plays can be done without that, too, I think they can be done in a very spare way. Just use your imagination, as I think she does. If you have other technologies at your fingertips that are available, then you would use them—like lights.[3] Yet, I think you could do the plays without them.

P. J.: As I read her work, especially *The Owl Answers* and *A Beast's Story*, and refer to a copy of a review which talks about your staging, the review mentions the kinds of lights that you used and projections. As a result of this review, and in light of what we have been saying, do you see anything in Kennedy, as a director, which leads you toward the epic, alienation, or a Brechtian kind of staging that invites the use of projections or things of that nature which you continue to employ with Kennedy?

FREEDMAN: The plays are cool, but they deal with very hot material that is presented in a very cool manner, almost objective manner. It is the accumulation of words and images that makes the play hot and your, or the audience's, imagination. So, in that sense the plays are alienating, in a kind of technical way. I don't think that Brecht is alienating, either. Those devices, now, are very powerful imaginative tools, not limiting tools. They distance only in a conventional old-fashioned manner.

P. J.: I know exactly what you are saying. It's all very exciting. The staging I saw at the Public, and I think that the bird was placed in midair....

FREEDMAN: The inspiration came from a sculpture that I saw in the Modern Museum of Art. I think it was a very early Giacometti sculpture and not anything that he pursued. But when I saw that piece of sculpture, I said, "That is the environment that *The Owl Answers* should be in." Then Ming Cho Lee created his own sense of that space. But that sculpture was the inspiration to me. And then again, Kennedy needs levels. She has levels going on, and in that, the angel is like a fragment of a fresco and that is what made me think it should be elevated in some way. I could do it many different ways depending on what materials were available. Unfortunately you could only get to produce them once; nobody would let you do them again. [Laughter.] I'd like to try them one after the other in different manners.

P. J.: There are many questions regarding the various versions of the script of *A Beast's Story*. The printed script that we have for *A Beast's Story* is different from that indicated in the program for *Cities in Bezique*; there were more beasts in the performance than are indicated as dramatis personae in the published version. You added some characters?

FREEDMAN: Really! I don't think so.

P. J.: Yes. Let me show you something.

FREEDMAN: Let me see it.

P. J.: Now this is a printed script.[4] Adrienne dismisses the play and would rather not talk about it. Now, when I reread the play over today, it seemed

The New York Shakespeare Festival production of *The Owl Answers* in *Cities in Bezique*, January–March, 1969, Gerald Freedman, director; Joseph Papp, producer. Photo by George E. Joseph.

very natural that you would add these extra characters because the play has a very Greek feel about it.

FREEDMAN: In my memory they were indicated. No, I don't think that I added them. I think that they were indicated in a play script [referring to a photograph with costumes from A Beast's Story], but you see those costumes were never used. I did exactly what Adrienne asked for and, when we got them on stage, they didn't add to the play. They subtracted; they really were "beasts." [Laughter.] So, we did it in rehearsal clothes which made the desired effect. Now this [indicating the Samuel French script] says "that the Beasts are real people, a black family. They perhaps could have an artificial power, perhaps artificial pale eyes which should be subtle." I don't think this is the script I read. I don't know if the production script was printed or not but this is not the script that I read. Just the title page, anyway.

P. J.: In reference to the staging of Beast's, there seems to be a kind of Greek approach you took; there seems to have been a chanting that you asked the actors to do in that production.

FREEDMAN: I don't remember. Images, projections, came from the way that the piece was outlined. I tried to do exactly what she says, "Flat means bright and sky means black." So that suggested to me children's drawings, like kids do. And that got me to thinking about...maybe I was just looking through some material of schizophrenics' drawings which are childlike. Maybe it was the drawing of schizophrenic children who worked out their emotional problems in art therapy. And so I used that, those kinds of images which seemed appropriate to the story. Now, because I did it in a three-sided theatre, we had three screens that were showing different images all the time, but it was all related to the text.

P. J.: You have directed opera.

FREEDMAN: Yes.

P. J.: Would you like to talk about Kennedy's dramaturgy in relation to an operatic form, in terms of the layering of the music?

FREEDMAN: Maybe that's why I have an affinity for it. I find it very musical, and she always is calling for music in some way and imagery.

P. J.: I guess, as a director, it would be fair to state that at least in these plays that there's a sort of motific structure.

FREEDMAN: What?

P. J.: A motific structure like Wagner where Kennedy repeats herself and it comes back like—

FREEDMAN: Yes, she does that.

P.J.: As a director, how do you handle, in Kennedy, moving from an original theme and then elaborating upon it?

FREEDMAN: Just try to repeat images. In this production of *Ohio State Murders*, I keep bringing in the character Robert Hampshire, even though he is not indicated in the script. He leaves the scene and looks back at her. Like the character of David, who becomes important, I give him some entrances that she hasn't indicated. First, from a distance and then a little closer and closer as he is coming closer in her life, which is like all these motifs. So I am trying to do visually what she is doing in her language. I try to reinforce that. Even though she doesn't say, "I want this guy to appear," that's what I pick up on from Kennedy's script. You just have to, as I said in these programs, listen to her with all your senses. You can't just use your brain, your intellect. You can't just use your ears to hear; you have to use your eyes to hear in a sense. In her autobiography, she gives the same importance to a philosopher, like Plato, as she does to Bette Davis.

P. J.: Yes she does.

FREEDMAN: And it's all very open, she has a very spacious imagination, and you have to bring that same openness to the material rather than trying to make something conventional out of it. When you let yourself be open to it, a lot of layers become apparent, and I am not even sure that Adrienne is conscious of it. I don't mean to do a disservice to her; she writes on an intuitive level and that is what happens.

P. J.: In regard to *The Ohio State Murders*, did you make any sort of additions?

FREEDMAN: Well, there are these images that I have added, and there were particularly a couple of phrases that I had characters repeat which she didn't indicate: "the illusion of truth."

P. J.: "The illusion of truth?"

FREEDMAN: "The illusion of truth," or "the illusion of chance," one of those phrases, and then another one, "the net closes." These are quotes from [Thomas] Hardy which is what the play is about. I thought they needed extra emphasis; so, I had the characters repeat them, all three, because it affects all three of them: the teacher, Robert Hampshire, the student and the elder Suzanne Alexander, and the boyfriend David Alexander. They each bring a different resonance to the same words, as does the audience. You know, it's in this piece.

And another one of the premises of this piece is, "What gave rise to your violent imagery?" And so I reemphasized ideas like that. So that the audience could keep track of them, to discover what the play was all about. So I had many images to develop like "watching the battleship the 'Potemkin.'" The characters talk about dismemberment, smashing. I bring that imagery up on the stage so the audience can see, and keep tying together, where her violent imagery comes from, and why she's attracted to these things. So those were directorial things. Again, I'm just doing what I think she wanted to do. I take it all from the text.

P. J.: Did you ever read a copy of the original *Cities of Bezique*?

FREEDMAN: Of course I did, yes. A lot of it was images. I don't quite remember the text—the images. I thought I could do a wonderful piece of it in a darkened room with a slot where one person could look through, and I could change images to do this piece. However, it didn't become practical for the Public Theater to do it. It would have been a wonderful performance piece, but I never got a chance to do it the way, I think, she wrote it. But the title was so fabulous, *Cities of Bezique*, that I decided to do these two plays under that title. *The Owl Answers* had been done before, but A *Beast's Story* had never been done. It had been commissioned by Lincoln Center, but it had never been performed. But *Cities of Bezique*—you know Bezique is a card game.

P. J.: I did not know that.

FREEDMAN: Yeah, it's a card game of chance and so her text actually had pictures in it. And cards turned over, and they made an interesting piece. I would have loved to do it, but I don't know a theatre company that could afford to do it. Maybe a museum can.

P. J.: Maybe a National Theatre Museum. Earlier you mentioned that you did not use Theoni Aldredge's original costumes as described in Kennedy's text and that you used rehearsal clothes instead. What sort of choices did you make?

FREEDMAN: Theoni edited the costumes, and they just looked like rehearsal clothes. Adrienne had written in the text that the beasts had long golden hair and that their bodies were covered with fur or something like that. We did it, and it came out looking pretty strange. The characters in the costumes looked like a lot of—well—they were "Smurfs." I said, "No, this can't be right; this is hurting the material." When Adrienne came to see it in the rehearsal, she agreed. So I just went back to rehearsal clothes, and it was very powerful, very powerful.

P. J.: Were the critics accepting of it?

FREEDMAN: They ranged the whole gamut. I think a lot of people did not know what they were seeing. Nor did they really realize that what they were watching was something which heretofore had no definition. Therefore I found that the journalists tended to do what they always do in that situation. They were either very guarded in their response or they dismissed it. I think at that point [in 1969], she was years ahead of us.

P. J.: Where do you think Adrienne's dramaturgy is going now?

FREEDMAN: Adrienne's writing is still not quite like anybody's. She's totally unique. She goes her own way. They are such evocative pieces that are so much fun for me to work on. I don't know what they're like for an audience to come in and see, you know.

P. J.: Now that we have the genre of performance art, it seems to have helped audiences approach Kennedy because we now are more open as audience members. We don't expect things the way we did previously in the theatre or from the theatre. In regard to *The Ohio State Murders*, it's sort of a narrative image-making without the classic antagonist/protagonist conflict that demands that we wait for the last curtain to get it resolved.

FREEDMAN: I always think of Adrienne's pieces as dance pieces. And so I feel like, in a sense, a choreographer, but I'm not just talking about movements, stage movements; it's choreographing impressions. Rhythm has a lot to do with communicating and that I like. I like the way that her scripts come to me rather than the printed versions. They tell me things; they tell me how her mind works. Just like the unique format of her autobiography; I mean that page "setup" is all-important to the information.

P. J.: You know, I bought a book about two days ago, when I first arrived here [in Cleveland] at the Cleveland Museum, *Ancestral Legacy*. It's about the African influence in African-American art. And it talks about the use of all of the arts in African rituals. The mask, the music, and all the components involved in the process of moving the audience/participant toward another frame of reality/consciousness. I see where Kennedy is connected to it. Ten years ago, I think I would have tried to synthesize Kennedy to a Western aesthetic, and she works well in that context. Yet, when you talk about African influences, it becomes exciting theatre.

FREEDMAN: Yeah. I think, if that's true, it would be very unselfconscious on the part of Adrienne.

Hazel Medina, who is the elder Suzanne in *The Ohio State Murders* and knows Adrienne's work well, likens the part to the African storyteller [the Griot], which is a tradition. And, of course, there is every bit of that. And I, as a director, am sitting there. Just as when somebody tells you a story, interestingly, you create images in your head; that's what I try to get on stage—these images that the stories put into my mind.

P. J.: I have a theory that there is a continuum. Adrienne talks about playwriting and making plays from dreams. And I believe that a continuum exists within the subconscious and links African-Americans to Africa. Kennedy, on some very mystical level, is in touch with that continuum. And I think that's a unique aspect of her writing, and it shows itself in her productions. The storyteller/Griot aspect that you talked about in the performance is a manifestation of this continuum.

On another level, I so marvel at her ability to understate the action. Three hours after I saw *The Ohio State Murders* yesterday afternoon, I was walking in the park and, all of a sudden, the images started baring themselves....

FREEDMAN: That's great.

P. J.: Of course, I'm slow.

FREEDMAN: No, I think that the play is too rich. I think that is a very wonderful response and a good response and not a slow response. And I would hope, to me, that is the perfect response. That the play keeps coming back to you, and you re-review it, you re-play it, in your own way. I think that's great. I would feel that it means that it was successful.

Notes

1. Biography adapted from the Great Lakes Theatre Festival biography, used with permission of Gerald Freedman, artistic director.

2. From Gerald Freedman's "Director's Notes," New York Shakespeare Festival, Public Theater, 1968–69 Season, *Cities in Bezique (Two Journeys of the Mind in the Form of Theater Pieces)*:

Adrienne Kennedy is a poet of the theater. She does not deal in story, character and event as a playwright. She deals in image, metaphor, essence and layers of consciousness. She uses theater materials to create a poem constructed of complex emotions and layers of time and reality that create a prism of refraction—story, event and character filter through by indirection, impression, and consciousness on the edge of awareness. The communication is not direct or simple.

I sometimes question whether it is theater. Then why do it? Adrienne Kennedy uses theater materials—actors, lights, sound, movement, masks, music, words. She requires new solutions and new techniques. The director and actor and other theater technicians are forced to search for new ways, to stretch their talents and skills in an expanded mind, a stretched imagination—a new theatrical experience.

At a later date (February 12, 1991), Freedman elaborated on his discussion of Kennedy's theatre to include *She Talks to Beethoven* with the following remarks:

In *She Talks to Beethoven*, Adrienne brings together Afro-American poetess, Suzanne Alexander, who is living in Accra, Ghana, in 1961 soon after independence has been won. Beethoven is there also. We hear snatches of Ghanese string music juxtaposed against Beethoven's music for *Fidelio*, which he is composing on his pianoforte and eventually conducting in public performances. Suzanne and Beethoven share anxieties and fears and physical disabilities. They are mutually pained by the imagined or real loss of loved ones. Beethoven's *Fidelio* libretto and music are echoed in passages of Afro-American poetry. The resonance of wars for freedom fought and won in 1805 and 1961 are mingled in the audience's imagination. It is all strangely unsettling and dream-like. Who but Adrienne Kennedy could create this extraordinary and yet quite normal-seeming confluence of people and patterns?

3. Although Freedman speaks about the concerns of the visuals and the electronic lightboards, the production that I witnessed on June 16, 1990, appeared to have overcome those obstacles.

4. The difference between the Samuel French script and the dramatis personae in the program at the Public Theater is primarily one of numbers of characters. There are more characters, potentially choruslike, listed as part of the performance script.

18

An Interview with Billie Allen

Paul K. Bryant-Jackson and Lois More Overbeck

On February 22, 1990, Bryant-Jackson and Overbeck interviewed Billie Allen, who created the role of Sarah in the performance of *Funnyhouse of a Negro* (1964) produced by Joseph Papp and directed by Michael Kahn. She also directed the play at the New York School of the Arts (1989).

Billie Allen began her career as a classically trained dancer and performed in Broadway musicals, television specials, concerts, and opera here and in Europe. Along with her role in *Funnyhouse of a Negro*, she is remembered as an actress for her performance in *A Raisin in the Sun* on Broadway and in *Every Night when the Sun Goes Down* at the American Place Theatre.

As associate artistic director of the AMAS Repertory Theatre, she directed many musicals, including *Miss Ethel Waters* and *The Crystal Tree*, with music by her husband, Luther Henderson. She directed *Brothers* by Kathleen Collins as a National Endowment for the Arts fellow for the Women's Project at the American Place Theatre (1984–85). She is associate director and coauthor of *Bearden on Bearden*, a film on the life and work of Romare Bearden, shown periodically on PBS and as an integral part of the retrospective exhibit of his life's work. At the George Street Theatre, she developed as a musical and directed *Little Ham*, a play by Langston Hughes, which will be presented in London (1992). As a member of the directors' unit of the Actors Studio, Allen has worked on a production with Noise, an avant-garde theatre in Tokyo (1989).

216

PAUL JACKSON: How did you happen to get the part [of Sarah in *Funnyhouse of a Negro*]?

BILLIE ALLEN: I remember exactly how it happened. I'd been acting for some time and someone called me, I think Michael Kahn, and arranged a meeting with Adrienne.

They sent me the play, *Funnyhouse*, to read, and it was a little strange at first. Then I read that line, "My mother...went to school in Atlanta."[1] I knew exactly who the character was, what she was. [Motioning to a picture in her apartment:] See that picture there, all those women finished Spelman. Four generations and the one on this side was in the first graduating class. She was a slave.

So, when I met Adrienne, she looked very, very remote [and] shy, and she said, "What do you think of it?" And I said, "Well I think we should buy her a straightening comb and do another play." I was laughing and just teasing because I was so moved about this play. And I couldn't begin by saying, well, "I was so moved by your play." She was a bit surprised but when she saw me laugh, she started laughing, and I said that my mother had finished school in Atlanta and that is when she said, "You don't do this and you don't do that because I am from Atlanta." [And then I said,] "We don't do that. I don't care what these other people's children do. We don't do that."

For me the whole play was a catharsis for my life. I was very disciplined. I began as a classically trained dancer, so I was very disciplined. I had been working with Lee Strasberg and we had been digging around here and digging around there, but I'd never been that deep.

LOIS OVERBECK: This play was demanding, then.

ALLEN: It was really very demanding. I couldn't do anything else but that play. We did it twice a night, since it was short and the union did not realize how demanding it was.

P. J.: [You mentioned your work with Strasberg] and that you were a dancer. Do you think [in] going that deep that your focus was a combination of the mental and the physical?

ALLEN: Definitely a combination, because I remember Jerry Robbins [Jerome Robbins] came to see the play and thought it was kind of a ballet, because in order to physicalize certain things you just let the body go with the moaning or the chanting.

P. J.: Did you find that you had to create a whole new kind of body vocabulary?

ALLEN: Well, no, just understanding Sarah. Understanding her created a different kind of body for me because she was very depressed, [and] did not have very much of a certain kind of self-esteem, yet, she has a certain fantasy, and in her fantasy she was chatting with those queens, and [in acting the part] you have your back arched and you have your fan and your airs, and that was wonderful.

L. O.: So you needed your body.

ALLEN: Oh yes.

L. O.: It wasn't really done all in your mind, although it was all in the lines.

ALLEN: But I felt I was so open. I became so vulnerable that I had to be very careful with my friends.

P. J.: What did the director have you doing on the stage after Sarah's long speeches?

ALLEN: She's in her room, she imagines the landlady is talking about her so she's listening. She's onstage and she is listening thinking this is an imaginary thing in her head. So she's listening at the drape and at the window.

L. O.: So she's moving, she's listening, and she's active.

ALLEN: Yes. She's very active. Sarah is trying to sleep, and these people are bothering her. She's in her bed or on her bed; I remember the bed was a raked bed, it was a hard raked platform with covers and I had to really struggle to not slide down and to keep in touch with that bed.

P. J.: In what other roles that you have played, could you see that sort of catharsis?

ALLEN: None. None.

P. J.: So, it was really a unique experience.

ALLEN: Yes. I don't get rid of it. And yet, when I think of working with it again, I have to always decide if I want to go to *that place*, even as a director. Well, I think you have to go there, there's no other thing to do and if you don't then you don't have anything, because that's what it is. During this time, I was seeing a therapist. I remember saying to him that I was going to do [the play] and he had to support me and that was that. And when he came to see the play, he came many times to see the play, he agreed that he knew that I had to do it. And he agreed that it was a very, very difficult thing to do, because even after you got it, and you could pull away from it, you still had to go to *that place*.

P. J.: [As a young "method" actress you might have felt the necessity to physically go to *that place*. Do you think that if now if you were to recreate Sarah, it would be the same type of experience or would you have the sort of mechanism to say "I'm going to draw this aesthetic line?"]

ALLEN: You think you have to go there. You think that you have to commit suicide every night. But by the end of the run, I knew that I did not have to do that.

P. J.: So then there was a growth process.

ALLEN: Oh, a wonderful growth process. I knew I wasn't going to put myself through that. I knew the audience had to go through it. I did *not* have to go through it, but I had to lead them to it. I loved that, but it was so frustrating because [just about the time] when I got to that point, we finished.

What interests me is that some people got very angry about this play. Some black people, some white people, especially some black people because they felt it was denigrating of blacks. They felt that, "Black man, black man, I should never have let a black man put his hands on me, the wild black beast raped me and now my skull is shining" [*Funnyhouse*, 4]. They felt, "Oh God, that's such a put-down to black men," when it really wasn't. But the words say, that it's my "nigger" mother and my "nigger" father and "niggers" this and "niggers" that, but it was her [Sarah's] psychotic anger. What [the play is] so clearly about [is] the depth of the damage of institutionalized racism.

L. O.: It could be said that white culture so "over-determines" her [Sarah], that she is left with lots of shells—

ALLEN: With nothing—

L. O.: But the more radically politicized critics at that time were very critical—

ALLEN: Oh, very critical.

L. O.: —of her work as being personal, and therefore not committed.

ALLEN: Oh, very critical. And they were critical of me, because that was before people let their hair go and do all kinds of wonderful Afros.

L. O.: I have one question. [In *Funnyhouse*] the heads keep getting dropped; how did that work?

ALLEN: We didn't drop heads. Nor did ravens fly.

L. O.: What did you do?

ALLEN: Well everyone painted on a mask and Lumumba's split skull—

P. J.: There were times when bald heads appear.

L. O.: Bald heads appear, and there is a mask.

ALLEN: Yes, a mask that's carried on a stick or bald heads may be lowered from a slide or something like that. But the whole thing is so visual. William Ritman did the sets for this production and his production was stark white: a stark white raked stage and a white grayish bed. I still have two or three black slips that I bought for *Funnyhouse*.

L. O.: When you directed *Funnyhouse* at New York University, how did you approach the staging of the play, particularly the jungle scene?

ALLEN: I thought I needed a choreographer, so I called up Louis Johnson. When I finished doing it, he said, "Oh girl, that is perfect." [The other characters]…just had to circle and countercircle trying to get her [Sarah] to kill herself. Chanting to her, egging her on, trying to get her to kill herself. The way I saw it—the only thing I can think of is Blanche DuBois |in...| her fragility, her vulnerability, |and| what she is trying to cover, |and| what she wants.

P. J.: What process did you use with your actors to develop character?

ALLEN: Well, we did all kinds of things; we did animal exercises, we did improvisations.

P. J.: Did you feel that there were certain shortcomings with Michael Kahn, a white man, directing *Funnyhouse*?

ALLEN: Well, I feel that Michael was smart enough to stand aside when it was necessary. I think that he was very smart in not trying to plot every move and every emotion, because he could see, I'm sure, that the more we did it the more we were discovering. And there were things that he had not thought of, and he was very smart to kind of keep his distance and yet shape it.

I loved working with Michael on this play. And (yet) as a black woman who directed it twenty years later, I don't think that we finished it downtown |in 1964|.

P. J.: I understand because I directed *People Who Led to My Plays* as a performance piece, and I really felt that at some point I had to say, "O.K., this is as far as I can go with this production because the material |just| seemed to keep on giving."

ALLEN: |It does.| It just goes and goes and goes, and I found that when I came back to it twenty years later that I had been thinking about it for twenty years without even knowing it.

L. O.: Were the students of the eighties in a different place than the audiences of the sixties?

ALLEN: Well, the students and the audience were in a different place. It was largely a student audience at NYU. One young woman said to me, "I just had to look away for the first time in my life, I've never had to look away from a stage. I had to look away, it was too much."

L. O.: So the core is still there.

ALLEN: The core is there, and it is even more universal because we know that we have so many young people, and people of all kinds of circumstances and socioeconomic strata, who are not reconciled unto themselves. And this applies to anything.

P. J.: Yes, but at the same time I think that it's also uniquely African-American.

ALLEN: Yes, I think so too. I think that when she writes, "white stallions roaming under a blue sky" |*Funnyhouse*, 14|, you see that. I feel that in some place in my psyche some part of me has been there and has seen that and connects with that. And every time I get to that passage, and every time I think [of] that passage I emerge as royalty.

L. O.: "Revelation in the midst of golden savannas, nim and white frankopenny trees, white stallions roaming under a blue sky" [*Funnyhouse*, 14]. Is there something in Kennedy's poetry that invites an imaginative response?

ALLEN: She [Kennedy] says, "At dawn he watched her rise at dawn, kill a hen for him to eat at breakfast, then go work down at the big house till dusk, till she died" [*Funnyhouse*, 14]. In a realistic play that's two acts, at least one: The mother beating her breast and the chicken blood all over the floor and God knows *what* these realistic authors would come up with and take you through.

Adrienne one night came up to me and she said, "Billie, you know, this reminds me so much of Greek drama." And that's how it felt. I could feel Euripides.

L. O.: As an actress, how do these interior monologues work compared to other interior monologues?

ALLEN: I'm sure that there are other wonderful [interior monologues]. I was remembering James Baldwin's monologue in *Blues for* Mr. *Charlie* for the young woman and that's quite deep and moving. But even that was more of masculine aesthetic. This [Kennedy's] is more of a feminine aesthetic...with the repetition and all.

L. O.: The repetition is everything.

ALLEN: The repetition allows you to go deeper and find another place. I just consider the whole play as her [Kennedy's] stream of consciousness and Sarah's.

P. J.: Do you think one actress can play all the parts of Sarah?

ALLEN: No. The point is, these are Sarah's selves that she cannot reconcile. They're *biting* into each other. [The] Duchess wants her place, and Victoria wants her place, and Jesus wants his recognition and Lumumba says you are all wrong. And if they don't fight, then we can't see it. I don't think an actress can do that.

It is also the yin and yang of Sarah. The masculine and feminine part of Sarah, too. There's Jesus and Lumumba and Queen Victoria and the Duchess [of Hapsburg].

L. O.: Both of these women came to power inadvertently and both of them held power for a long time.

ALLEN: A *long* time and shrewdly.

L. O.: Both of them reigned in an era of colonization—very powerful images.

ALLEN: Very powerful.

L. O.: The multiple voices in this play are tangible presences. In *The Owl Answers*, there is the costume change where characters walk out, literally, of their costumes. I don't know whether you would say one is a growth or development from the other, but, at this particular point, there seems to be a *fusion* of character.

ALLEN: She has it in all of her plays. And it works quite well for her because I think she's so skilled at that fusion. I think that's her strength.

I wanted to ask her if she always knew exactly what each line meant and the repetition especially, but I didn't dare even though I could have. I know that some authors do; they are specific about every little thing. But I think that one of the beauties of this work is that it repeats, and you can do what you want to do about it, and if you let it happen, even if you don't do anything about it, you are swept with the rhythm.

L. O.: There is one thing that Clive Barnes said about *Cities in Bezique*: "Undoubtedly, Miss Kennedy intends a great deal more than she means."[2]

ALLEN: Yes, she does. If you are going to see her play, you are going to work. If you are going to get in it, or be a part of it, and get anything out of it, you are going to work.

P. J.: When you got into rehearsal of *Funnyhouse*, how interactive was the process?

ALLEN: She came to rehearsal, and we were struggling. And one day I looked over there, and I said, "you are 'haunting my conception, diseasing my birth,'" which is one of her lines....[Cf. *Funnyhouse*, 21: "haunting my conception, diseased my birth."]

P. J.: Did she make any changes?

ALLEN: Only through Michael, and by this time they had culled it and shaped it together.

I think each director with each play has to decide what they're trying to do and what they want to say with these words. It is the director's play. The point of view, I think is decided, and then you decide how best to serve it. But because I think the whole thing is *her* interior, and when we make that, we don't have to get too specific or you lose that.

I know about Kennedy, that if you change words, you don't understand. It is all there, and it is *all* done.

L. O.: Why do you think that Kennedy's plays are not often produced?

ALLEN: I think they are not being done that often because they are inaccessible to a lot of people. I get thousands of calls and letters asking to see my notes and suggestions because people don't know where to start. And I can understand this. Because even if they knew, after they trust their instinct, there's no precedent. I think they are slightly inaccessible. I think to some people that this particular play, *Funnyhouse*...is offensive.

P. J.: Too real?

ALLEN: Too real. "Black man, black man, my mother says, I never should have let a black man put his hands on me. The wild black beast raped me and now my skull is shiny" [Funnyhouse, 4]. That is too real. And on a certain level derogatory, and too insensitive to a certain [audience].

P. J.: In reality, Kennedy placed the "color" dialogue into the public forum years before Spike Lee, and yet it [the dichotomy] has always been there.

ALLEN: Yes, but when it comes out and says [it], it is very different. You know nobody had owned up to it, and nobody had come out and said it in public. The Anglo aesthetic and standard of beauty—we don't really know how deep, deep and damaging it is.

L. O.: Was this a radical statement in 1964?

ALLEN: I don't think that it was radical, but the point is that it was radical for a black woman. It wasn't radical at all. But I think ultimately the nineties are more prepared for Funnyhouse than the sixties.

[Billie Allen has added the following comments as a coda to her interview.]

In the play, Funnyhouse of a Negro, Adrienne Kennedy delves into the black psyche, exposing our universal demons to the scrutiny of the light. She forces us to look at them and deal with them.

Hair, for example, had not been dealt with in the theatre. Our hair, that grows from us and is a part of us, has always been an ongoing battle: too curly, too straight, too kinky, too thin, too thick.

Sarah, in Funnyhouse, says, "My one defect is that I have a head of frizzy hair—unmistakably Negro kinky hair—and it is undisguisable." I felt this way about my own hair at that time. Creating the role of Sarah in Funnyhouse, I wore my hair long—brushed back and clamped tightly. At a certain point in the play I unleashed it: it sprang forth, gushing from my head like a fountain, alive and visible to the public. Many black women and men were ashamed of my doing this and wondered what "possessed" me. I was possessed by the rhythm, the ancient rituals called up from the depths by Adrienne. I began to love my hair: for me this was a catharsis for life.

Adrienne Kennedy dared to step into the avant-garde surrealistic theatre, her strong images, poetry, repetition of phrases, and nonlinear form soaring to new heights.

Notes

1. Funnyhouse of a Negro, in Adrienne Kennedy in One Act (Minneapolis: University of Minnesota Press, 1988), 6; hereafter cited in the text.

2. Clive Barnes, "Theatre: 'Cities in Bezique' Arrives at the Public," New York Times, Jan. 13, 1969, 26.

19

Developing a Concert for the Spoken Voice: *Solo Voyages*, and an Interview with Robbie McCauley

David Willinger

All theatrical adventures are determined as much by what happens between the people working on them as by the quality of the material, the ideals that impel them, or the good intentions with which they are begun. Such was the case in the creation of *Solo Voyages*.

Joe Chaikin suggested that we fashion a one-person performance from fragments of Adrienne Kennedy's plays for the actress, Gloria Foster. I, at the time, had heard of Adrienne Kennedy, but had never read anything she had written, works that were not readily available in print. After the first page, I became an instant convert to Adrienne's brilliant explorations in form, character, and language. She was the playwright I had always been looking for and never found, one who used contemporary American iconography in surreal and expressionist structures forged through subjectivity.

Joe had worked with Adrienne on several occasions. His production of *A Movie Star Has to Star in Black and White* at the New York Shakespeare Festival was followed up by treatments of her work in workshop, when Robbie McCauley experimented with it in the Winter Project and where portions of Adrienne's work were used in *Tourists and Refugees* (a work by the Winter Project directed by Chaikin; it included writings solicited from various authors). Joe called Adrienne proposing this new project, and she was at once enthusiastic. Further impetus was added by Gloria Foster, who was delighted by the idea of doing a one-woman show of Adrienne's work. Later, Gloria Foster bowed out of the project. Robbie McCauley, who had performed in *Movie Star* and had done such intimate work with Adrienne's texts in the Winter Project, was delighted to undertake the project as its sole performer.

As dramaturg, the first step was for me to do a preliminary cutting from the various plays. I was attempting to make a verbal collage. There would be no character per se, only disembodied voices emerging from the virtuoso performer...to create a "concert of Adrienne's voices."

Once the cutting was completed, I showed it to Joe who liked it and urged me to pass it on to Adrienne. Imagine my dismay when, on reading it, Adrienne forbade us to go further, insisting we abandon the project as she did not want anyone tinkering with her words, after all. Not only did this spell the abortive end to an exciting collaboration, but I walked away with the guilt-ridden feeling that I had betrayed the intentions of the very artist I esteemed most highly.

As most people who follow avant-garde theatre know, Joseph Chaikin suffered a serious stroke in 1984, and his speech was severely impaired for a time. Driven by a feeling compounded of terror at a life bereft of work and the will to prove to the world that he was still capable, he sought among his former collaborators for one who would now work with him on the first project following his stroke.

I agreed to do something with him, but what was it to be? We entertained various options, and then he suggested that we might make another attempt at the Adrienne Kennedy project. I reminded him how unequivocally Adrienne had forbidden us to proceed several years earlier. But he urged me to call her: "Now...I...think, yes." When I did *very* reluctantly call Adrienne, she promptly agreed.

Ultimately Margot Lewitin of the Interart Theatre welcomed the project, which was now known as (my title) *Solo Voyages*. But Interart turned out not to have sufficient funds to mount the show, a situation that became a continual, nagging concern. *Solo Voyages* was ultimately funded within the framework of Peter Sellars's ambitious and adventurous scheme of bringing the best of America's avant-garde theatre groups to Washington's Kennedy Center.

Early on, in the preproduction phase, I served primarily as dramaturg. However, after Joe's stroke, I was assigned the title of "assistant director," one that those who have collaborated with Joe subsequently have refused, preferring to be known as "Codirector." While Joe established the basic mise-en-scène and acting style, I worked with Robbie on refining her playing over the course of rehearsals, my work subject, of course, to Joe's approval.

At the beginning, Joe suggested I resuscitate the earlier cutting I had done. We read it over together, after which he invited Robbie to bring in a cutting of her own; she did so, and it was this version, with small revisions, that was the text that was used. This latter version did not intermingle parts of the various plays; rather it distilled passages from three of the plays—*The Owl Answers*, *A Rat's Mass* (despite Adrienne's avowed disenchantment with this play, Joe was attached to it primarily owing to its intriguing verbal imagery around "Nazis"),[1] and *Movie Star*—into three quite separate "movements" of the larger work. In this framework, discrete characters were only suggested, but did not vanish altogether. Something suggested within Adrienne's works, namely that all her characters are actually emanations from one sensibility and are perhaps all facets of a single persona, became explicitly so in *Solo Voyages*. Robbie, the stand-in or spokesperson for the main sensibility, would never totally transform into this or that character, but would become invested, now with this tone, now with that, always maintaining a strong, recognizable performer's identity. The work was reminiscent of a diary or, as the title suggested, an inner journey.

This structure did not change appreciably during the course of the rehearsals. The element of music was also introduced very early on with Skip LaPlante and his homemade instruments; also Robbie suggested Edwina Lee Tyler, a drummer, who became as much of a presence in the scenic drama as Robbie.

We began working around a table, with Robbie reading at random from the text and experimenting with varying degrees of entering into the life of the characters. When we eventually moved our rehearsals to the Interart stage, there was only a very subtle development away from the atmosphere of "reading" the text. The first part, *The Owl Answers* section, was especially inactive in the physical sense. Joe held firmly to the choice that Robbie not leave the stool on which she was seated, so this portion of the play or "movement" (in the musical sense of the word) became rather similar in that sense to Joe's own work in *Tongues* (written by him and Sam Shepard), which he had performed sitting in a chair. The simplicity and immobility of the mise-en-scène was meant, Joe later maintained, to echo the Japanese Noh theatre style.[2] The character shifts were accomplished almost entirely with subtle changes of voice and rhythm and tilting of the head in various directions.

The second section, from *A Rat's Mass*, was somewhat more active, though still spatially circumscribed. I suggested that Robbie perform it largely squatting, taking from the image of someone cowering in a fallout shelter, hidden away from a conflagration raging on the outside. Thus, Robbie, her back and knees bent, would shift from side to side and back to center again, as she spoke in the three voices of the brother, sister, and the white girl, Rosemary.

And A *Movie Star*, the third section, was the freest physically, and the one most directly addressed to the audience, as Robbie strode throughout the space, adding a "gestus" to incarnate each of the movie stars: Bette Davis, Jean Peters, and Shelley Winters. For example, a puff at an imaginary cigarette and an arm stiffly crooked at the elbow, but held away from the body, was all it took to evoke Bette Davis. She wouldn't do a full camp imitation of each "star," only take on a hint of their vocal rhythms and attitudes. The transitions between the three "movements" were filled with the simple image of Robbie walking in place, further suggesting a journey. Robbie walking accompanied by Edwina's congas mounting to a crescendo was also the culminating image of the piece.

While Robbie performed the first section downstage right, on her stool, and the second, center stage, Edwina Lee Tyler was firmly planted all the way upstage left with her drumset nestled on a gnarled tree stump in front of her. In her African garb and strong-featured face with pitch-black skin, she became a witty, pounding instrumental voice responding with counterpoint to Robbie's actual one. Skip LaPlante and his battery of homemade instruments was positioned alongside the audience, in sight but out of focus, as was Dianne Houston, the stage manager, who called the show in full view of the audience, perched on a stool with a headset intercom.

From the first we had conceived the show with some manner of effigies participating—dolls, masks, puppets. Joe commissioned Ronnie Asbell's extremely colorful and fanciful puppets for the show. When Jun Maeda, resident set designer of La Mama, later on appeared and began constructing his evocative black rippling cyclorama into which were embedded a series of bas-relief contemplative masks, all of Ronnie Asbell's puppets were in attendance. But Maeda had no intention of incorporating puppets that had no relation whatever to his design.

Even from the early days of the Open Theater, one of the hallmarks of Chaikin's method was to eliminate any element that threatened to calcify the work,[3] although the relentless divestment of inessentials often brings with it dropping of personnel and stripping people of assigned functions, a process that can be quite painful. In this case Ronnie Asbell was understandably distraught as Joe now proved ready to jettison the whole lot of her puppets. He finally conceded that three of the twenty would appear and pass by in the space upstage right of Robbie's stool in *The Owl Answers* portion of the play.

The most impressive part of the production, from my point of view, was the way in which Robbie McCauley, throughout the potentially catastrophic peripeties of money, puppets, alternating directors, shifting dates of opening, and near cancellations, maintained her still center and firm determination to continue with her creative work. She was like a boulder in a hurricane, imperturbably certain of her task. If any single person were responsible for the show's integrity, it was she.

I did not go with the production to Washington, but saw the performance there in its second week. A dancer, Jowale Willa Zollar, was added as an alter ego to the character, Clara, doing free-form movements in "dialogue" with Robbie's speaking the text and Edwina's percussion. Joe Chaikin's and Sam Shepard's play, Is This Real?, was also on the bill, with Chaikin as actor.

Reviews of the New York production varied. Alisa Solomon, in the Village Voice, noted that

> Chaikin has constructed a Kennedy chamber piece, and though Solo Voyages lacks the bloody emotional texture of the plays themselves, it marks the welcome return of two of our most important theatrical imaginations.... Kennedy distributes her incantatory memory poems among fictional and archetypal characters; Chaikin has reined them in, assigning the various speakers' lines, and some stage directions, to one actress. He's smoothed over some of the crazed grisliness of Kennedy's dramatic spirit, while drawing out the sorrow, yearning, and intellectual complexity of her language....Solo Voyages works...impressionistically.[4]

Mel Gussow's review in the New York Times remarked on Solo Voyage's resemblance to Tongues and Savage/Love and the Eastern atmosphere to which the production aspired.

> In each case, poetic language, music, solo performance and design blend and give a theatrical immediacy to an interior monologue....In Solo Voyages we are asked to tune ourselves to the playwright's inner ear....Together, Mr. Chaikin as director and Miss McCauley keep monodrama from becoming monotonous....Miss McCauley gives a varied, expressive performance, substituting in large measure for the absence of other actors on stage.[5]

In the Post, Marilyn Stasio began with praise but ultimately undercut it. She mentioned the set with appreciation: "The faces buried in Jun Maeda's walled set supply validation for the solo voyager's paranoid nightmares," and "Ronnie Asbell's body puppets corroborate her fantasies and add dimension to them." But she closes with a negative response to the Noh style: "It's odd, then, that neither McCauley's intense performance nor Chaikin's carefully textured presentation of it manages to hit any emotional nerves. This Voyage takes us to lofty intellectual places worth visiting, but never into the valley of the heart."[6] While Julia Just's review in the Westsider finds little to like, she concludes that "Kennedy's writing, nevertheless, remains compelling."[7]

The following is an interview I conducted with Robbie McCauley (March 9, l990); it offers a different point of view on the evolution of *Solo Voyages*. In addition to her work on plays by Adrienne Kennedy, Robbie McCauley most recently directed A *Tempest*, an adaptation of Shakespeare's *Tempest* by Aimé Césaire at Ubu Repertory Theatre. Her work as a performance artist, which is based in content-as-aesthetic, has been extremely influential. She has toured throughout the United States with a serial autobiographical work: *Indian Blood, My Father and the Wars*, and *Sally's Rape*. She has developed performances with actors about historical events at various sites, including Buffalo, Boston, and Western Mississippi. Her performance work grows out of a long career in the theatre, where she was best known for her performance on Broadway in *For Colored Girls.* . . .

DAVID WILLINGER: What were your explorations of Adrienne's work like in the Winter Project, and how did they feed into your work in *Solo Voyages*?
ROBBIE MCCAULEY: It started way back before A *Movie Star Has to Star in Black and White*. And Joe expressed to me at that time the possibility of working on a piece with Adrienne's text, my acting instrument, and his directing. This came out of a long history of my working on Adrienne's texts. The first so-called professional piece I did in New York was *Cities in Bezique* (*The Owl Answers* and *A Beast's Story*) at the Public. And I felt at the time I had a connection to the text which went beyond its being a play for a specific occasion. I felt a connection to the writer—to the author's images. So now looking back, I see a very clear connection being born—*Cities in Bezique* and that progression to *Movie Star* to *Tourists and Refugees*.
D. W.: How did your acting approach to Adrienne's work differ from that when you started in her plays (*Owl Answers, Beast's Story, Movie Star*) and the monodrama we put together, *Solo Voyages*?
MCCAULEY: What's interesting in her work is that the characters—Clara or Beast Girl—are one character. It's a matter of listening. It's something Joe turned me on to. He said, "You have many voices." So in *Solo Voyages*—probably because it was he who made the suggestion earlier—I was listening to the other voices in myself. Whereas in the other plays, it was a matter of listening to the other characters. But the principle was the same.
D. W.: As someone who worked with Joe Chaikin before his stroke and then afterwards, in *Solo Voyages*, could you identify the similarities and differences in his directing in the two periods?
MCCAULEY: It was inspirational. His work was slower after the stroke, but just as clear, and that was inspirational to me. There are other parts to it of course, but the communication between actor and director—which is so rare and accounts for a lot of what makes Joe so special—that was

there. For instance, it was a very active piece of work, and yet I was sitting most of the time. It was his clarity of concept that made me seem more active.

D. W.: What, if you will, was the *spine* of *Solo Voyages*, which was, after all, a theatre piece that was glued together from parts of other works?

McCAULEY: The image of the journey—voyage, journey. One day Joe used the word "conductor." That provided the through-line. And it was a trip both inside and outside the character of Clara, all these journeys.

D. W.: How about the choice that was made to distance yourself from the panicked and hysterical emotional life that so obviously pervades the texts?

McCAULEY: In all my work, emotion is always present. And the dialogue about whether it sinks or heightens in a piece, there's no either/or answer. The answer is in the balance. And here the conductor image helped a lot. And I was emotionally connected to all those images. I was able to be there emotionally and be clear through the conductor image.

D. W.: How about the contribution of the musicians: Edwina and Skip?

McCAULEY: They were other characters, and especially Edwina heightened the emotional life. This was Joe's concept, and it really worked. The drum and all the varieties of strings which Skip was using supported the emotional range of the piece. It was quite a brilliant "concept:" the music and the musicians were other characters. We worked moment to moment with the music the same way an actor works moment to moment.

D. W.: Anything else you want to add?

McCAULEY: It was such a fortunate circumstance. To be able to work with Adrienne's texts that way. And I think she was really generous to allow it. And to have Joe directing. So it was a special experience for me as an artist. The approach to the music of the piece—I've carried it (kind of unconsciously)—I've carried it into everything else I've done since. The connection between text and music and concept. Of course there were many problems, but that's not what I remember when I think of *Solo Voyages*.

Notes

1. From an unpublished interview about *Solo Voyages* between Joseph Chaikin and Ruby Cohn; provided by Bill Coco.

2. Ibid.

3. Eileen Blumenthal, *Joseph Chaikin: Exploring the Boundaries of Theater* (London: Cambridge University Press, 1984), 14-15.

4. Alisa Solomon, *Village Voice*, Oct. 1, 1985.

5. Mel Gussow, *New York Times*, Sept. 20, 1985, C3.

6. Marilyn Stasio, *New York Post*, Sept. 28, 1985, 15.

7. Julia Just, *Westsider*, Oct. 3, 1985, 2.

Selected Bibliography

Works by Adrienne Kennedy

Plays

Adrienne Kennedy in One Act. Includes *Funnyhouse of a Negro, The Owl Answers, A Lesson in Dead Language, A Rat's Mass, Sun, A Movie Star Has to Star in Black and White*, and adaptations of *Electra* and *Orestes.* Emergent Literatures. Minneapolis: University of Minnesota Press, 1988. |The definitive edition of the plays.|

Funnyhouse of a Negro: A Play in One Act. New York: Samuel French, 1969. Reprinted in *Black Drama: An Anthology,* ed. William Brasmer and Dominick Consolo (Columbus, Ohio: Merrill, 1970); *Contemporary Black Drama: From "A Raisin in the Sun" to "No Place to Be Somebody",* ed. Clinton F. Oliver and Stephanie Sills (New York: Scribner, 1970); Stanley Richards, *Best Short Plays of 1970* (Philadelphia: Chilton, 1970); and *Adrienne Kennedy in One Act.*

The Owl Answers. Poet Lore 60 (Autumn 1965): 195–211. Reprinted in *New American Plays,* vol. 2, ed. William M. Hoffman (New York: Hill and Wang, 1968); *Black Theatre USA: 45 Plays by Black Americans, 1847–1974,* ed. James V. Hatch and Ted Shine (New York: Free Press, 1974); and *Adrienne Kennedy in One Act.*

A Rat's Mass. In *The Off Off Broadway Book: The Plays, People, Theatre,* edited by Albert Poland and Bruce Mailman. Indianapolis, Ind.: Merrill, 1967. Reprinted in *New Black Playwrights,* ed. William Couch, Jr. (Baton Rouge: Louisiana State University, 1968); *More Plays from Off-Off Broadway,* ed. Michael Smith (New York: Bobbs- Merrill, 1972); and *Adrienne Kennedy in One Act.*

A Lesson in Dead Language. In *Collision Course,* edited by Edward Parone. New York: Random House, 1968. Reprinted in *Adrienne Kennedy in One Act.*

The Lennon Play: In His Own Write, adaptation of the writings of John Lennon. In collaboration with John Lennon and Victor Spinetti from Lennon's *In His Own Write* and *A Spaniard in the Works.* London: Cape, 1968; New York: Simon and Schuster, 1968. Reprinted in *Best Short Plays of the World Theatre, 1968–1973,* ed. Stanley Richards (New York: Crown, 1973.)

Cities in Bezique: Two One-Act Plays |The Owl Answers and A Beast Story|, New York: Samuel French, 1969. Reprinted in *Kuntu Drama: Plays of the African Continuum,* edited and with an introduction by Paul Carter Harrison (New York: Grove Press, 1974).

Sun: A Poem for Malcolm X Inspired by His Murder. Scripts 1, no. 1 (November 1971): 51-54. Reprinted in *Spontaneous Combustion: Eight New American Plays,* ed. Rochelle Owens, *Winter Repertory,* no. 6 (New York: Winter House, 1972); and *Adrienne Kennedy in One Act.*

A Movie Star Has to Star in Black and White. Wordplays 3 (Performing Arts Journal Publications, 1984): 51–68. Reprinted in *The Norton Anthology of American Literature,* 3rd ed. (1989); and *Adrienne Kennedy in One Act.*

An Evening with Dead Essex. Theater 9, no. 2 (Spring 1978): 66–78.

Electra and *Orestes*. In *Adrienne Kennedy in One Act*.
She Talks to Beethoven. *Antaeus* 66 (Spring 1991): 248–58.
The Alexander Plays: She Talks to Beethoven, The Ohio State Murders, The Film Club. Minneapolis: University of Minnesota Press, 1992.

Unpublished plays

Pale Blue Flowers (1955)
Boats (1969)
Lancashire Lad (1980)
Black Children's Day (1980)
Diary of Lights (produced, 1987)

Fiction

Adrienne Cornell |pseud.|. "Because of the King of France." *Black Orpheus: A Journal of African and Afro-American Literature*, no. 10 (1963): 30–37. Reprint. Nendeln: Kraus Reprint, 1972.
Deadly Triplets. Minneapolis: University of Minnesota Press, 1990.

Autobiographical Writing

"Becoming a Playwright." *American Theatre* 4 (February 1988): 26–27.
"A Growth of Images." edited by Lisa Lehman. *Drama Review* 21 (December 1977): 41–48.
People Who Led to My Plays. New York: Knopf, 1987.
"Preface." *Adrienne Kennedy in One Act*, ix.
"A Theatre Journal." In *Deadly Triplets*, 99–124. Minneapolis: University of Minnesota Press, 1990.

Interviews

"Adrienne Kennedy." In *Interviews with Contemporary Women Playwrights*, edited by Kathleen Betsko and Rachel Koenig, 246–58. New York: Morrow, Beech Tree Books, 1987.
Diamond, Elin. "An Interview with Adrienne Kennedy." *Studies in American Drama, 1945–Present* 4 (1989): 143–57.
Dunning, Jennifer. "Kennedy Decides That the Classroom's the Thing."
    New York Times, December 29, 1977, sec. 3, p. 13.
Kennedy, Adrienne. "Where Are the Women Playwrights?" *New York Times*, May 20, 1973, sec. 2, p. 1.
Kennedy, Adrienne, and Margaret B. Wilkerson. "Adrienne Kennedy: Reflections." *City Arts Monthly*, February 1982, 39.

Selected Theatre Reviews

"A Beatle at the National Theatre." *Times* (London), January 19, 1968, 6.
"John Lennon Play, *In His Own Write*, Is Staged in London." *New York Times*, June 10, 1968, 50.
"Miss Kennedy Adapts Beatle Books." *Village Voice*, December 21, 1967.
"New Kennedy Play." *New York Herald Tribune*, August 25, 1965.
"The 1981 Juilliard Season." *Theatre Crafts* 15 (August/September 1981): 109.
"Off-Broadway Reviews: *Cities in Bezique*." *Variety*, January 19, 1969, 75.
"Teatro: Atti unici americani." *L'Unità*, June 23, 1966.

"Theater: A *Rat's Mass*: Death Images Dot Play about Prejudice." *New York Times*, March 11, 1976, 42.

Barnes, Clive. "*Cities in Bezique* Arrives at the Public." *New York Times*, January 13, 1969, sec. 1, p. 26.
————. "Irreverence on London Stage." *New York Times*, July 9, 1968, 30.
————. "A *Rat's Mass* Weaves Drama of Poetic Fabric." *New York Times*, November 1, 1960, sec. I, p. 39.
Billington, Michael. "A Racial Dilemma." *Times* (London), April 29, 1968, 13.
Cooke, Richard P. "The Theater: World of Fantasy." *Wall Street Journal*, January 14, 1969.
Clurman, Harold. "Theatre." *Nation*, February 10, 1964, 154.
Duberman, Martin. "Theater 69." *Partisan Review* 36 (Winter 1969): 483-500.
Ermatinger, J. Lance. "Of Women and Other Things" and "Best since Zoo Story," *Off-Off*, no. 5 (April 1969): n.p.
Esslin, Martin. "Two Trifles and a Failure." *New York Times*, July 14, 1968, sec. 2, p. 4.
Evett, Marianne. "*Ohio State Murders* at the GLTF Workshop." *Plain Dealer* (Cleveland), May 31, 1990.
G., C. "Jeunes Américains." *Les Nouvelles Litérraires*, March 7, 1968.
Gautier, Jean-Jacques. "Spectacle Shepard-Kennedy." *Le Figaro*, March 11, 1968.
Gottfried, Martin. "*Cities in Bezique*." *Women's Wear Daily*, January 13, 1969, 63.
Gussow, Mel. "Stage: *Solo Voyages*, Play Excerpts." *New York Times*, September 20, 1985.
Kerr, Walter. "Some Day Adrienne Kennedy Will..." Review of *Cities in Bezique*, *New York Times*, January 19, 1969, sec. 2, p. 3.
Lane, John Francis. "Rome Off-Broadway." *Rome Daily American*, June 26–27, 1966.
Lemarchand, Jacques. "*Drôle de baraque* d'Adrienne Kennedy au Petit-Odéon." *Figaro Litérraire*, March 25, 1968.
Marash, David. WNEW radio review of *Cities in Bezique*, January 14, 1969.
Massa, Robert. "Bits." *Village Voice*, April 22, 1981.
Oliver, Edith. "The Theatre." *New Yorker* 39 (January 25, 1964): 76–78.
————. "Off-Broadway." *New Yorker* 44 (January 25, 1969): 77.
Oppenheimer, George. "*Funnyhouse of a Negro* at the East End." *Newsday*, January 15, 1964, 2.
————. "On Stage: *Cities in Bezique* Is Haunting though Confusing." *Daily Item* (Port Chester, N.Y.), January 13, 1969, 21.
P., A. "Tanto di capello all buona volontà." *Specchio*, July 3, 1966.
Paget, Jean. "Spectacle: Shepard-Kennedy." *Combat*, March 19, 1968.
Poiror-Delpech, B. "*Drôle de baraque*, d'Adrienne Kennedy." *Le Monde*, March 19, 1968.
Rich, Frank. "Stage: 'Lancashire Lad' for Children." *New York Times*, May 21, 1980, sec. 2, p. 30.
Sainer, Arthur. "Gavella Orchestrates a Sigh." *Village Voice*, November 29, 1976, 97, 99.
Silver, Lee. "*Cities in Bezique* Has Grim Sights and Sounds." *Daily News*, January 13, 1969, 46.
Simon, John. "Whirled without End." *New York*, February 3, 1969, 54.
Solomon, Alisa. "Sojourner's Truths." *Village Voice*, October 1, 1985, 98.
Taubman, Howard. "The Theater: *Funnyhouse of a Negro*." *New York Times*, January 15, 1964, 25.
Tennen, Steve. "Off-b'way Shows." *Show Business*, January 15, 1969.
Rudin, Seymour. "Theatre Chronicle: Winter-Spring 1969." *Massachusetts Review* 10 (1969): 586–87.
Vice. "Le Prime Roman: San Saba: Tre attit unici di autori ameriani." *Il Messaggero*, June 23, 1966.

Wardle, Irving. "Tormented Fury." *Times* (London), May 27, 1970, 14.
———. "Unknown Plays for New Directors." *Times* (London), June 19, 1968, 11.
Watts, Richard, Jr. "The Gift of Adrienne Kennedy." *New York Post*, January 13, 1969, 24.
———. "Two on the Aisle." *New York Post*, January 13, 1969, 24.
Zolotow, Sam. "London Will See a Beatle's Play." *New York Times*, February 27, 1968.

Related Works

Abramson, Doris E. *Negro Playwrights in The American Theatre, 1925–1950.* New York: Columbia University Press, 1969.
Benston, Kimberly W. "Cities in Bezique: Adrienne Kennedy's Expressionistic Vision." *College Language Association Journal* 20 (December 1976): 235–44.
Blau, Herbert. "The American Dream in the American Gothic: The Plays of Sam Shepard and Adrienne Kennedy." *Modern Drama* 27 (1984): 520–39. Reprinted in Blau, *The Eye of Prey: Subversions of the Postmodern.* Theories of Contemporary Culture, no. 9. Bloomington, Ind.: University of Indiana Press, 1987.
Brasmer, William, and Dominick Consolo, eds. *Black Drama: An Anthology.* Columbus, Ohio: Merrill, 1970.
Brown, Lorraine A. "'For the Characters Are Myself': Adrienne Kennedy's *Funnyhouse of A Negro.*" *Negro American Forum* 9 (1975): 86–88.
Case, Sue-Ellen. *Feminism and Theatre.* New York: Methuen, 1988.
Cohn, Ruby. *New American Dramatists, 1960–1980.* New York: Grove Press, 1982.
Curb, Rosemary K. "Fragmented Selves in Adrienne Kennedy's *Funnyhouse of a Negro* and *The Owl Answers.*" *Theatre Journal* 32 (May 1980): 180–95.
———. "'Lesson I Bleed.'" In *Women in American Theatre,* edited by Helen Krich Chinoy and Linda Walsh Jenkins. New York: Crown, 1981; Theatre Communications Group, 1987.
———. "Re/cognition, Re/presentation, Re/creation in Woman-Conscious Drama: The Seer, the Seen, the Scene, the Obscene." *Theatre Journal* 37 (October 1985): 302–16.
Diamond, Elin. "Mimesis, Mimicry, and the 'True Real.'" *Modern Drama* 32 (1989): 58–72.
———. "Toward a Politics of Identification: Brecht, Freud, and Kennedy." Forthcoming.
Elwood, William R. "*Mankind* and *Sun*: German-American Expressionism." *Text and Presentation,* Comparative Drama Papers, vol. 11 (1991): 9–13.
Fabre, Geneviève. *Drumbeats, Masks, and Metaphor: Contemporary Afro-American Theatre.* Translated by Melvin Dixon. Cambridge, Mass.: Harvard University Press, 1983.
Fletcher, Winona L. "Who Put the 'Tragic' in the Tragic Mulatto?" In *Women in American Theatre,* edited by Helen Krich Chinoy and Linda Walsh Jenkins. New York: Crown, 1981; Theatre Communications Group, 1987.
Forte, Jeanie. "Realism, Narrative, and the Feminine Playwright: A Problem of Perception." *Modern Drama* 32 (1989): 115–27.
Giddings, Paula. "Bookmarks." *Essence* 19, no. 26 (November 1988): 26.
Grossman, Samuel L. "Trends in the Avant-Garde Theatre of the United States during the 1960's." Ph.D. dissertation, University of Minnesota, 1974.
Harrison, Paul Carter, ed. *Kuntu Drama: Plays of the African Continuum.* New York: Grove Press, 1974.
———. *The Drama of Nommo.* New York: Grove Press, 1972.
Hatch, James. "Speak to Me in Those Old Words, You Know, Those La-La Words, Those Tung-Tung Sounds (Some African Influences on the Afro-American Theatre)." *Yale/Theatre* 8 (Fall 1976): 25–34.
Hay, Samuel A. "African-American Drama, 1950-1970." *Negro History Bulletin* 36 (1973): 5–8.
Houghton, Norris. *The Exploding Stage: An Introduction to Twentieth Century Drama.* New York: Weybright and Talley, 1971.

Keyssar, Helene. *Feminist Theatre: An Introduction to Plays of Contemporary British and American Women*. London: Macmillan, 1984; New York: Grove Press, 1985.

Kintz, Linda. "The Dramaturgy of the Subject(s): Refining the Deconstruction and Construction of the Subject to Include Gender and Materiality." Ph.D. dissertation, University of Oregon, 1986.

Lewis, Allan. *American Plays and Playwrights of the Contemporary Theatre*. New York: Crown, 1965; rev. ed., 1970.

Miller, Jeanne-Marie A. "Images of Black Women in Plays by Black Playwrights." *College Language Association Journal* 20 (June 1977): 494–507. Reprinted in *Women in American Theatre*, ed. Helen Krich Chinoy and Linda Walsh Jenkins (New York: Theatre Communications Group, 1987).

Mitchell, Loften. *Black Drama: The Story of the American Negro in Theatre*. New York: Hawthorne Books, 1967.

Murray, Timothy. "Screening the Camera's Eye: Black and White Confrontations of Technical Representation." *Modern Drama* 28 (1985): 110–24.

Ogunbiyi, Yemi. "New Black Playwrights in America, 1960–1975." Ph.D. dissertation, New York University, 1976.

Olauson, Judith. *The American Woman Playwright: A View of Criticism and Characterization*. Troy, N. Y.: Whitson, 1981.

Oliver, Clinton F., and Stephanie Sills, eds. *Contemporary Black Drama: From "A Raisin in the Sun" to "No Place to Be Somebody."* New York: Scribner, 1971.

Overbeck, Lois More. "Adrienne Kennedy." *Contemporary Authors: American Dramatists*. Vol. 3. Detroit, Mich.: Gale Research, 1989.

Poland, Albert, and Bruce Mailman. *The Off Off Broadway Book: The Plays, People, Theatre*. Indianapolis, Ind.: Bobbs-Merrill, 1972.

Simon, John. *Uneasy Stages: A Chronicle of the New York Theater, 1963–1973*. New York: Random House, 1975.

Sontag, Susan. "Going to the Theater (and the Movies)." *Partisan Review* 31 (Spring 1964): 284–94.

Talbot, William. "Every Negro in His Place." *Drama Critique* 7 (Spring 1964): 92–95.

Taubman, Howard. *The Making of the American Theatre*. New York: Coward McCann, 1965.

Tener, Robert L. "Theatre of Identity: Adrienne Kennedy's Portrait of the Black Woman." *Studies in Black Literature* 6 (Summer 1975): 1–5.

Thomas, Cathy. "The Daughter and Her Journey of Self-Definition in the Familial Plays of Adrienne Kennedy." A.B. honors thesis, Harvard University, 1985.

Turner, Darwin T. "Negro Playwrights and the Urban Negro." *College Language Association Journal* 12 (September 1968): 19–25.

Wilkerson, Margaret B. "Adrienne Kennedy." *Dictionary of Literary Biography*. Vol. 38, 162–69. Detroit, Mich.: Gale Research, 1985.

Williams, Mance Raymond. *Black Theatre in the 1960's and 1970's: A Historical-Critical Analysis of the Movement*. Contributions in Afro-American and African Studies, no. 87. Westport, Conn.: Greenwood Press, 1985.

Zinman, Toby. "'In the presence of mine enemies': Adrienne Kennedy's An Evening with Dead Essex." *Studies in American Drama, 1945–Present* 6 (Spring 1991): 3–13.

Contributors

Kimberly W. Benston is professor of English at Haverford College. His books include *Baraka: The Renegade and the Mask* (1978), *Speaking for You: The Vision of Ralph Ellison* (ed.) (1987), and the forthcoming *Faces of Tradition*.

Paul Bryant-Jackson is chair and assistant professor of theatre and drama at Spelman College. He has adapted and directed a performance of *People Who Led to My Plays*. He has contibuted a bibliographical essay on Amiri Baraka to *Contemporary Authors*, vol. 3, *American Dramatists* (Gale Research, 1989), and serves as contributor and adviser to a forthcoming book on the director, to be published by Greenwood. He is currently at work on a book that investigates the relationship between form and Aframerican dramaturgy.

Rosemary Curb, professor of English and women's studies at Rollins College, Winter Park, Florida, has published essays in books including *Lesbian Texts and Contexts: Radical Revisions* (1990), *Making a Spectacle: Feminist Essays on Contemporary Women's Theatre* (1988), *Women In American Theatre* (1987), and *The Many Forms of Drama* (1985). She has contributed biographical essays and subject entries to *The Feminist Companion to Literature in English* (1991), *Notable Women in American Theatre* (1989), *A Dictionary of Black Theatre* (1983), and *Dictionary of Literary Biography: Twentieth Century American Dramatists* (1981). Essays have also been published in several theatre and women's journals. With Nancy Manahan, curb edited *Lesbian Nuns: Breaking Silence* (Naiad Press, 1985).

Elin Diamond is associate professor of English at Rutgers University, New Brunswick, New Jersey. The author of *Pinter's Comic Play* (1985), she has published numerous articles on feminist and theatre theory in EHL, *Theatre Journal*, *Modern Drama*, TDR, and *Art and Cinema*. She is completing a new book, *Feminist Stagings: Unmaking Mimesis* (Routledge, forthcoming).

William R. Elwood is dean of graduate studies at Emerson College in Boston. He was formerly chair of the Department of Theatre and Drama at the University of Wisconsin-Madison, where he taught theatre history and dramatic literature. He held two Fulbright-Hays Grants for study at

the Freie Universtät in Berlin (1966–67) and at Ludwig Maximilian Universität in Munich (1975–76). His major research interest is in German
expressionism. His published works include "Incoherence as Meaning:
From the Real to the Expressive," *Comparative Drama Papers*, 1988; "Hasenclever and Brecht: A Critical Comparison of Two Antigones," *Educational
Theatre Journal*, 1972; and "Expressionism and Deconstructionism: A Critical Comparison," *Comparative Drama Papers*, 1990. His translations include
The Sell-Out (*Der Mitmacher*) by Friedrich Dürrenmatt, published in *Modern
International Drama*, 1985.

Jeanie Forte is an independent scholar and an instructor at DeAnza
College in Cupertino, California. Her writings in feminist performance
have been published in numerous journals and anthologies, including
Theatre Journal, *Theater*, and *Modern Drama*. Her book, *Women in Performance
Art: Feminism and Postmodernism*, is forthcoming from the University of
Indiana Press.

Elinor Fuchs is a New York theatre critic whose articles have appeared
in the *Village Voice*, *American Theatre*, *Performing Arts Journal*, and other
publications. In addition, she teaches in the Theater and Film Studies
Department of Emory University. She has contributed chapters to several
edited volumes, including *Strindberg's Dramaturgy* (1988) and *Sacred Theatre*
(1989). Her books include *Plays of the Holocaust: An International Anthology*
(1987) and, with Joyce Antler, the coauthored documentary play, *Year One
of the Empire* (1973). A volume of her essays, *The Death of Character: Theater
after Modernism*, will be published by Indiana University Press.

Deborah R. Geis is assistant professor of English at Queens College,
CUNY, where she specializes in modern and postmodern drama and
women's studies. She has published essays on Fornes, Shange, Rabe,
and Mamet, and is completing a book entitled *Postmodern Theatric(k)s:
Monologue in Contemporary American Drama*.

bell hooks is associate professor of English and women's studies at
Oberlin College and the author of *Ain't I a Woman: Black Women and Feminism*
(1981), *Black Feminist Thoery from Margin to Center* (1984), *Talking Back: Thinking
Feminist and Thinking Black* (1988), *Yearnings: Race, Gender, and Cultural Politics*
(1990), and (with Cornel West) *Breaking Bread: Insurgent Black Intellectual Life*
(1991).

Lois More Overbeck is research associate with the Graduate School of
Emory University. She is associate editor of *The Correspondence of Samuel
Beckett* and editor of *The Beckett Circle* (1984–89). Her bibliographical essay
on Adrienne Kennedy is published in *Contemporary Authors*, vol. 3, *American*

Dramatists (Gale Research, 1989). She has published essays on modern drama in collections including *Drama Conference Papers* (1985), *Myth and Ritual in the Plays of Samuel Beckett* (1987), *Women in Beckett* (1990), *Approaches to Teaching Ibsen's "Doll House"* (1985), and *David Storey* (1992).

Robert Scanlan is the literary director of the American Repertory Theatre in Cambridge, Massachusetts. He directs frequently in the United States and abroad, and is a lecturer in dramatic arts at Harvard University where he also teaches playwriting and dramaturgy at the Institute for Advanced Theatre Training. He has written widely on the works of Samuel Beckett and modern drama. He is currently working with Derek Walcott and Galt MacDermot on the premiere production of *Steel*, a new musical about steel bands in Trinidad.

Werner Sollors is the Henry B. and Anne M. Cabot Professor of English at Harvard University. Previously he taught at the Freie Universität in Berlin and at Columbia University. Among his publications are the books *Amiri Baraka/LeRoi Jones: The Quest for a "Populist Modernism"* (1978) and *Beyond Ethnicity: Consent and Descent in American Culture* (1986). He is currently at work on a study of the theme of black-white couples and their descendants in literature.

Howard Stein has recently retired as chair of the Oscar Hammerstein II Center for Theater Studies at Columbia University. His previous academic appointments include dean of theatre and film at SUNY Purchase, chair of the Theater Department of the University of Texas at Austin, associate dean and professor of playwriting at Yale School of Drama, and head of the playwriting program at the University of Iowa. He has published *A Time to Speak* (1974), as well as a number of articles of criticism and commentary. He is the present editor of *The Best Short Plays* series, and is working on a second book, *Why Don't They Write Plays Like They Used To?*

Margaret B. Wilkerson is professor and chair of the Department of African American Studies at the University of California at Berkeley. Wilkerson, who holds a Ph.D. in Dramatic Art from Berkeley, is editor of *Nine Plays by Black Women* (New American Library, 1986) and is currently writing a literary biography of Lorraine Hansberry to be published by Little, Brown.

David Willinger studied with Joseph Chaikin in the Center for Theatre Practice (formed by Chaikin, Meredith Monk, and Francoise Kourilsky). In 1985 they collaborated on *Solo Voyages*, a production based on the writing of Adrienne Kennedy, featuring Robbie McCauley. It was presented at Interart Theatre, in association with the American National Theatre at the Kennedy Center, opening on September 11, 1985. Willinger directed a production of Adrienne Kennedy's *Diary of Lights*, a musical without songs, at CitiRep at Davis Hall, City College, New York, June 5–14, 1987. Willinger's authorial/directorial pieces include *Andrea's Got Two Boyfriends*, *Malcolm's Time*, *Frida y Diego*, and *The Crusade*, which have played such theatres as La Mama and Theatre for the New City. He has translated and edited five volumes of plays, most recently *Ghelderode* and *Four Works for the Theatre by Hugo Claus*. A recipient of a Fulbright Research Grant, he teaches theatre at City College and the Graduate Center, CUNY.

Index

Compiled by Eileen Quam and Theresa Wolner